The Best
BARBECUE
ON EARTH

GRILLING ACROSS 6 CONTINENTS AND 25 COUNTRIES, WITH 170 RECIPES

Rick Browne, PhB

TEN SPEED PRESS

Berkeley | Toronto

This book is dedicated to my wife, Kate, my incredible family,
my many friends, and the thousands of wonderful people
all over the earth who shared their smiles, their delicious recipes,
and their friendship with me. God bless you all.

Ten Speed Press
PO Box 7123
Berkeley, California 94707
www.tenspeed.com

Distributed in Australia by Simon and Schuster
Australia, in Canada by Ten Speed Press Canada,
in New Zealand by Southern Publishers Group, in
South Africa by Real Books, and in the United
Kingdom and Europe by Publishers Group UK.

Photographs on pages 16 and 17 courtesy of
    Christopher Robert Dennis Browne.
Jacket and text design by Toni Tajima
Food and prop styling by Carol Ladd (pages 10, 19,
    30, 39, 46, 57, 66, 77, 84, 93, 100, 111, 120, 131,
    136, 149, 160, 170, 182, 193, 203, 211, 220, 237,
    and 242)

Library of Congress Cataloging-in-Publication Data
on file with the publisher

Printed in Thailand
First printing, 2008

1 2 3 4 5 6 7 8 9 10 — 12 11 10 09 08

Contents

Introduction

IN SEARCH OF THE BEST BARBECUE ON EARTH

During the last seven years, in my pursuit of America's "best" barbecue, I've heard the same thing repeated, oh, about a zillion times, by folks from coast to coast and border to border: "Barbecue is American! No one barbecues like we do!" Both phrases are often said with the kind of pride appropriate to a new father bragging about his future-Nobel-Prize–winning newborn twins.

And while I hate to dispute American excellence in anything, I have to disclose that just about everyone on the planet grills, barbecues, smokes, or cooks food outdoors. Barbecue is, in fact, a universal language.

Of course we have to define barbecue. Purists insist that true "barbecue" *must* involve all the following: 1) cooking meat indirectly 2) for a long time 3) using smoke 4) over a low temperature wood or charcoal fire. To me, barbecue means food cooked outdoors over a heat source, period. I think putting a steak right over a hot fire is barbecuing, too, as is adding a packet of wood chips for smoky flavor or cooking over an electric element, a solar-heated grill, a campfire log, or a propane gas flame. So you will find a range of preparations and techniques in this book, and I'll call them all barbecue.

"Barbecue" is both a noun and a verb. When people around the globe invite friends for an outdoor meal, it's a noun; when we describe how they are cooking the food over flame or coals, it's a verb. Simple, right? Food, fire, and friendship.

Thinking about the universality of barbecue gave me the idea to write a book where I could gather and share grilling and barbecue recipes and techniques from as many countries as I could manage to visit (this ended up being twenty-five countries, across all six continents). What did I find? Well, the Japanese grill chicken yakitori on sticks of bamboo over coals in a small hibachi; Mancunians (that's people from Manchester, England) grill their homemade sausages over charcoal; Brazilians cook beef, pork, chicken, sausage, and lamb on swordlike skewers; the Spanish slow-cook black Iberian pork in 800-degree ovens; a billion Chinese light up fires to cook pork *char siu* on long forks. In addition, the Portuguese coat chickens with a fiery *piri piri* sauce and grill it over open flames or burning piles of charcoal; Jamaicans rub jerk seasonings into the flesh and slow-cook the bird over smoldering pimiento wood; Singapore's Makansutra (a gathering of dozens of hawker food stands) features the world's best satay over open fires; South Africans use hardwoods in their *braai* stands to char up their *boerewors*; and Turkish cooks skewer chunks of lamb and eggplant for flavorful shish kebabs.

And, of course, everyone thinks their barbecue is the best. I agree. It's just that there are a whole world of bests out there, and try as I might I just couldn't taste them all. But I tried awfully hard.

I bring you here the best of the best barbecue I discovered on my round-the-world travels, serving you up some delicious appetizers, main courses, side dishes, and even desserts, all adapted for American home grillers. I got my ideas and recipes from backyard cooks, restaurant chefs, and other foodies I met along the way, and by asking questions of street food cooks (often through an interpreter), butchers, spice vendors, cooking school teachers, and just about anyone else I could collar who seemed to know what they were doing foodwise. Then I played with my new recipes at home and surprisingly found little difficulty in getting exotic spices, condiments, or grains, either online, in the "ethnic food" sections of local grocery stores, or in stores that serve Asian and Latino customers.

After looking at dozens of menus, restaurant and market displays, local cookbooks, and magazines, and the home backyard barbecues we were invited to in many places, I included those dishes that I felt best characterized each country's cooking styles—or those that I had eaten along the way that stayed in my mind and on my tongue.

The next few pages are dedicated to laying out what I'll modestly call THE secret to perfect grilling every time. With the passport of good skills at the grill, you'll be ready to eat your way around the world, one barbie, hibachi, or *braai* at a time.

Grilling is a much more refined culinary art than, say, throwing your meat on the hot barbecue grill and turning it once or twice so it doesn't burn (too much anyway). As a novice barbecuer, I sinned plenty, using all the excuses you may have uttered yourself: "That black crispiness? Oh, that's just a new blackened barbecue sauce technique I'm trying, honey"; or, "No, Chris, those aren't hockey pucks—they're Daddy's burgers. They'll taste fine, trust me"; and, of course, "This grill just doesn't work right. Everything burns. Here I turn my back for just the last quarter of the game and. . . ."

A better way to grill is to use a combination of direct grilling—the aforementioned throwing the food on a hot grill—and indirect grilling, moving the food away from the hottest part of the grill, cooking it slowly, and thereby keeping it juicy, tender, and loaded with flavor. Here's how it's done.

INDIRECT GRILLING

When working with briquettes or wood pieces, place the combustible materials on one side only at the bottom of the barbecue. Leave the other side empty (for now) and start your fire as you normally would (hopefully with an electric fire starter or kindling, not flammable chemicals, which can add a petroleum flavor to the food you are cooking).

When the fuel is covered with a thin film of white ash, use barbecue mitts to set a 9- by 12-inch metal or foil pan on the bottom of the empty side. Fill the pan with 1 to 2 inches of water, replenishing as you cook. The water evaporates during the cooking process and the steam helps keep the food above it moist. Note: some folks like to throw herbs, citrus slices, onion peels, etc., into the water to "flavor" the steam. I personally don't think this does anything other than give you a colorful, spicy pan of water, but if you wish, give it a try.

While the coals or wood pieces are heating, clean the grill (if you didn't do so after your last barbecue immolation). If you have an expensive copper grill brush, for heaven's sake use that. If you don't, take a 12- by 12-inch piece of aluminum foil, wad it up loosely into a ball, and, using long tongs, use it to scrape off the grill after it's been heated over high heat for 2 to 3 minutes. The hot fire the next time you cook will take care of any remaining stuck-on food particles.

At this point, you should also oil the grill rack. Fold a paper towel into a 2- by 2-inch square. Using long tongs, dip it into a small bowl of cooking oil, then rub it across the grill surface, covering the entire grill rack, re-dipping as necessary. You could also keep one barbecue basting brush handy just for this purpose, dipping the brush into the oil, and brushing across the rack (natural or silicone bristles only—not plastic, please, unless you want a melted mess at the end of the handle!). Some adventurous folks like to try to spray a nonstick spray across the heated grill surface. Not a good idea unless you want a wall of flames shooting toward you, catching the spray can on fire and barbecuing—*whoosh*—your face! Instead, remove the grill from the barbecue, spray, then return it to the barbecue. Or simply turn off the gas, spray the grill, then turn the gas back on.

Once the oiled grill is on the barbecue, add the food you wish to cook. I often start out with the meat, poultry, fish, or veggies placed on the "hot" side of the grill (the side with the coals). This way I can sear the food for a short time over the higher heat, perhaps 2 to 3 minutes per side. Then (depending on the recipe), I'll move the food to the "cool" side of the grill. ("Cool" is a relative term here: the "hot" side of the grill may be at 600° to 700°F, while the "cool" side may be as high as 200° to 350°F, or thereabouts.) Most times a "cool" temperature of 275° to 350°F is a good target. (If you can hold your hand, palm-side down, 6 inches over the grill for 4 to 5 seconds, it's about 250° to 350°F.)

The cool side of the grill, you remember, is also over the pan of water, which keeps flames from shooting up and engulfing the food, something that can happen in the latter stages of direct grilling. Presto, change-o! Now you're *indirect grilling* with charcoal (or whatever).

If you have a gas grill, the process is much the same. Most gas barbecues have at least two burners, and that's all you need. If it's a two-burner grill, turn on only one burner. Place your water pan over the unlit burner and—ta-da!—you've got your gas grill set up. (Because of the height of some burners, you may have to put bricks on either side of the unlit burner to hold the water pan.) Clean and oil the rack (see above), and when the grill is ready, add the food you wish to cook, first placing the food on the hot side to sear, and then on the cool side to cook for the rest of the time. Voilà! You're *indirect grilling* with gas.

If you've got more burners, you can be a bit more creative. With a three-burner setup, you can turn on both outside burners (to the same temperature, please). Place the water pan under the grill and over the middle burner, again, searing on the hot side and cooking for the majority of time on the cool side.

Using this method, you can cook virtually anything on a barbecue that you can cook in your kitchen oven. I've made soufflés and custards; baked bread, cakes, and pies; and perfectly cooked dishes that might have been incinerated over direct heat. And the slower, lower-temperature cooking, after the meat has been seared to keep the juices inside, produces the best results for those expensive cuts of meat that you cook on special occasions. Remember that a barbecue is just a sort of outdoor oven. It has a heat source like an oven, it's an enclosed box like an oven, and you can (somewhat anyway) control the heat like an oven.

Though I've developed these recipes to be made on a barbecue grill, most, if not all of them, can also be accomplished in a kitchen stove, or on rangetop burners or griddles (gas please, electric just doesn't work that well). After all, a barbecue is nothing but that oven taken outdoors—remember Grandma's woodstove?

Stay away from using glass pans or cookware in the barbecue, as the risk of cracking seems to be greater over open flame. However, I love and highly recommend using cast-iron skillets and Dutch ovens in the barbecue. Cast iron was made for cooking with fire and flame and produces wonderful results, especially with today's cast-iron cookware, which is often pre-seasoned and, if properly used, is about as easy to cook with as a good nonstick pan. Aluminum pans, either reusable or disposable, also work well when you're cooking on the grill.

If you are working with a charcoal grill, the secret to long cooking times is to add charcoal or briquettes (8 to 10 at a time) about every hour or so, to keep the temperature steady. But DON'T add them right from the bag. Instead, preheat them in a barbecue chimney, small metal pan, or small, inexpensive barbecue so that when you add them, they are up to temperature. Adding unlit fuel to your grill will cause the temperature to lower dramatically and thus change the cooking time of the food.

COOKING-TO-TEMPERATURE

For most of the recipes for barbecuing meat, fish, and poultry in this book, I list the temperature to cook to ("cook to medium-rare, 145°F") instead of cooking purely by time ("cook ribs for 35 minutes"). I advocate that barbecuers *cook to temperature* rather than practice the very fallible, *time-to-cook* method of grilling, smoking, and barbecuing. Using a thermometer gives you a better chance of success with a very accurate means of checking the doneness of your barbecue, and only a few times will I throw in some time suggestions, where I think it's appropriate and safe.

Time to cook is prone to culinary disaster because of a whole range of factors: thickness of the food; temperature of the food when you began cooking; temperature variables inside the barbecue; temperature changes as the wood,

charcoal, or briquettes cool; varying outside air temperature; varying outside humidity; heat loss from the barbecue itself; how often you lift the lid and release built-up heat; how long food will sit after you remove it from the barbecue before serving it.

So if you don't have a meat thermometer, get one. Actually, get two: a "manual" one that you stick into the food whenever you want to check the temperature, and a battery-operated one with a cable that you stick into the food inside the barbecue to keep track of temperature while you cook. Most of these have audio signals to tell you you're near, or at, the right temperature.

What's the right temperature? Well:

- Cook your beef steak to medium-rare (145°F), medium (160°F) medium-well (165°F), or your favorite degree (that's code for "if you want to burn it to leather, go right ahead").
- Pork should be cooked to: medium-light (155°F), medium (160°F), medium-well (165°F), or your favorite degree. (Why "medium-light" instead of "medium-rare"? Because there's something about the word "rare" while discussing pork that scares people silly.)
- Lamb should be prepared to medium-rare (145°F), medium (160°F), medium-well (165°F), or your favorite degree.
- Poultry should be cooked until a meat thermometer inserted in the thigh reads 180°F, and the breast 160°F.
- Seafood is best cooked until a meat thermometer inserted in the thickest part of the fish reads 140°F.

ThanQUE for listening.

ARGENTINA

A Day of Asado, or One Less Cow

One of the most barbecue-oriented countries on the planet, Argentina shines like a glowing bed of *asado* coals among real barbecue aficionados. When my television crew and I visited Buenos Aires to tape an episode of *Barbecue America: The World Tour*, we found out why. Man, oh man, do they eat beef there—twice or three times a day is not unusual, and they get through more beef than any country on earth, an unbelievable 150 pounds a year per capita (the average American devours 67 pounds). Depending on who you talk to, the national dish is one of a dozen or so cuts of beef, all cooked on a *parrilla* (pronounced "parizha").

During our trip to Buenos Aires, we were watched over by a goddess. Not a mythological, ethereal, or heavenly kind of goddess. A flesh-and-blood, blonde, steak-eating, beer-drinking, stick-shift-driving, charming, witty one. Maria Marcela Sorondo is her name, and she took us under her wing to show us the delights of one of the world's most vibrant cities.

Before we had even met, Marcela wrote to me: "You must come to my home for an *asado*. We do them every Friday night, and many of my family and friends will be there." I took her up on it, and it was a night I will never forget.

9 p.m. We arrive at Marcela's home in the *partido* of San Isidro, city of Martinez, to meet her husband, Alex; son, Augustin; daughter, Mercedes; and a handful of their close friends.

9:02. I have a glass of Argentine cabernet sauvignon in my hand and a plateful of *picadita* (cheese, salami, peanuts, and olives), Argentine hors d'oeuvres, in front of me.

9:15. Augustin, who manages three ranches and who must have been a stand-up comic in another life, rolls up his sleeves and starts the fire in the *parrilla* with thin strips of wood, newspaper, and lump charcoal.

9:55. After a chilled Quilmes beer, I watch as Augustin pronounces the fire right for cooking and puts small, plump chorizo sausages, kidneys , sweetbreads, red pepper, large onions, and potatoes in foil on the back of the grill. A plate of large empanadas is passed around. The meat-and-spice-filled flaky pastries disappear in seconds. They are by far the best I've had on my entire trip to a part of the world where empanadas are universally superb.

10:15. A handful of intestines, which have been soaking in brine, are added to a hotter part of the fire. I look dubiously at the tubular curls that are starting to sizzle.

10:30. Augustin's sister, Mercedes, a charming, bubbly lass who is a well-known local ceramicist, brings out a tray of Creole sausages, strips of bone-in short ribs, slices of spiced provolone cheese, and some blimp-sized blood sausages to start cooking. The black sausages also cause me to look dubious. But I happily drown my doubt with another cold beer and a couple more pieces of the salami.

10:45. Marcela and Alex emerge from the kitchen, she carrying a tray of more meat (no kidding) including a large hunk of beef tenderloin, a tri-tip, and a large piece of flank steak. Alex, who used to cook the *asado* but now enjoys watching his son do the work, is carrying more bottles of cabernet.

10:50. Small French-bread rolls appear and are quickly filled with the plump chorizo sausages and passed around. They last only seconds.

11:00. Marcela hands Augustin yet another tray of meat (Holy cow! We're going to eat a whole cow!) containing a different cut of flank steak and strips of boneless short ribs. Cheering erupts as Augustin points to the table and suggests we sit and begin to eat. My joy is tempered by the fact that first course includes the intestines, sweetbreads, and kidneys. I warily nibble small pieces of kidney and intestine, then gleefully give the rest of this offal food (offal as in innards, not awful) to Augustin's "assistant" Rodrigo Balbiani, who downs them just as gleefully. The sweetbreads, however, are superb, tender, flavorful, and juicy, and don't get passed to anyone.

11:15. Next from the *parrilla* comes a platter sizzling with the short ribs, the grilled cheese, and the blood sausage. Now let me say one thing right now. I have lived quite well for my sixty-plus years without ever eating sausage made from blood, and here are two kinds offered up to me. The Argentine variety of *morcilla* (made with a filler of rice and onions and seasoned with paprika and other spices) confirms everything I have ever thought about sausages made primarily of congealed blood. But being the adventurer, I also take one bite of the sweet, or Basque, kind, which includes raisins and which is, well, sweet. This I love. Surprise, surprise, surprise! The texture is a little like squishy meat, sure, but the taste is delicious and I finish quite a large sausage in three to four bites.

11:30. I thought we were through, forgetting the other quarter cow still cooking on the *parrilla*, but am jolted to reality by yet another

tray of cooked meat. This time the duo of flank steaks appear, surrounded by the Creole sausages, more chorizo, and the tri-tip (served "juicy," or as we call it "rare.") Juicy? Yes. Rare? Yes. Delicious? Absolutely!

By the way, in case you wondered, the red peppers, potatoes, and onions have been brought over too, and were quickly done away with. We have already cleaned out several bowls of lettuce salad, sliced tomatoes, grated carrots, and potato salad, which were on the table when we started the feast. Add several baguettes of French bread that were used to soak up the red and pink meat juices, and I am getting quite full, thank you.

11:45. As I giddily accept one more glass of cabernet, I have a fleeting moment of panic when I think I see three people coming toward the table with yet another tray of meat. Oh my Lord, they're real, and so is the tenderloin—still steaming and dripping pink juices, glowing medium-rare and juicy in the center—and several slabs of the short ribs (both the bone-in and the boneless), crunchy and charred on the outside, gloriously pink inside.

Midnight. I can barely lift my fork to listlessly stab a small slice of the tenderloin and one small bone of the *asado*, but I am brushed back by the knife-and-fork-wielding sharks around me. I hurriedly take a picture before the protein completely vanishes.

Here I am, a professional cook who usually holds his own at any table, vanquished. I'm ready to throw in the towel, the napkin, and the tablecloth in ignominious eating defeat. We have been eating for more than three solid hours, consuming enough meat to feed Miami, quaffing innumerable bottles of wine and beer, downing countless bowls of vegetables and starches—and they all still look hungry.

1 a.m. As I say good-bye to my new friends, I keep a wary eye on the *parrilla*, fearing that someone will find "just one more" piece of meat that has been forgotten. But the only thing left is the memory of a wonderful evening with generous and friendly people, and the distinct feeling that because of our *asado* for twelve, there was now one less cow on earth.

BEEF EMPANADAS

Empanadas are individual turn-overs (although some are pie-sized) with a pastry crust filled with chicken, meat, seafood, vegetables, or fruit. Food stands all over Buenos Aires sell these tasty snacks. This recipe calls for lard, which is richer than many other fats and makes superbly tender, flaky pastry. You can substitute solid vegetable shortening, but the taste will not be the same.

CRUST

- 2 cups flour
- 2 teaspoons baking powder
- $1/2$ teaspoon salt
- 2 tablespoons cold lard
- 1 egg
- $1/2$ cup milk, plus additional for brushing the pastry

FILLING

- 2 large onions, coarsely chopped
- 1 pound ground beef
- 3 tablespoons lard
- 1 tablespoon sweet paprika
- $1/4$ teaspoon crushed red pepper flakes
- $1/2$ teaspoon cumin
- Salt
- Freshly ground black pepper
- 2 hard-boiled eggs, chopped
- $1/4$ cup dark or golden raisins
- $1/4$ cup chopped green or black olives

To make the crust, sift together the flour, baking powder, and salt in a large bowl; add 2 tablespoons of the lard and crumble between your fingers to combine. In a small bowl, beat the egg, add the milk, and add both to the flour mixture. Mix with a wooden spoon until the dough forms a ball. Divide the dough into 8 parts, form the parts into balls, and roll the balls out on a floured surface into 3- to 4-inch circles, each about $1/8$ inch thick. Set aside.

To make the filling, combine the onions and ground beef in a large bowl and set aside. In a saucepan, heat the 3 tablespoons lard, paprika, and red pepper flakes, stirring constantly, until well mixed. Let stand a minute, then pour the seasoned lard over the meat mixture; add cumin, season with salt and pepper, and stir to combine. Let cool completely.

Prepare a charcoal or gas grill for indirect grilling (it is not necessary to use a drip pan with this recipe). Preheat to 400°F.

To form the empanadas, place 1 heaping tablespoon of filling onto each dough round; divide evenly and add to each round the hard-boiled egg, raisins, and olives.

Wet the edges of the dough with cold water. Fold each round in half over the filling, sealing with the tines of a fork; brush with milk.

Transfer the pastries to a baking sheet, place on the barbecue over indirect heat, and bake for 20 minutes, turning several times, until the empanadas are just turning brown on the edges. Remove from the barbecue and serve.

SERVES 4 TO 6 AS AN APPETIZER

CHIMICHURRI SHORT RIBS

In Argentina, you don't ask for ketchup for your burgers, steaks, roasts, and just about any other meat: you ask for chimichurri *sauce, a mélange of oil and vinegar with chopped herbs, spices, garlic, and onion. Every family and every chef has their own recipe. This is one of my favorites; it uses lemon juice instead of vinegar for the acid kick.*

SAUCE

- 6 cloves garlic, peeled and coarsely chopped
- 1 white onion, coarsely chopped
- 2 bunches Italian parsley, stems trimmed
- Juice from 2 large lemons
- $1/2$ teaspoon crushed red pepper flakes
- $1/4$ teaspoon cayenne
- $1/2$ cup olive oil
- $1/2$ teaspoon salt
- $1/4$ teaspoon freshly ground black pepper

RIBS

- $1/2$ cup coarsely ground black pepper
- $1/4$ cup firmly packed light brown sugar
- $1/4$ cup sweet paprika
- $1/2$ teaspoon garlic powder
- 2 tablespoons kosher or sea salt
- 6 pounds beef ribs, trimmed
- 2 bottles of your favorite beer

Preheat a charcoal or gas grill to 300°F. Make sure the grill rack is clean.

To make the *chimichurri* sauce, in a food processor, process the garlic and onion until finely chopped. With the motor running, add the parsley, lemon juice, red pepper flakes, and cayenne. Pour in the olive oil in a slow, steady stream. Continue to process the mixture until it is smooth and quite thick, about 5 minutes. Use a rubber spatula to scrape the sauce into a bowl, add the salt and pepper, cover, and set aside.

In a small bowl, combine the pepper, brown sugar, paprika, garlic powder, and salt and mix well.

Rub the ribs with the spice mixture and transfer them to a covered roasting pan or Dutch oven. Pour beer around the beef (not over it), cover the pan, and cook over direct heat on the barbecue for 3 hours.

Remove the ribs from the pan and cut into individual portions. Remove the grill rack from the grill and oil it thoroughly with cooking spray. Transfer the ribs back to the grill over direct heat, close the grill cover, and cook for 5 minutes longer, or until crusty and tender. Serve with *chimichurri* sauce.

SERVES 4 TO 6

GRILLED FLATIRON STEAK WITH CHIMICHURRI SAUCE

You can also use flank steaks in this recipe; flank steaks are very popular in South America, but many North Americans disdain them because they are "too thin" or "cook too fast." So I'm calling for the thicker flatiron steak. Or if you'd rather spend the money you can use a rib-eye, sirloin strip, or New York strip steak. Any of these are great with this herby, garlicky chimichurri sauce.

1	cup (1 handful) wood smoke chips (oak, hickory, or pecan, or your choice)
1	cup extra-virgin olive oil
15	cloves garlic, peeled
1/3	cup sherry vinegar
1/4	cup loosely packed chopped fresh parsley
1/4	cup loosely packed chopped fresh cilantro
1/4	cup loosely packed fresh oregano
3	tablespoons fresh thyme
	Salt
	Freshly ground black pepper
1/4	cup (half a stick) butter
2	(1 1/2-pound) flatiron steaks

Place the wood chips in a large bowl or can, cover with water, and soak for at least 2 hours.

For the *chimichurri* sauce, in a food processor, combine the olive oil, garlic, vinegar, parsley, cilantro, oregano, thyme, 1 teaspoon salt, and 1/2 teaspoon pepper. Process until smooth, then scrape into a bowl, cover, and set aside.

Preheat a charcoal or gas barbecue to 375°.

In a cast-iron saucepan, melt the butter either on the stovetop or over direct heat on the grill until it begins to turn brown, about 2 minutes. Add the *chimichurri* sauce and cook, stirring, for 2 to 3 minutes, until it's bubbling. Remove the pan from the heat and keep it warm.

Sprinkle the steaks with salt and pepper and let stand at room temperature for 5 minutes.

Meanwhile, put the soaked wood chips on a piece of heavy-duty aluminum foil and fold it over like an envelope to enclose the wood. Using a pencil, poke 3 or 4 holes in the top of the foil envelope (don't poke all the way through). Place the foil directly on the coals or gas jets and when the wood inside starts to smoke, transfer the steaks to the grill rack over direct heat, cover the grill, and cook until juices form on the top of the steaks, about 4 minutes per side for medium-rare. Remove the steaks from the grill, cover with foil, and let stand for 5 minutes.

To serve, slice the steaks thinly across the grain and drizzle with the *chimichurri* sauce. Serve with extra sauce on the side.

SERVES 6 TO 8

STUFFED GRILLED BASS

This recipe is from the tropical north where Argentina, Brazil, and Paraguay meet. This preparation is usually done with local freshwater fish called suribi *or* pacu. *You can easily substitute sea bass, grouper, halibut, or salmon for the striped bass used here, and for a richer flavor use heavy cream instead of the milk. If you do not know how to bone a whole fish, get your fishmonger to do it for you.*

1 whole (3-pound) striped bass, cleaned and boned

   Salt

   Freshly ground black pepper

1 onion, finely chopped

2 cloves garlic, finely minced

3 tablespoons chopped fresh parsley

$1/2$ cup fresh bread crumbs

$1/4$ cup milk

2 tablespoons olive oil, plus additional for brushing

2 tablespoons butter, melted

1 cup dry white wine

   Lemon wedges, for garnish

Prepare a charcoal or gas grill for indirect grilling (it is not necessary to use a drip pan with this recipe). Preheat to 400°F. Grease a roasting pan large enough to hold the fish.

Season the inside of the fish with salt and pepper. Set aside.

In a mixing bowl, combine the onion, garlic, parsley, and bread crumbs, season with salt and pepper, and moisten the mixture with the milk.

Stuff the cavity of the fish loosely with the bread-crumb mixture. Secure the cavity with toothpicks. Brush olive oil on the fish and transfer it to the grill over direct heat, cooking, 2 to 3 minutes per side, until nicely marked on both sides.

Transfer the fish to the prepared pan. Add the butter, the 2 tablespoons of olive oil, and the wine. Place in the barbecue, cover the grill, and cook over indirect heat for 20 to 25 minutes, until the fish feels firm when pressed with a finger, and a meat thermometer inserted in the thick part of the fish reads 140°F.

Spoon the juices from the pan over each serving and serve immediately with lemon wedges on the side.

SERVES 4 TO 6

NOTE: Rub your hands with salt and lemon juice to remove odor after handling a fish. But when you are shopping for seafood, heed an old saw: "Fish should smell like the ocean. If they smell like fish, it's too late."

CHEESY GRILLED VEGETABLES

This dish is usually made with an Argentinian cheese called sardo, *which is available online and in specialty stores. I substitute Gruyère since it's much easier to find. You could also use Cheddar for a bit more sharpness. As a general rule, select the smallest possible zucchini that can be used for the recipe, because larger ones are less flavorful and can have bitter overtones.*

6   firm plum tomatoes

1   red bell pepper, stemmed, seeded, and quartered

1   large onion, quartered lengthwise

2   small zucchini, halved lengthwise

2   tablespoons olive oil

1   tablespoon chopped fresh basil

1/2   teaspoon dried thyme

1/2   teaspoon minced garlic

1   teaspoon kosher salt

     Freshly ground black pepper

4   large eggs

1/2   cup whole milk

1   cup shredded sardo or Gruyère cheese

1   cup fresh bread crumbs

2   tablespoons grated Parmesan cheese

Prepare a charcoal or gas grill for indirect grilling (it is not necessary to use a drip pan with this recipe). Preheat to 350°F. Make sure the grill rack is clean and oil it thoroughly with nonstick cooking spray. Spray a 10-inch cast-iron skillet with cooking spray and set aside.

Lightly brush the tomatoes, bell pepper, onion, and zucchini with the olive oil. Place the vegetables on the grill rack and cook over direct heat, turning several times, until vegetables start to brown on the edges but are still firm. Keep vegetables separate on the grill as the zucchini will be finished first, then the tomatoes, then the bell peppers, then the onions. Set aside until cool enough to handle. Remove the skins from the tomatoes and peppers, and cut all the vegetables into 1/2-inch pieces. Drain the tomatoes on paper towels.

Transfer the vegetables to a large bowl. Add the basil, thyme, garlic, salt, and pepper, stirring to combine.

In another large bowl, whisk together the eggs and milk, stir in the *sardo* cheese, and add the mixture to the vegetables, stirring to combine. Pour into the prepared skillet. Sprinkle the top evenly with the bread crumbs and the Parmesan.

Transfer the skillet to the barbecue and cook over indirect heat until the edges of the mixture are browned and the center is set, about 20 minutes.

Let cool to room temperature, cut into wedges, and serve.

SERVES 4 TO 6

NOTE: *Sardo*, a sharp cow's-milk cheese, is used in many Argentinian dishes. It's shredded on pasta, sprinkled on hearty soups or on steamed or grilled vegetables, and even shaved and sprinkled on barbecued steaks.

ALFAJORES

In Buenos Aires, every food stand has these layered cookies for sale. It seems like everyone eats several every day, and no wonder—they're delicious. Some coat the cookies with chocolate, but I love the plain cookies with the dulce de leche filling. Meaning "milk candy" in Spanish, dulce de leche is a caramel-like candy syrup seen everywhere in Argentina, and, for that matter, in South and Central America. It is used to make candy, frosting, ice cream, flan, and cakes, and is even spread on toast for a sweet treat.

¹/₂	cup (1 stick) butter
1	cup sugar
1	egg
2	egg yolks
1	teaspoon vanilla
2	teaspoons grated lemon zest
1¹/₂	cups cornstarch
¹/₂	cup flour
1	teaspoon baking powder
¹/₄	teaspoon salt
1¹/₂	cups Dulce de Leche, at room temperature (recipe follows)

Preheat a charcoal or gas grill to 350°F. Grease a large baking sheet.

In a large mixing bowl, combine the butter and sugar and beat by hand or electric mixer until pale and fluffy, about 5 minutes. Add the egg and egg yolks, one at a time, beating well with each addition. Beat in the vanilla and zest until well blended.

In another mixing bowl, sift together the cornstarch, flour, baking powder, and salt. Add to the butter mixture and mix well.

Drop batter by small spoonfuls onto the prepared baking sheet, 2 inches apart (the cookies spread while baking). Transfer the baking sheet to the barbecue over direct heat and cook until they just begin to turn golden, about 15 minutes.

Remove immediately and transfer to a work surface. Spoon 1 tablespoon of the dulce de leche on half of the cookies. Top each filled cookie with a second cookie, making a sandwich.

MAKES 20 SANDWICH COOKIES

DULCE DE LECHE

1 (14-ounce) can sweetened
    condensed milk

Preheat a charcoal or gas grill to 425°F.

Pour the sweetened condensed milk into an 8-inch round pie pan or square cake pan. Cover with aluminum foil and place the pan into a shallow pan filled with 1 inch of water. Transfer the pans to the barbecue over direct heat and cook for about 1 hour, until the milk is a thick, tan-colored syrup. Let cool before using. The dulce de leche will keep in the refrigerator for a week or so.

MAKES ABOUT I¹/₂ CUPS

AUSTRALIA
Don't Fork the Snags, Mate!

"Australian barbecues aren't what they used to be. No longer are they slash-and-burn affairs held in the backyard under the clothesline, with the women standing at one end of the yard talking about babies, and the men standing at the other talking about cars and football, drinking cold tinnies and eating cremated lamb chops and soot-black snags."

TERRY DURACK, *The Independent*, London

Yes, it's true. Barbie has grown up in Oz. What used to be backyard humdrum, charred beyond recognition and drowned in chilled cans of Aussie suds, now features fine wines, exotic entrées, complex sauces, and garnishes from around the globe.

There's still plenty of shrimp on the barbie, but nowadays it's Malaysian spotted prawns marinated in Chinese hoisin and Japanese sake, served on a bed of baby arugula, dusted with lemon myrtle, and drizzled with a honey-onion-macadamia-nut sauce or chermoula-marinated barbecued lamb loin with spiced fig, vegetable couscous, and harissa jam.

Everybody barbecues in Oz. There are thousands of parks, beaches, and campgrounds in Australia, and most have free or coin-operated gas and/or electric barbecues, many with covered shelters, picnic tables, and running water available. What a great concept!

Australians prefer faster-cooking, open, flattop gas grills, as opposed to the slower-cooking covered charcoal grills. (This trend toward gas barbies was boosted by legislation banning backyard fires in major cities.)

Trolly barbies, portable grills on wheels, have become, by far, the most popular outdoor cooking appliances. Also popular are bush barbies, for sojourns in the outdoors, and the stainless steel barbies mounted on the rails and aft decks of yachts featured prominently all over Sydney, Adelaide, and Hamilton Island harbors.

At the Sydney Fish Market, the largest of its kind in the Southern Hemisphere, you can take a seafood barbecue class that's so popular, it's repeated four or five times a month just to keep up with demand.

Other than seafood, Aussies love to grill steaks, pork, turkey, sausages, chicken, lamb, sausages, and veal. But since it's Australia, you'll find plenty of emu and ostrich, bright red meats that look more like steaks; crocodile, milky white and very much like firm fish or chicken; and wallaby and kangaroo, which look and taste like top-grade beef steaks. If presented with a witchetty grub, a 4- to 5-inch gray-white worm about as thick as your thumb (eating of which is a rite of passage for tourists), be sure to ask for it grilled. I think it tastes like a grainy, peanut butter–flavored sausage. But raw, it's slimy and wriggly and tastes like a raw potato.

But maybe above all else, Aussies love their "snags," or "mystery bags," and many seem to think they share a national gift for sausage barbie cookery. Greg Squire, a chef in Cairns, invited us to his home for an "Aussie barbie," where he advised me with great solemnity: "Snags should never be pricked, always use

tongs to turn them. The skin's job is to keep the meat juicy and a burst skin is either a sign of a bad sausage or a bad cook using a fork."

So when, on my recent visit to Adelaide, Jacob's Creek Winery chef Robert Yates put me in charge of a grill covered with lamb chops, beef steak, pork steaks, scallops, barramundi, calamari, oysters, octopus, and of course snags, I knew what to do to prove my skills.

I didn't fork the snags.

PRAWNS IN ORANGE-GINGER SAUCE

Tiger prawns are noted for their firm, sweet flesh and are also the most popular species for prawn farmers because of their rapid growth rates. They are easily distinguished by the black-and-white stripes across their bellies, which turn dark red when cooked. The brown tiger prawn variety is endemic to Australian waters.

1/2	cup (1 stick) butter
1	cup freshly squeezed orange juice (juice of about 3 oranges)
2	tablespoons dry sherry
1	teaspoon grated orange zest
2	green onions, minced, white and green parts only
1	teaspoon grated fresh ginger root (see Note)
12	giant tiger prawns, shelled and deveined (tails intact)
	Spinach leaves, for serving
1	orange, thinly sliced, for garnish

Combine butter, juice, sherry, zest, green onion, and ginger in a saucepan and cook over medium-low heat, stirring, until butter is completely melted. Let cool to room temperature.

Put the prawns in a 1-gallon resealable plastic bag and add half of the orange juice sauce; seal the bag, pressing out the air, and refrigerate for 1 hour. Cover remaining sauce to use for basting.

Preheat a charcoal or gas grill to 375°F. Make sure the grill rack is clean and oil it thoroughly with nonstick cooking spray.

Drain the prawns and discard the marinade. Transfer the prawns to the prepared grill rack, and cook for 2 minutes per side, liberally basting. Most of the prawns will be done at this point, but continue basting and turning any larger ones until they are pink and just cooked through.

Remove the prawns from the heat immediately, as they will get tough if overcooked. Transfer the remaining basting sauce to a serving bowl.

Line a warmed platter with spinach leaves and transfer the prawns to the platter. Garnish with orange slices and serve with the sauce as a dip.

SERVES 4 TO 6 AS AN APPETIZER

NOTE: Fresh ginger can be kept for several weeks in the salad drawer of the refrigerator. Dried ginger should be "bruised" before using by beating it to open the fibers, then infused in the cooking liquid, and removed before serving.

BACON AND EGG PIE

Sixteenth-century European peasants could rarely afford to serve pork. So when visitors arrived, it was customary to hang up the bacon as a way to show off, because it was a sign of wealth that a man could "bring home the bacon." Small slices were shared with guests and everyone would sit around "chewing the fat." Versions of this recipe date from the first days of the Australian colonies when none of the immigrants or landed convicts had much money and dishes like this were cooked up and fed whole families.

$3/4$	cup flour
1	teaspoon salt
2	tablespoons cold butter, cut into small pieces
1	tablespoon cold lard, cut into small pieces
2 to 3 ounces ice-cold water	
$1/2$	pound bacon, cut into small pieces
3	tablespoons chopped fresh parsley
1	small onion, grated
$1/2$	cup grated Swiss cheese
2	large tomatoes, peeled and sliced thinly
$1/4$	teaspoon salt
$1/2$	teaspoon lemon or orange zest
	Freshly ground black pepper
6	eggs
2	tablespoons heavy cream

Sift the flour into the bowl of a food processor, add the salt, butter, and lard, and process until crumbly, about 2 minutes. With the motor running, dribble in the cold water. When the mixture starts to clump, turn the motor off and check the consistency of the dough. If it is damp and forms a ball when you squeeze, it's perfect; if it crumbles, keep processing on low speed with a little extra water until it forms clumps.

Remove the dough, divide it in half, forming it into 2 balls; wrap the dough in foil or plastic wrap and chill for 20 minutes.

Meanwhile, prepare a charcoal or gas grill for indirect grilling (it is not necessary to use a drip pan with this recipe). Preheat to 350°F.

Grease a 9-inch pie plate. On a lightly floured surface, roll out half the dough to an 11-inch round, about $1/8$ inch thick, and fit it into the prepared pie pan.

Roll out the remaining dough to a 10-inch round.

Spread the bacon over the dough in the pan; add the parsley, onion, and half of the cheese. Arrange half the tomato slices on top, and sprinkle with the salt, zest, and pepper. Break 5 of the eggs on top of the tomato slices, breaking each yolk with a knife so it runs. Top with the remaining cheese and tomato. With a brush moisten the edges of the pastry with cold water, and place the remaining pastry round on top. Using a fork, gently crimp the edges, sealing the dough.

In a small bowl, beat the remaining egg with the cream. Make 3 small slashes in the top of the pie and glaze with the egg mixture.

Transfer the pie to the grill over indirect heat and cook for 1 hour, or until nicely browned on top. Remove the pie from the grill, let stand for 10 minutes, then serve.

SERVES 6

WHOLE BARBECUED SNAPPER WITH GREEN CURRY SAUCE

Grilling a whole fish is really pretty easy. The skin acts to hold everything together, protecting the meat from the flame, keeping the flesh moist, and is then discarded. This recipe is from Neil Perry of the Rockpool Restaurant in Sydney. If you can't find kaffir lime leaves, you can leave them out. Use your favorite bottled Thai green curry sauce, and serve this with white rice. If you don't know how to clean a whole fish, have your fishmonger do it for you.

1   whole (1-pound) line-caught red snapper, cleaned, head and tail intact

2   tablespoons vegetable oil

1¼   cups Thai green curry sauce

4   kaffir lime leaves, crushed (optional)

2   green Thai or serrano chiles, split and deseeded

5   Thai or regular basil leaves

Napa cabbage leaves, blanched

Preheat a charcoal or gas grill to 375°F. Make sure the grill rack is clean and oil it thoroughly with nonstick cooking spray.

Make 3 slashes through the skin on each side of the fish and rub the vegetable oil into the skin.

Transfer the fish to the prepared grill rack and cook over direct heat for approximately 5 minutes on each side, until the flesh turns opaque and begins to brown on the edges. Remove from the grill, cover, and keep warm.

In a saucepan, slowly bring the green curry sauce to a simmer. Add the kaffir lime leaves, chiles, and basil and simmer for 5 to 7 minutes.

Line a platter with the cabbage leaves, top with the fish, and serve with the sauce alongside.

SERVES 4

PEPPER-ORANGE STANDING RIB ROAST

A standing rib roast comprises seven ribs starting from the shoulder (chuck) down the back to the loin. Each rib feeds about two people, so if you have a party of eight, buy a four-rib roast. It is given the name "standing" because it is most often roasted in a standing position, that is, with the ribs stacked vertically. Remove the bones, slice the meat into thick steaks, and you have rib-eyes. A chef in Adelaide introduced me to orange granules, and I was delighted by the strong orange flavor, even better than dried zests. In the U.S., they are available online.

- 1 ($8^1/_2$-pound) standing rib beef roast

  Extra-virgin olive oil

  Kosher salt
- 4 large cloves garlic, thinly sliced
- $3/_4$ cup ($1^1/_2$ sticks) unsalted butter, at room temperature
- 2 tablespoons freshly ground black pepper

  Pinch of cayenne pepper
- 3 tablespoons dried orange granules or dried orange zest
- 1 tablespoon finely chopped fresh parsley
- $2^1/_4$ cups beef broth
- $1/_2$ cup dry red wine
- 2 tablespoons finely minced fresh orange zest, or dried orange granules

  Sprigs of parsley or cilantro, for garnish

Place the roast, fat-side up, in a large roasting pan and brush the exposed ends of the meat with olive oil; sprinkle all over with salt. Using a sharp knife, make small cuts in the meat and insert garlic slices into the cuts.

In a small bowl, combine 1 stick of the butter with the black pepper, cayenne, 2 teaspoons of salt, orange granules, and parsley. Cover and refrigerate half the butter mixture. Spread the remaining butter over the fat side of the roast. Cover and refrigerate for 12 to 24 hours.

Prepare a charcoal or gas grill for indirect grilling (it is not nec-essary to use a drip pan with this recipe). Preheat to 350°F.

Transfer the roast, in the roasting pan, to the barbecue and cook over indirect heat until the internal temperature at the thickest part of the meat reaches 125° to 130°F for medium-rare, about $2^1/_2$ hours.

Transfer the roast to a heated platter, cover it loosely with foil, and let stand for 20 minutes.

Strain the pan juices into a small bowl and skim off the fat. Pour the pan juices back into the roasting pan and transfer to the grill or to the stove top. While stirring, add the broth and the wine and bring to a boil over high heat, scraping up any browned bits that have stuck to the pan and cooking until the liquid is reduced by half. Remove from the heat, pour into a saucepan, and whisk in the reserved butter mixture, orange zest, and remaining butter.

Slice the prime rib and serve on a heated platter with the sauce on the side. Garnish the platter with the parsley.

SERVES 8

AUSSIE CARPETBAG STEAK

Many attribute this unique steak preparation to Australia, where it is very popular among local chefs. However, it was probably "invented" in the United States by Frenchman Louis Diat in his 1941 cookbook Cooking à la Ritz. *Serve the steak with mashed potatoes and grilled red and yellow bell peppers. If you wish, you can use chervil vinegar instead of the apple cider variety in the béarnaise sauce, and grate in some fresh nutmeg.*

- 1 tablespoon Worcestershire sauce
- 2 teaspoons prepared mustard
- 1 tablespoon freshly squeezed lemon juice
- 16 small raw oysters, shucked
- 4 (1/2-pound) rib-eye fillets, 1 1/2 to 2 inches thick
- 8 slices smoked bacon
  Salt
  Freshly ground black pepper
- 1 cup Béarnaise Sauce (recipe follows)
- 1 tablespoon chopped fresh parsley, for garnish

In a bowl, combine the Worcestershire, mustard, and lemon juice. Add the oysters and gently stir to coat. Let stand for 30 minutes.

Preheat a charcoal or gas grill to 400°F. Make sure the grill rack is clean and oil it thoroughly with nonstick cooking spray.

Insert a very sharp knife into the side of each steak, cutting into the meat to form a pocket three-quarters of the way through the steak.

Stuff 4 oysters and 1 tablespoon of the oyster marinade into each of the steaks. Wrap each steak with 2 pieces of the bacon and secure the opening with toothpicks. Season with salt and pepper.

Transfer the meat to the grill and cook over direct heat for 4 to 5 minutes per side for medium-rare, or until the internal temperature reaches 145°F.

Serve immediately topped with béarnaise sauce.

SERVES 4

THIRTY-SECOND BÉARNAISE SAUCE

- 1 tablespoon cider vinegar
- 2 tablespoons finely chopped fresh tarragon
- 3 egg yolks
  Juice of 1 lemon
  Pinch of cayenne pepper
- 1 cup (2 sticks) butter, melted

In a small saucepan, bring the vinegar and tarragon to a boil, remove from the heat and let stand for 5 minutes to steep.

In a food processor, combine the egg yolks, lemon juice, cayenne, and the vinegar mixture. Process for 30 seconds at high speed while slowly adding the butter through the feed tube.

If the sauce gets too thick and begins to clump, add 1 tablespoon of water at a time, scraping down sides between additions, until it is smooth and clings to the back of a spoon.

MAKES ABOUT 1 1/4 CUPS

BLACK PEPPER EMU STEAKS

Emu is a red meat, almost beefy, but lower in fat and cholesterol. If you don't have emus in your backyard, there are several places on the Internet to get steaks, ribs, roasts, and fillets.

- $1/2$ cup cracked black pepper (see Note)
- $1/4$ cup olive oil
- 4 (4- to 6-ounce) emu or ostrich steaks (sometimes called flat fillets)
- $1/2$ teaspoon flaked or kosher salt
- $1/2$ cup plus 2 tablespoons Cognac
- 1 cup heavy cream

Spread the peppercorns on a flat plate or work surface. Lightly coat both sides of the steaks with olive oil. Press the emu steaks into the peppercorns and sprinkle with $1/4$ teaspoon of the salt.

Preheat a charcoal or gas grill to 375°F. Make sure the grill rack is clean and oil it thoroughly with nonstick cooking spray. Place a large cast-iron skillet over medium heat on a side burner of your grill or on the stove top to heat.

Transfer the steaks to the grill and cook over direct heat until the internal temperature reaches 145°F for medium-rare, 2 to 3 minutes per side.

Transfer the steaks to the hot cast-iron skillet, placing the skillet on the hottest part of the grill or on the side burner over high heat. Add $1/4$ cup of the Cognac and cook until reduced by about half.

Transfer the steaks to a serving platter, sprinkle with 2 tablespoons of the Cognac, cover, and keep warm,

Add the cream to the skillet and cook, stirring, over high heat until the cream boils and thickens; remove from heat and add the remaining $1/4$ cup Cognac and the remaining $1/4$ teaspoon salt, stirring to combine.

Spoon the sauce over the steaks and serve.

SERVES 4

NOTE: If you only have whole peppercorns and don't have a mortar and pestle, place peppercorns in a resealable plastic bag, place the bag on a hard surface and gently tap on the peppercorns with a hammer. Remember you're not trying to powder them, just crush them.

CORNFLAKE POTATOES

A close friend in Melbourne cooked these for us on his backyard barbie, using Kellogg's brand cornflakes, manufactured right in Melbourne, not in the U.S. in my hometown of Battle Creek, Michigan. You can very happily use this technique on fish fillets or fish steaks as well: try baking or barbecuing salmon, halibut, or even mahi mahi in a cast-iron skillet using this recipe.

- 1 (1-pound) bag frozen hash browns
- 1 (8-ounce) container sour cream
- $1 1/2$ teaspoons cumin
- 1 can condensed cream of mushroom, cream of chicken, or cream of celery soup
- 1 tablespoon dried onion soup mix
- 2 cups shredded Cheddar cheese
- $1/4$ cup butter, melted
- $1 1/2$ to 2 cups cornflakes, lightly crushed

Prepare a charcoal or gas grill for indirect grilling (it is not necessary to use a drip pan with this recipe). Preheat to 350°F. Grease a 12-inch cast-iron skillet.

Combine the hash browns, sour cream, cumin, cream of mushroom soup, onion soup mix, and cheese, and transfer to the prepared cast-iron skillet.

In a small bowl, pour the melted butter over the cornflakes; sprinkle the corn flake mixture on top of the hash-brown mixture. Transfer the skillet to the barbecue over indirect heat, close the grill lid, and cook for about 1 hour, or until the potatoes are browned on the edges.

SERVES 4 TO 6

GRILLED PAVLOVA WITH THREE-BERRY COMPOTE

Probably no other dish in the Southern Hemisphere has inspired such a culinary controversy as to its origin, as both New Zealand and Australia claim ownership. The ballerina Anna Pavlova had toured both countries in 1926. Subsequent to her visit, Chef Davis Gelatine of New Zealand published a recipe in 1927. A similar but slightly different recipe was published in 1935 by Chef Bert Sachse of the Esplanade Hotel in Perth. This is a luscious dessert, whatever its birthplace. Meringues can be stored, uncovered, at room temperature for up to 8 hours, while the compote can be stored in an airtight container in the fridge for up to 1 day.

- 6 egg whites
- 1 1/2 cups granulated sugar
- 2 tablespoons white vinegar
- 1 teaspoon vanilla extract or favorite liqueur
- 1/4 teaspoon cream of tartar
- 2 tablespoons cornstarch
- 3 cups fresh raspberries
- 1 tablespoon confectioners' sugar
- 2 cups strawberries, hulled and quartered
- 2 cups fresh blueberries
  Whipped cream
  Fresh mint, for garnish
- 2 kiwifruits, peeled and thinly sliced, for garnish

Prepare a charcoal or gas grill for indirect grilling (it is not necessary to use a drip pan with this recipe). Preheat to 275°F. Line 2 large baking sheets with parchment paper.

In a large bowl, beat the egg whites until they form soft peaks. Gradually beat in the sugar, 1/2 cup at a time, until the egg whites are stiff and glossy. Beat in the vinegar, vanilla, and cream of tartar. Using a fine mesh sieve, shake the cornstarch over the top and, with a spatula, fold into the egg whites.

On the prepared baking sheets, form the meringue into 8 ovals about 3 1/2 inches long by 2 1/2 inches wide. Transfer the baking sheets to the barbecue and grill over indirect heat for 50 to 60 minutes, until the meringues are crisp outside but still soft inside. Remove from the grill and let cool to the touch.

In a food processor or blender, puree 1 cup of the raspberries, then press the liquid through a sieve into a saucepan. Stir in the sugar and cook the mixture over low heat until just heated though, then stir in the strawberries, the blueberries, and the remaining raspberries, mixing well. Let cool.

To serve, spoon 2 to 3 tablespoons of the compote onto each plate, then top with a meringue. Serve with freshly whipped cream, slices of kiwifruit, and fresh mint leaves.

SERVES 8

BRAZIL

Protein, Passion, and the Passador

It was both a nightmare and the most fantastic dream I've ever had.

They came gliding up to the table, each one armed with a long, sharp sword. On each sword were impaled hearts or kidneys, livers, spleens, intestines, tongues, ribs, loins, necks, heels, knuckles, or slabs of shoulder.

They approached my table, swords held high, razor-sharp knives at the ready, slashing and spearing pink-tinged meat onto my plate, then moving off at a run. Seconds later more swords flashed through the dim light, and more flesh was sliced off and plopped in front of me. An endless stream of nattily dressed warriors

appeared and retreated in rapid succession, like the relentless parade of brooms in *The Sorcerer's Apprentice*, until my plate was piled high with smoky charred meat.

When I could barely see across the table, I begged waiters to stop, but they kept coming in an endless procession.

Then I spotted a magic disk on the table—one side bright green, the other ruby red with "*Aguarde*" and "Hold On" inscribed in large black letters in the center. Desperately I waved it at the approaching phalanx, finally sticking the disk to my forehead as I pleaded with the legion of sword-carriers to show mercy. Magically they began to slow, then turned en masse and glided away from the table. I closed my eyes to rid myself of the nightmare, only to jolt awake. My nightmare was over.

But wait a minute, I *was* in a restaurant, and there *was* a huge pile of meat on a plate in front of me, and a cameraman was sitting across from me filming all the while. It wasn't a dream. It was lunch.

A Brazilian-style lunch at a *churrascaria*, that is. A place where you can literally eat all day, as long as you don't wave the red disk (or white flag). And, incidentally, a style of restaurant that has begun to appear around the U.S.—heaven for carnivores, a lower, hotter, unfriendlier place for vegetarians.

I was at Na Braza, an upscale restaurant in the center of Porto Alegre, the bustling capital of the state of Rio Grande de Sul and a city that sets itself apart from São Paulo and Rio and Brasilia. It's its own kind of place—to heck with the rest of the country. Known for its rugged individualism, the city is like its native gauchos, and as close to a frontier town as a modern South American city of one and a half million can be.

The word *churrascaria* comes from the Portuguese word for barbecue (*churrasco*), and these restaurants feature fiery rotisseries, spinning merrily along, grilling up beef and just about anything else that makes up a cow, as well as pork, chicken, vegetables, even fruits. The method of serving, however, is what sets the Brazilian *churrascaria* apart from any other dining experience. *Passadores* (meat waiters) carrying *rodizios* (long rotisserie skewers) go to each table laden with barbecue that's carved tableside. The secret is to know when to call a halt to the proceedings. If you don't signal, they keep coming.

Most *churrascarias* also offer a wide assortment of salads, side dishes, and other delicacies. At Na Braza, pickled onions, beets, and quail eggs were served buffet-style, surrounded by more than a dozen varieties of sliced fresh fruit, grilled eggplant, thinly sliced and deliciously vinegar-marinated cucumbers, smoked sun-dried tomatoes, four or five kinds of lettuce, chilled white asparagus, grilled red and green peppers, garbanzo bean salad, potato salad, coleslaw, marinated artichoke hearts, lovely juicy sliced tomatoes layered with mozzarella, green bean salad, corn relish, pea and carrot salad, and fresh spinach leaves—you get the picture.

But it's the meat, especially the wondrously tender beef, that is the star of the show here. In addition to the more unusual (to us, anyway) cuts, there were mouth-watering sirloin and rump steaks (the most-favored of all Brazilian cuts), pink-centered rib-eye roasts, strip loins, succulent tri-tip, meaty beef ribs, tenderloin, sausages, even ground beef (our favorite, a ground meat deliciously sprinkled with pine nuts). Brazil produces about 7 million metric tons of beef each year from a total population of 165 million head. And, like other South American beef, Brazilian cows almost never see a North American–style feedlot: 96 percent are grown to finish under a hormone-free regime on grass pastures.

The red *Aguarde* (Hold On) disk still stuck to my forehead, I trembled in fear as a lone waiter approached, a huge menu tucked under his arm, a conspiratorial and determined look on his face. I laughingly pointed to the disk, and he responded with a chuckle of his own.

"Señor, this is the dessert menu!"

The disk came off.

LITTLE BEEF BARBECUES

Brazilians have the fourth highest consumption of beef, per capita, of any country on earth—behind Argentina, the U.S., and New Zealand. So this appetizer, served with cold beer, is right up their alley. These "little beefs," as opposed to the rather large steaks and portions of beef served at churrascarias in Brazil, was suggested by a cook at the Porcão restaurant in Recife when my wife asked for a smaller portion.

1	pound beef tenderloin
2	tablespoons olive oil
2	tablespoons freshly squeezed lemon juice
1	tablespoon minced parsley
1	tablespoon minced onion
	Salt
	Freshly ground black pepper
$^1/_2$	pound bacon

Cut the beef tenderloin into 1-inch slices, then into cubes about 1 inch square. Place the beef in a large resealable plastic bag, then add the olive oil, lemon juice, parsley, and onion, and season with salt and pepper. Seal the bag, pressing out any air. Let stand in the refrigerator for at least 4 and no more than 12 hours.

Preheat a charcoal or gas grill to 375°F. Make sure the grill rack is clean and oil it thoroughly with nonstick cooking spray.

Cut the bacon slices in half crosswise, and wrap each piece of beef with a half-slice of the bacon. Thread the meat onto steel skewers, spacing them $^1/_2$ inch apart.

Transfer the skewers to the barbecue and cook, turning often, for 3 to 5 minutes, until browned on all sides.

SERVES 4 TO 6 AS AN APPETIZER

CITRUS SALMON FILLETS

This recipe was inspired by my visit to the Grilled Dourado Festival at Iguaçu Falls, one of the most spectacular sights in South America (the falls, that is, not the festival). Dourado is very similar to our salmon, so I'm substituting it here. You can also substitute whole trout, either the lake or ocean variety, if salmon isn't your cup of tea (er, fish). This is a wonderfully easy dish to prepare and can be served with roasted potatoes and fresh asparagus or Brussels sprouts.

4	(5- to 6-ounce) salmon fillets, with skin
	Zest and juice from 1 large lemon
	Salt
	Freshly ground black pepper
	Zest and juice from $^1/_2$ large orange
2	tablespoons brown sugar
1	tablespoon chili powder
1	large clove garlic, finely minced
1	teaspoon finely chopped parsley
2	tablespoons butter, melted

In a shallow dish large enough to hold the salmon, combine the orange and lemon juices, season with salt and pepper, then add the salmon, turning to coat. Let stand at room temperature for 30 minutes, turning the fillets once or twice.

Preheat a charcoal or gas grill to 425°F. Cover the grill rack with a large piece of heavy-duty aluminum foil and spray well with nonstick cooking spray.

In a small bowl, combine the orange and lemon zest, brown sugar, chili powder, and garlic. Rub the mixture onto the skinless side, or top, of each of the salmon fillets.

Add the parsley to the melted butter. Transfer the fish to the prepared grill rack and drizzle the butter mixture over the fish. Cook for 9 to 12 minutes, until just medium-rare. When the fillets have become translucent, the edges are beginning to brown, and the fish flakes easily, it is done.

SERVES 4

ROAST LOIN OF PORK WITH FAROFA

Manioc, which also goes by the name "cassava" or "tapioca plant," is native to the Amazon River basin of Brazil, and was one of the first cultivated plants in the Western Hemisphere. Farofa, or toasted manioc flour, is Brazil's quintessential side dish and can be found at virtually every meal, including breakfast. You can get manioc flour (also known as tapioca flour) in natural foods stores and online. It is sweet and mild, and acquires a nutty taste when you toast it.

- 1 (4- to 5-pound) boneless pork loin
  Juice of 2 limes
  Salt
- 1 large onion, cut into thin slices
- 5 tablespoons vegetable oil
- 4 tablespoons chopped green onions (green and white parts)
- 4 tablespoons chopped parsley
- 3 tablespoons butter, softened
- 4 cups milk, warm
- 2 cups manioc flour
- 1/4 to 1/3 cup water
- 1 large onion, grated
- 2 tomatoes, peeled, seeded, and chopped
- 1 hard-boiled egg, chopped
- 1/4 cup raisins
- 1/4 cup chopped prunes
- 1/4 cup walnuts, coarsely chopped
  Parsley sprigs, for garnish

The day before roasting, cut several shallow slashes in the top of the loin. Squeeze the lime juice over the meat and season it with salt. Place the meat in a resealable plastic bag with the sliced onion, 4 tablespoons of the oil, half of the green onions, and half of the chopped parsley. Seal the bag and refrigerate for 8 to 12 hours.

Prepare a charcoal or gas grill for indirect grilling and preheat to 350°F. Make sure the grill rack is clean and oil it thoroughly with nonstick cooking spray.

Remove the meat from the bag, wipe off the marinade and rub 2 tablespoons of the butter on all its surfaces. Transfer the meat to the prepared grill rack over direct heat, and brown on all sides until nicely marked, about 4 to 6 minutes per side.

Place a Dutch oven on the cool side of the grill. Add the meat and the milk, cover the pot, and continue cooking for 1 to 1 1/2 hours until the meat reaches an internal temperature of 160°F. Let the pork rest for 5 minutes before slicing.

To prepare the farofa, place the manioc flour in a bowl, stir in enough water to evenly moisten the flour. Heat the remaining 1 tablespoon of butter and the remaining 1 tablespoon of the oil in a large saucepan over medium heat. When the butter is melted, add the grated onion and the tomatoes, sautéing until the onion is translucent, about 3 minutes.

Add the moistened manioc to the pan and stir to incorporate, then cook for 3 to 4 minutes. Remove the pan from the heat and stir in the remaining parsley and green onions, and the egg, raisins, prunes, and walnuts.

Slice the pork and serve it on a warm platter with the farofa on the side, garnished with parsley sprigs.

SERVES 8 TO 10

CHURRASCARIA MARINATED STEAKS WITH CHILE-LIME SAUCE

The grills used by churrascaria restaurants in Brazil vary from eight-foot-tall stainless rotisserie racks over gas flames, to huge concrete pits where the meat is suspended over charcoal on steel rods, to pits simply dug in the earth, framed by wooden logs, where the meat is on wooden skewers placed across the logs.

- 5 jalapeño peppers, stemmed, seeded, and chopped
- 2 teaspoons kosher or flake salt
- 2 white onions, chopped
- 12 cloves garlic, chopped
- 4 ($^1/_2$-pound) sirloin steaks, $1^1/_2$ inches thick
- $^1/_2$ cup freshly squeezed lime juice (about 3 limes)
- $^1/_3$ cup dry red wine
- 2 teaspoons dried oregano
- 1 bay leaf
- 1 teaspoon freshly ground black pepper
- 1 cup loosely packed coarsely chopped Italian parsley

Combine the jalapeños, 1 teaspoon of the salt, half the onions, and one-third of the garlic in a blender or food processor, and process until a paste is formed. You'll have about $^1/_2$ cup. Refrigerate until ready to use.

Place the steaks in a large baking dish. Mince the remaining onion and garlic. In a bowl, whisk together the lime juice, wine, minced onion and garlic, oregano, bay leaf, remaining 1 teaspoon salt, and the pepper. Pour the marinade over the steaks, turning to coat each steak evenly. Cover and refrigerate, turning every couple of hours, for 4 to 6 hours.

Preheat a charcoal or gas grill to 450°F. Make sure the grill rack is clean and oil it thoroughly with nonstick cooking spray.

Remove the jalapeno-onion-garlic sauce from the refrigerator and set aside to bring to room temperature.

Remove the steaks from the marinade and wipe off the excess. Transfer the steaks to the grill over direct heat, and cook for 5 to 6 minutes per side, to an internal temperature of 145°F for medium-rare.

Remove the steaks and place on a heated platter, cover with foil, let stand for 5 minutes. Serve with the sauce.

SERVES 4

SÃO PAULO CURRIED BANANAS

This dish has a delightful roasted banana flavor that is wonderfully accented by the curry. You can substitute plantains, which are starchier, firmer, and less sweet than bananas, and thought by many to be richer in flavor and more easily digested. You can use either green or black plantains, but I prefer the more intense flavor of the black ones. Serve this dish over rice with barbecued pork or beef.

$1/2$	cup (1 stick) butter
2	tablespoons curry powder
8	green (unripe) bananas, peeled and sliced $1/2$-inch thick
1	teaspoon hot sauce
1	cup coconut milk
1	tablespoon brown sugar
	Salt
	Freshly ground black pepper
1	egg, lightly beaten
	Steamed rice

In a large saucepan, melt the butter over medium-high heat. Add the curry and cook for 2 minutes, stirring constantly.

Add the bananas to the pan, cooking over medium-high heat for 3 to 4 minutes, until the bananas start to brown. Add the hot sauce, coconut milk, and brown sugar, and season with salt and pepper. Decrease the heat to low and simmer, stirring often, for 30 minutes. Stir in the egg, cooking for 3 minutes longer, stirring often, until the egg is cooked and incorporated into the mixture. Serve over rice.

SERVES 4 TO 6

COCONUT CUPCAKES

Coconut cupcakes are a very popular sweet in Brazil—I saw them in restaurants and bakeries and even at roadside stands. You can find unsweetened coconut in most Asian markets, but this dessert calls for the sweet packaged variety as well—which is as close as the baking aisle of your supermarket. I like using the unsweetened variety on top for a bit of a tang, and the sugar sprinkled on is sweet enough.

$1/4$	cup ($1/2$ stick) butter, softened
$1^1/2$	cups sugar
1	teaspoon orange zest
$1/2$	teaspoon ground cinnamon
$1/4$	teaspoon ground cloves
8	egg yolks
2	egg whites
1	cup all-purpose flour
1	cup sweetened flaked coconut
$1/4$	cup butter, melted
$1/4$	cup unsweetened flaked coconut

Prepare a charcoal or gas grill for indirect grilling and preheat to 375°F.

Whip the egg whites until they triple in volume and are frothy. Set aside. In a large bowl, combine the butter, 1 cup of the sugar, orange zest, cinnamon, and cloves, and beat until light and fluffy. Beat in the egg yolks 1 at a time, until smooth. Fold in the egg whites, gently stirring until the batter is smooth.

Add the flour, $1/2$ cup at a time, and stir until fully incorporated. Add the 1 cup of sweetened coconut and stir to incorporate. Liberally spray the cups of a muffin pan with nonstick cooking spray. Fill each cup of the pan halfway.

Place the muffin pan into a large baking pan, adding boiling water to reach halfway up the sides of the muffin pan.

Transfer the pan to the unheated side of the grill and cook for about 40 minutes, or until the cupcakes are slightly brown on top.

Remove the pan from the heat. Brush the hot cupcake tops with butter and immediately sprinkle over the remaining $1/2$ cup of sugar and the unsweetened coconut. Transfer the cupcakes to a wire rack to cool.

MAKES 12 CUPCAKES

CANADA
O Canada, Eh?

Many Americans view their neighbor to the north as a sort of Upper United States, populated by people who say "zed" for the last letter of the alphabet, actually know what millimeters and kilometers are, and probably have a team of huskies in their backyards. Certainly these north-of-the-border folks must paddle around in birch-bark canoes, chew blubber, and cook beaver over a campfire, eh?

(A note on the "eh?": you will notice this tiny word used liberally throughout this text. Eh? Many Canadians—the author included when he's been there for more than a couple of days—end a surprising number of their sentences with this verbal question and/or declaration, eh? We guard this oral tradition and even jest about it among ourselves, but woe to those who disdain it. They're toast, eh?)

We Canadians started eating well very early when indigenous people brought forth foods from the plains, rivers, and forests. We roasted polar bear, boiled reindeer, heated up moose soup, fried beaver, charbroiled squirrel, and seared woodchuck. From the surrounding oceans and teeming rivers came whale roast, steamed muskrat haunches, staked-out salmon, roasted clams and oysters, and grilled trout, pike, and perch.

We hunted porcupine, caribou, buffalo, ptarmigan, quail, grouse, black and brown bear, deer, caribou, elk, antelope, wildcat, cougar, and rabbit. And we fished the Maritimes amid huge schools of cod, shallows filled with lobsters, and crab pots almost too heavy to hoist, eh? The oceans and rivers freely gave up a bounty of lobster, oysters, shrimp, river eel, lake trout, lotte (monkey fish), mussels, and even salmon roe, along with the rest of the fish, eh?

As farming spread across the prairies, game was no longer commercially hunted, at least for public consumption, and was replaced by Alberta beef, farmed buffalo, venison, and reindeer, pheasants, partridge, and quail, grouse, and, of course, good old domesticated poultry.

While the style of Canadian barbecue seems virtually a mirror-image of American barbecue, I would argue the American style is actually a mirror of Canada's. Why? Because Canadians grill up a lot more game (rabbit, venison, pheasant, as examples) than their U.S. counterparts. I think Canadians grill more vegetables as well, with carrots, onions, cabbage, zucchini and summer squash, asparagus,

and root vegetables like turnips, parsnips, and salsify turning up at local barbecues. Ever seen salsify on the grill, eh? It's beauty.

Canadian barbecuers have organized themselves (into the Canadian Barbecue Association) and have done very well at some of the most prestigious American contests like Memphis in May, Jack Daniels, and the American Royal. They even host some fantastic barbecue contests in major cities (Vancouver, Calgary, Toronto, and Ottawa) and smaller ones (Barrie, Paris, and Whistler) alike.

So Canadian barbecue isn't that different from U.S. barbecue in terms of grilling technique—it's more about the diversity in what we grill. With a small population (at press time, 3 million less than the population of California alone) and vast natural resources, we just have more good stuff to go around.

But don't despair, America. You still have better comedians, eh? Oh wait, you don't. . . . Er, better beer? No, not that either. Hmmm, give me a minute. I'll think of something, eh?

(In the interest of full disclosure, author Rick Browne was born and raised in Brantford, Ontario, and lived in Toronto, then Montreal, Quebec, before coming to the U.S.)

CANADIAN BACON ROAST WITH A PECAN-WALNUT CRUST

A Canadian bacon roast is nothing like bacon; it's from the rib-eye of the pork loin, is amazingly moist and tender, and is as good a barbecue meat as you can get. Because there's no fat on it, you must be careful not to overcook it. I'm using the roast here as an appetizer, but it makes a wonderful main course with roasted buttered potatoes, green beans with mushrooms, or freshly picked corn on the cob. It's also great sliced in sandwiches the next day.

- 2 teaspoons chopped fresh rosemary
- 1/4 teaspoon thyme
- 2 teaspoons minced garlic
- 1 teaspoon salt
- 1/2 teaspoon freshly ground black pepper
- 4 tablespoons olive oil, plus more to spray
- 3 tablespoons dark brown sugar
- 1 (4- to 5-pound) boneless Canadian bacon roast
- 1 cup (1 handful) wood chips
- 1/8 teaspoon ground cloves
- 1/4 pound pecan halves, chopped
- 1/4 pound walnut halves, chopped
- 1 cup chopped fresh mango
- 1/4 cup finely chopped red bell pepper
- 1 green onion, thinly sliced, white and green parts
- 2 tablespoons freshly squeezed lime juice
- 1/2 jalapeño pepper, seeded and minced
- 1 tablespoon chopped fresh cilantro or basil

For the rub, combine rosemary, thyme, garlic, salt, pepper, 1 tablespoon of the olive oil, and the brown sugar in a food processor and pulse until you have a thick paste. Rub the paste into the pork roast, covering it completely, then wrap the meat tightly with plastic wrap and refrigerate for 2 to 4 hours.

Place the wood chips in a bowl or can, cover with water, and soak for at least 2 hours.

For the nut crust, in a shallow dish large enough to hold the pork loin, mix together the cloves, pecans, and walnuts and set aside.

For the salsa, in a large bowl combine the mango, bell pepper, green onion, lime juice, jalapeño, and cilantro, blending the ingredients well. Store in the refrigerator in a covered bowl or container until ready to serve, but no longer than 3 days.

Prepare a charcoal or gas grill for indirect grilling, placing a drip pan under the cool side of the grill rack (see page 3). Preheat to 250°F. (You can also use a water smoker; if doing so, follow manufacturer's directions.) Spray a roasting pan with nonstick cooking spray.

Mist the pork roast with olive oil from a sprayer, being careful not to disturb the marinating paste. Roll the pork in the nut mixture, using your fingers to gently press the nuts into the surface of the meat. Then put the meat into the prepared roasting pan.

Put a handful of soaked wood chips on a piece of heavy-duty aluminum foil and fold it over like an envelope to enclose the wood. Using a pencil, poke 3 or 4 holes in the top of the foil envelope (don't poke all the way through). Place the foil directly on the coals or gas jets and when the wood inside starts to smoke, transfer the roast to the grill, placing it on the cool side above the drip pan. Cover the grill and cook, adding briquettes to the fire and water to the drip pan as needed. The meat is done when the internal temperature reaches 155°F, about 2 to 2 1/2 hours. Transfer the meat to a large platter or cutting board, and let the roast rest, covered with foil, for 15 minutes.

Cut the roast into bite-sized pieces, garnish each piece with a spoonful of salsa, and serve as an appetizer.

SERVES 6 TO 8 AS AN APPETIZER, WITH LEFTOVERS

SMOKE-GRILLED LIME SALMON

Some of the best salmon on earth come from the cold waters off the eastern and western coasts of Canada. When buying salmon at the market, make sure the eyes are bright, clear, almost alive; the gills reddish, and the skin moist with shiny, tightly adhered scales. Fresh salmon will give slightly when you press it with a finger, then spring back into shape.

- 1 cup (1 handful) wood chips
- 1 teaspoon grated lime zest
- 1/4 cup freshly squeezed lime juice
- 1 tablespoon vegetable oil
- 1 teaspoon Dijon mustard
- 1/2 teaspoon salt
- 1/2 teaspoon pepper
- 1 teaspoon brown sugar
- 4 (1/2-pound) salmon steaks, 1 inch thick
- 1/3 cup toasted sesame seeds
- 1 lime cut in 1/8-inch slices, for garnish
- Chopped parsley, for garnish

Place the wood chips in a bowl or can, cover with water, and soak for at least 2 hours.

In a shallow dish, combine the lime zest, juice, oil, mustard, salt, pepper, and sugar, then add the fish, turning to coat both sides. Cover and marinate the fish at room temperature for 1 hour, turning occasionally.

Remove the fish steaks from the marinade, drain, and sprinkle with sesame seeds, reserving the marinade. Pour the marinade into a saucepan and bring it to a boil for 5 minutes.

Preheat a charcoal or gas grill to 375°F. Make sure the grill rack is clean and oil it thoroughly with nonstick cooking spray.

Put a handful of soaked wood chips on a piece of heavy-duty aluminum foil and fold it over like an envelope to enclose the wood. Using a pencil, poke 3 or 4 holes in the top of the foil envelope (don't poke all the way through). Place the foil directly on the coals or gas jets and when the wood inside starts to smoke, place the salmon steaks on the prepared grill rack over direct heat. Cover and cook, turning the steaks and basting them with the boiled marinade 2 to 3 times, for 16 to 20 minutes, until the fish begins to flake when tested with a fork. Transfer the steaks to a heated platter, garnish with lime and parsley, and serve.

SERVES 4

GROUSE WITH APRICOT SAUCE

You can substitute Cornish hens or pheasant, but nothing tastes quite like grouse. The best source would be a friend who hunts grouse and will share his harvest with you. Serve this dish with wild rice and grilled glazed carrots.

- 1   (6-ounce) box cornbread stuffing mix
- 1½   cups hot tap water
- ¼   cup plus 2 tablespoons butter
- 2   (2- to 3-pound) ruffed grouse, cleaned and plucked, thawed if frozen
- 2   tablespoons olive oil
- 1   teaspoon salt
- 1   cup apricot jelly
- ¼   cup freshly squeezed apricot juice (or nectar)
- 2   teaspoons freshly squeezed lemon juice
- ¼   teaspoon ground allspice
    Freshly ground black pepper

Prepare a charcoal or gas grill for indirect grilling, placing a drip pan under the cool side of the grill rack (see page 3). Preheat the grill to 225°F. Make sure the grill rack is clean and oil it thoroughly with nonstick cooking spray.

In a bowl, combine the stuffing mix with any seasoning packet from the box, the water, and ¼ cup of the butter. Loosely pack the stuffing into the birds' cavities. Brush the birds' skin with the olive oil and sprinkle with ½ teaspoon of the salt.

In a small saucepan, combine the jelly, apricot juice, the remaining 2 tablespoons of butter, lemon juice, allspice, and the remaining ½ teaspoon of salt. Cook over low heat, stirring, until the jelly is melted, about 5 to 6 minutes. Set aside ⅔ cup for the sauce. Use the rest for basting.

Transfer the grouse to the prepared grill rack over indirect heat (you may wish to use a roasting pan, but I prefer direct roasting because it gets more grilling flavor into the birds). Brush some of the apricot basting mixture onto the grouse. Cover the grill and cook for 1½ to 2 hours, replenishing briquettes and refilling the water-filled drip pan as necessary, until the grouse are browned all over and the liquid from a fork stuck in the thigh runs clear. Internal temperature should be 160°F in the breast.

Serve the grouse whole or cut in half with kitchen shears, spooning some of the reserved sauce over the birds.

SERVES 2 TO 4

GRILL-ROASTED VENISON LOIN WITH ROSEMARY AND DRIED CHERRIES

Tart cherries like Montmorency and Morello are seldom sold fresh in your local grocery store—you would need to find a farmers' market at just the right time of year to purchase them fresh. They can be found frozen, canned, or dried for use throughout the year. The loin or backstrap of a deer is very much like filet mignon, or beef tenderloin. Allow 4 to 5 ounces of meat per serving. Since venison is so lean, you will be surprised by how little it takes to fill you up.

$1^1/_2$ teaspoons chopped fresh rosemary

1 large clove garlic

$^1/_2$ teaspoon salt

$1^1/_2$ teaspoons extra-virgin olive oil

1 (2-pound) boneless venison loin

Salt

Freshly ground black pepper

$^1/_2$ cup dry red wine

$^1/_2$ cup dried tart cherries

$^1/_2$ cup beef broth

$^1/_2$ cup water

1 teaspoon cornstarch

2 tablespoons black currant jelly

With a mortar and pestle, combine 1 teaspoon of the rosemary, the garlic, and salt, grinding until you have a paste; stir in $^1/_2$ teaspoon of the oil.

Pat the venison dry and transfer it to a shallow roasting pan; rub with the remaining olive oil, then the paste. Season well with salt and pepper, cover, and chill for 20 minutes.

Prepare a charcoal or gas grill for indirect grilling, placing a drip pan under the cool side of the grill rack (see page 3). Preheat to 375°F. Make sure the grill rack is clean and oil it thoroughly with nonstick cooking spray.

Let the venison come to room temperature. Transfer the meat to the prepared grill rack and grill over direct heat, turning once, about 10 minutes total. Move the meat to the indirect side of the grill, and cook for 20 to 25 minutes longer, until the internal temperature at the center registers 135°F for medium-rare. Transfer the meat to a plate and cover it tightly with foil,

then let it rest for 10 minutes before serving.

Combine the wine and cherries in a large skillet and boil over medium-high heat, stirring continuously. Combine the broth, water, cornstarch, and the remaining $^1/_2$ teaspoon of rosemary in a bowl and add to the skillet. Simmer, stirring, until thickened, about 5 minutes. Whisk in the jelly and season with salt and pepper to taste.

Cut the venison against the grain into $^1/_4$-inch-thick slices and serve with the sauce.

SERVES 4 TO 6

NOTE: If you prefer moist, juicy meat without pink centers, simply grill the venison loin to medium-rare, then place it in a 200°F oven for 5 to 15 minutes, depending on the thickness of the cut. Internal temperature should be about 135°F for medium-rare, or 140°F for medium.

GRILLED VEGETABLES WITH CREAMY SAUCE

I first tried this dish at my grandmother's home in Gravenhurst, Ontario (always loved that name, though as a child I called it Gravyhurst). Her garden provided just about every vegetable that they ate. She grilled these on a flat-top grill on her woodstove (yes, it was a while ago), so I moved them to the modern equivalent of the woodstove: the barbecue grill.

4	carrots
2	zucchini
2	tablespoons extra-virgin olive oil
2	tablespoons mayonnaise
2	tablespoons sour cream
1	clove garlic, minced
1	teaspoon dried savory
$^1/_2$	teaspoon grated lemon zest
	Juice of 1 lemon
$^1/_4$	teaspoon salt
$^1/_4$	teaspoon pepper
	Dash of hot sauce
2	tablespoons sliced toasted almonds, for garnish
1	tablespoon chopped fresh parsley, for garnish

Scrub the carrots and cut into 2- by $2^1/_2$-inch pieces. Slice the zucchini diagonally into $^1/_2$-inch-thick slices. In a large bowl, toss the vegetables with the olive oil until well coated.

Preheat a charcoal or gas grill to 375°F. Make sure the grill rack is clean and oil it thoroughly with nonstick cooking spray.

Place the vegetables on the prepared grill rack over direct heat. Grill for 4 to 6 minutes for the zucchini, 8 to 10 minutes for the carrots, until brown and tender, turning often. Watch the carrots, as their natural sugars cause them to burn easily.

In a large bowl, combine the mayonnaise, sour cream, garlic, savory, lemon zest and juice, salt, pepper, and hot sauce, and stir until completely mixed. Add the cooked vegetables to the mayonnaise mixture, tossing well to coat.

Spoon the grilled vegetables onto a warmed serving platter and sprinkle with the toasted almonds and parsley.

SERVES 4 TO 6

ASPARAGUS WITH APPLE VINAIGRETTE

In addition to being delicious, asparagus is a virtual health-food dream. It's high in folic acid, is a good source of potassium, fiber, vitamin B_6, vitamins A, and C, and thiamin, has no fat, contains no cholesterol, and is low in sodium. This recipe is so good that we've used it several times as our whole dinner, especially when the new spring asparagus hits the market.

$^3/_4$	cup coarsely chopped apples (about 2 medium or 1 large), preferably Macintosh or Red Delicious, not peeled
1	cup water
1	tablespoon honey
$^1/_4$	cup red wine vinegar
1	clove garlic, minced
1	teaspoon Dijon mustard
1	tablespoon freshly squeezed lemon juice
$1^1/_2$	teaspoons brandy
	Olive oil
	Salt
	Freshly ground black pepper
$1^1/_2$	pounds asparagus, trimmed

Preheat a charcoal or gas grill to 375°F. Make sure the grill rack is clean and oil it thoroughly with nonstick cooking spray.

Combine the apples, water, and honey in a saucepan, bring to a boil, lower the heat, and simmer about 10 minutes, until the apple is tender but not mushy. Remove the pan from the heat and cool until just warm, then place the apple mixture in a food processor and puree.

Add the vinegar, garlic, mustard, lemon juice, and brandy to the apple puree and blend until combined, 1 to 2 minutes. With the motor running, add 2 tablespoons of the olive oil and blend until smooth, then season with salt and pepper.

Brush the asparagus with olive oil, place on the prepared grill rack, and grill over direct heat until the stalks are just becoming tender and nicely marked, about 3 to 4 minutes.

Arrange the stalks on individual serving plates and drizzle generously with the apple vinaigrette.

SERVES 4

MAPLE CREAM PIE

There are four distinct grades of maple syrup: Grade A light amber is very light, has a mild, delicate maple flavor, and is the best grade for making maple candy. Grade A medium amber is a bit darker, has a bit more maple flavor, and is the most popular grade of table syrup. Grade A dark amber is darker yet, with a stronger maple flavor. Grade B, sometimes called cooking syrup, is very dark, and many people use it for table syrup because of its strong maple flavor.

- 1/3 cup heavy cream
- 1/2 cup pure maple syrup
- 1 egg
- 1 tablespoon freshly squeezed lemon juice
- 1/4 teaspoon salt
- 1/3 cup firmly packed brown sugar
- 1/4 cup flour
- 1 (9-inch) piecrust, prebaked
  Whipped cream, to serve (see Note)

Prepare a gas or charcoal grill for indirect cooking (it is not necessary to use a drip pan with this recipe). Preheat to 350°F.

In a large bowl, whisk together the cream, maple syrup, egg, lemon juice, and salt until thoroughly combined.

In a smaller bowl, combine the sugar and flour, stirring well. Whisk the flour mixture into the cream mixture, making sure there are no lumps. Pour the filling into the baked piecrust.

Transfer the pie to a cookie sheet and place it on the grill over the indirect side, close the grill lid, and cook over indirect heat for 45 minutes, until the filling is almost set, the edges of the crust are golden brown, and the center of the pie is slightly golden. The center of the pie will rise and be somewhat loose, but this will set and firm up as the pie cools.

Remove the pie from the heat and let cool completely. Serve with generous dollops of whipped cream.

SERVES 4 TO 6

NOTE: To create the best topping, cream must be whipped when very cold. Refrigerate the mixing bowl and beaters prior to whipping, and consider filling a larger bowl with ice to serve as a base to keep the mixing bowl cold while whipping, particularly on hot days. Use heavy cream with a 30 to 40 percent butterfat content for best results.

ENGLAND

London and Manchester:
A Tale of Two Cities

It was the worst of times, but now it's the best of times.

The best of times for English cookery, that is, once deemed the worst cuisine on the planet by much of the culinary world. France's former president Jacques Chirac was once quoted as saying, "The only thing they [the British] have done for European agriculture is mad cow."

Aucun monsieur, c'est pas exact! Although pub food (toad in the hole, mushy peas, bangers, and fish and chips) is still thriving in the UK, most restaurant menus could easily stand apron-to-apron with any other cuisine. Even *la cuisine de France*!

My television crew and I visited two English cities on a mission to sample grilling and barbecue, so we hit the streets looking for telltale smoke and found quite a few happy surprises.

Our first stop was Manchester, settled by the Romans around AD 79, who liked it so much they stayed for the next three centuries. By the early 1300s, there was already a thriving textile trade and by 1600, imported cotton, mostly from American plantations, was fuelling Manchester's growth. By the nineteenth century, Manchester had become one of the world's great industrial cities.

Today, after many troubled decades, it has been rejuvenated, and the rebounding economy has made modern-day Manchester England's "second city. " During our short visit, we were impressed by the city's delightful fusion of historic and modern, with pubs like Mr. Thomas's Chop House dating from 1870 and the ultra-modern, ultra-chic restaurant Grill on the Alley, where on one can order an eight-ounce Kobe beef steak (yes, from Japan) for a lively fifty pounds. (For those who haven't been "across the pond" recently, that's about $100 U.S.).

Cuts of meat here are called "fill-its," never "fill-ays" (so there, M. Chirac) or rump steaks, and are usually grilled over gas flames; however, a few enterprising chefs are starting to use charcoal or wood.

Nontraditional menu items on our Mancunian dining tour included ostrich fillet, baby back ribs, lamb cutlets, grilled curry lobster, sashimi tuna loin, seared marinated beef carpaccio, charred organic salmon, and (yes, in England!) beef and pork fajitas. And, oh yes, lots and lots of fish and chips.

One of the most delightful experiences we had, despite two days of sporadic drizzle, was our visit to St Ann's Square, where from an assemblage of tents were sold grilled sausages (the blood variety), hamburgers (exclusively from English White Beef), assorted meat pies, long coils of farm-produced sausages, mild to fiery local chutneys, various cheeses, jams and jellies, and tons of other edible goodies.

Manchester's restaurants do a fair amount of grilling, mostly indoors though. But we discovered a few places, like Dukes 92, where they haul out their grill in the summer and cook up burgers, kebabs, and vegetables right on the banks of a canal.

In London, we ran into quite a few restaurants that have actual outdoor barbecue grills, where they cook up everything hoofed, winged, and finned for their customers.

The Gun pub and restaurant is a prime example, located at the Docklands in Coldharbour, once an industrial port of ancient warehouses and rotting wharves that has been rebuilt into a whole new high-rise city overlooking the bustling harbor. The Gun serves up "Portuguese Alfresco Dining" on a wooden deck with views of the Thames and the Millennium dome. It's one of the few London area restaurants with a real charcoal grill that's a featured part of the outdoor ambiance.

The night I visited, Chef Micky O'Connor started us off with an "amuse" of fennel froth (an airy liquid filled with bubbles, tasting of whatever was cooked in the liquid), with a very light foccacia with herbed garlic butter (these bite-sized tastes are usually called "amuse-bouche," which means "delight the mouth" in French; here they drop the "bouche." (Touché, M. Chirac.) Hello, this is English cooking? My party then settled in and ordered more not-what-you'd-expect items: smoked eel ravioli with lobster froth; grilled Aberdeen Angus rib-eye steak with snails and a homemade wild mushroom pasty; and grilled sea bream and sea bass, both served up with Jersey royal potatoes in a pesto sauce. Hardly your steak and kidney pie.

And then there was the barbecue atop Harrods department store. Yes, the very generous management decided that since we were filming our visit to the Food Halls, they'd set up a grill for some proper English sausages on the roof of the 4.5-acre building. The tour of the Food Halls captivated my imagination, appetite, and wallet. I would rank it as one of the

top sights in Britain, or perhaps the world, when it comes to displays of food: twenty-eight restaurants, one hall just for chocolates, another for pastries, a huge charcuterie, another hall for fresh produce, additional halls for tea and coffee, a huge ice cream store, a Krispy Kreme donut shop, a hall dedicated to hard candies, and another hall filled with hundreds of cheeses, patés, and prepared foods. In addition, the art nouveau "rooms" are works of art themselves with incredible tile murals that rival those in Vienna, Barcelona, or Paris (aha, again, M. Chirac!). Leave two to three hours for your tour; you'll need it.

Then it was off to the Fish Works in nearby Richmond, where chef/owner Gary Rossen runs a barbecue cooking school when he's not grilling up fresh fish for his customers. "We're chock-a-block full whenever we have classes," he shared. "People just have a fear of fish when it comes to the barbecue, so we're here to teach them how to do up a proper fish grill." Every shrimp, scallop, and sea bream he grilled for us was perfectly lightly charred on the outside, tender, moist, and flavorful inside.

Throughout Britain, and in London in particular, home barbecue and grilling are catching on. There are now local barbecue contests; a team from London won the prestigious Jack Daniel's World Championship two years ago, and more and more British households have a kettle grill in their backyards. Homemade brick barbecues are also becoming popular.

While hamburgers, sausage, chicken, beef, lamb, and fish are still the most popular 'cue fare, culinary changes are creeping (no, rushing) in. So don't be surprised if you attend an English barbecue and are served chorizo flamed in medrono (a Portuguese spirit); chicken *piri piri*; tiger prawns cooked in their shells with garlic, chiles, and fresh herbs; whole dourade (sea bream); sea bass and lamb *espetada* (hanging skewer); seared scallops, pancetta, and polenta, with black olive sauce; warm baby mozzarella with aubergine (eggplant), caviar, and smoked cherry tomato relish; or the ever-popular grilled English asparagus with a poached truffled duck egg.

But Anglophiles, don't despair. Fish and chips and mushy peas are still available at the local take-away.

BANGERS ON A LANCE

British sausages were called bangers during World War II because they contained so much water they often exploded when cooked. Today in England, sausages are featured in 49 percent of barbecue meals, ahead of beef burgers (38 percent) and poultry (37 percent). According to the website www.sausagefans.com, the first week of November is British Sausage Week in the UK; the British Sausage Appreciation Society has more than 7,000 members; Britons spent a sizzling $963 million buying sausages in 2004; and in England alone there are over 470 varieties to choose from.

    Juice of 1 lemon
6   tablespoons honey
3   tablespoons tomato paste
$1/2$ cup apple cider
    Salt
    Freshly ground black pepper
8   large homemade or butcher shop pork link sausages
8   slices bacon, halved crosswise
16 large button or crimini mushrooms
1   tablespoon olive oil

Preheat a charcoal or gas grill to 375°F. Make sure the grill rack is clean and oil it thoroughly with nonstick cooking spray.

In a small saucepan, combine the lemon, honey, tomato paste, cider, $1/2$ teaspoon of salt, and $1/4$ teaspoon of pepper, and cook over low heat, stirring constantly, until the sauce is completely blended.

Pinch each sausage in the middle and twist to make 2 short sausages, then cut the two halves apart with a sharp knife. Season each of the 16 mini-sausages with salt and pepper. Wrap each one with a half slice of bacon and spear the sausages onto 4 skewers, alternating with the mushrooms.

Brush each skewer with the olive oil, place on the prepared grill rack, and cook over direct heat for 10 to 15 minutes, turning from time to time and basting with the sauce.

Transfer to a heated platter, drizzle with the remaining sauce, and serve on toothpicks.

SERVES 4 TO 8 AS AN APPETIZER

PUMPKIN SEED–CRUSTED SALMON

Pumpkins were first brought back to England from the American colonies and soon became very popular, even though they were called "pompions" by the folks there. This recipe was inspired by a dish I had at a restaurant in Bourton-on-the-Water in the Lake Country. Serve this dish with mashed sweet potatoes and green beans with mushrooms.

$2/3$ cup shelled, roasted, and coarsely ground pumpkin seeds
$1/2$ cup fresh fine rye bread crumbs
1   tablespoon chopped fresh parsley
2   tablespoons walnut oil
1   teaspoon salt
1   ($1^1/2$- to 2-pound) salmon fillet, skin on
    Olive oil

Combine the pumpkin seeds, bread crumbs, parsley, walnut oil, and salt in a wide shallow pan.

Rinse the salmon and pat it dry. Lightly brush the salmon with olive oil, then place it, flesh side down, in the seed mixture. Press down to make sure the crust mixture coats the whole fillet. Refrigerate for 20 minutes.

Preheat a charcoal or gas grill to 375°F. Make sure the grill rack is clean and oil it thoroughly with nonstick cooking spray.

Transfer the salmon, skin-side up, to the prepared grill rack and grill for 3 minutes; turn and grill 5 minutes longer, or until fish flakes easily when tested with a fork, and is beginning to brown.

SERVES 4 TO 6

STILTON-STUFFED MUSHROOMS WITH HERB BUTTER

A cheery historical side note: some famous victims of mushroom poisoning include the Buddha, the Roman emperors Tiberius and Claudius, Tsar Alexander I of Russia, Pope Clement II, and King Charles V of France. These decadent stuffed mushrooms won't hurt you at all—unless you can't stop eating them.

- ¹/₄ cup (¹/₂ stick) butter
- 5 shallots, chopped
- 6 slices white bread, torn
- 4 ounces Stilton cheese, crumbled
- 1 tablespoon chopped fresh sage
- 2 tablespoons chopped fresh parsley
- 2 cloves garlic, minced
- 12 large open cap mushrooms, such as shiitakes or portobellos, stems removed

Paprika

Prepare a charcoal or gas grill for indirect grilling (it is not necessary to use a drip pan with this recipe). Preheat to 375°F. Cover the grill rack with heavy-duty aluminum foil.

Melt the butter in a saucepan, add the shallots, and cook until soft, 3 to 4 minutes.

Place the bread in a food processor and reduce to crumbs. Add the shallots, Stilton, sage, parsley, and garlic. Process briefly until well combined.

Press the stuffing lightly into the caps. Transfer the mushrooms to the prepared grill, cover, and cook over indirect heat until the mushrooms wilt and the stuffing begins to brown, 14 to 18 minutes.

Remove the mushrooms from the foil with a spatula, sprinkle with paprika, and serve as an appetizer with a chilled white wine.

SERVES 4

NOTE: For a quick and tasty English snack, try Stilton rarebit: blend Stilton cheese with a little cider and diced apple, spread on toast, grill the toast until the cheese melts, serve with a glass of port.

OLDE COUNTRY RABBIT

"Fryer" or "young rabbit" refers to a rabbit weighing more than $1^{1}/_{2}$ pounds and less than $3^{1}/_{2}$ pounds, and under 12 weeks of age. The flesh is tender, fine-grained, and a bright pearly pink color. Young rabbits may be cooked in much the same way as young poultry—they are tender and don't need the long cooking times that the older ones require. You can have your butcher quarter the rabbit for you.

1 young (3- to $3^{1}/_{2}$-pound) rabbit, cut into quarters

$^{1}/_{2}$ cup chopped crimini or button mushrooms

2 cloves garlic, crushed

1 teaspoon minced fresh chives

1 teaspoon chopped fresh parsley

4 juniper berries, crushed

$^{1}/_{4}$ cup plus 2 tablespoons olive oil

3 tablespoons English gin

$^{1}/_{2}$ teaspoon salt

$^{1}/_{2}$ teaspoon freshly ground black pepper

1 cup apple cider

Make several deep incisions in each quarter of the rabbit with the tip of a sharp knife. Set aside.

In a mixing bowl, combine the mushrooms, garlic, chives, parsley, juniper berries, 2 tablespoons of the olive oil, gin, salt, and pepper, and stir until well blended.

Transfer the rabbit to a resealable plastic bag and pour the marinade over the meat. Shake and turn the bag to coat the pieces thoroughly; marinate for 4 to 6 hours in the refrigerator, turning the pieces from time to time.

Preheat a charcoal or gas barbecue to 375°F. Make sure the grill rack is clean and oil it thoroughly with nonstick cooking spray.

Combine the remaining $^{1}/_{4}$ cup of olive oil and apple cider in a spray bottle; set aside.

Remove the rabbit from the plastic bag and discard the marinade.

Transfer the rabbit to the prepared grill rack and cook over direct heat, turning from time to time and periodically spraying with the cider mixture, for 15 to 20 minutes, until the meat is cooked through to an internal temperature of 160°F.

Remove the rabbit from the grill, cover it, and let stand for 5 minutes. Serve with grilled sweet potatoes and grilled Brussels sprouts.

SERVES 4

STILTON STEAKS

True Stilton can only be made by six authorized creameries in Leicestershire, Nottinghamshire, and Derbyshire. Together these creameries churn out over a million cheeses a year. Also called a "cowboy steak" in England, the French-cut rib-eye is juicy and rich in flavor, all the way to the bone. Rich marbling melts and actually self-bastes the meat as it cooks, and delivers a succulent prime-rib taste. Only buy bone-in rib-eyes, as leaving the bone in results in amazing flavor. Superior beef and real Stilton cheese: what combination could be more quintessentially English or more gob-smackingly delicious?

- 1 cup butter, softened
- 3 tablespoons extra-virgin olive oil
- 3 large shallots, diced
- 3 green onions, white and green parts, diced
- 1/2 cup crumbled cooked bacon (about 8 strips)
- 1/2 cup crumbled English Stilton cheese or other strong blue cheese
- 1 tablespoon A.1. steak sauce
- 1 tablespoon Worcestershire sauce
- 4 (10-ounce) bone-in rib-eye steaks
  - Kosher or flake salt
  - Freshly ground black pepper

Melt 1 tablespoon of the butter in a skillet with 2 tablespoons of the olive oil over medium heat and sauté the shallots and green onions until soft, about 4 minutes.

Transfer the shallot mixture to a bowl, add the remaining butter, the bacon, Stilton, A.1. and Worcestershire sauces and mix thoroughly with a fork; let cool.

On a work surface, mound the butter mixture in the middle of a sheet of aluminum foil, forming it into a long tube by wrapping the foil around the mixture and rolling it back and forth on the work surface. Chill 2 to 2^1/$_2$ hours, until firm.

Prepare a charcoal or gas grill for indirect grilling, placing a drip pan under the cool side of the grill rack (see page 3). Preheat to 375°F. Make sure the grill rack is clean and oil it thoroughly with nonstick cooking spray.

Brush the steaks lightly with the remaining tablespoon of olive oil and season with salt and pepper. Transfer the steaks to the prepared grill rack and grill, covered, over direct heat for 3 minutes per side, then transfer to the indirect ("cool") side and grill 2 minutes per side, until the internal temperature reaches 145°F for medium-rare.

Remove the steaks from the grill to a warmed serving platter, place a generous pat of Stilton

butter on each one, cover with foil, and let stand for 5 minutes.

Serve immediately.

SERVES 4

BEEF WELLINGTON

An urban gustatory legend has it that this dish is named for Arthur Wellesley, the first Duke of Wellington, the man who crushed Napoleon at Waterloo. But there is no written proof of its origin, and since it's also claimed by the French, and the Irish, its genesis remains one of the great unsolved culinary mysteries. It is a luxurious and elaborate dish, worth making at least once in your life. Serve it with steamed broccoli, sautéed green beans, honey-glazed carrots, and garlic mashed potatoes.

1   (6-pound) beef tenderloin

5   tablespoons butter, melted

   Salt

   Freshly ground black pepper

1   tablespoon olive oil

2   tablespoons Madeira

1   cup minced crimini or button mushrooms

1   teaspoon dried thyme

1   teaspoon minced shallots

1   (17.4-ounce) package frozen puff pastry

1/2   pound best-quality goose or duck liver paté

1   egg

2   teaspoons of milk

   Parsley sprigs, for garnish

Prepare a charcoal or gas grill for indirect grilling, placing a drip pan under the cool side of the grill rack (see page 3). Preheat to 425°F. Make sure the grill rack is clean and oil it thoroughly with nonstick cooking spray.

Using kitchen string, tie the tail of the tenderloin under the meat so that you have an even-diameter roast, head to tail.

Brush the meat with 3 tablespoons of the melted butter, then season lightly with salt and pepper. Place the meat on the prepared grill rack over indirect heat and cook for 30 to 40 minutes, until it reaches an internal temperature of 120°F (very rare).

Remove the tenderloin from the grill and let stand for 30 minutes.

In a skillet over medium-high direct heat, heat the oil and the remaining butter; add the wine, mushrooms, thyme, and shallots, and sauté, gently stirring, until the mixture is dry and the mushrooms are soft, about 10 to 15 minutes. Remove from the heat and set aside.

Meanwhile, on a floured surface, roll out 2 sheets of the pastry dough to 14 by 12-inch rectangles. Combined, they should be large enough to enclose the entire tenderloin.

Place 1 of the sheets of dough on a baking sheet, and place the meat lengthwise in the center of the dough. With a rubber spatula, spread the paté on top of the tenderloin; top with the mushroom mixture.

Beat the egg together with the milk in a small bowl and brush the edges of the pastry with the egg wash. Cover the meat with the second sheet of puff pastry, cutting off any excess pastry to leave a 1-inch border all around the meat. Dip a fork into cold water and press down along the edges to seal.

Brush the top and sides of the pastry envelope with the egg wash and transfer the baking sheet to the grill over indirect heat. Cook, covered, for 10 minutes, then lower the temperature to about 375°F by opening vents or lowering gas flames, and cook for an additional 20 to 25 minutes, until the crust is golden.

Remove the baking sheet from the barbecue; let the meat rest, covered, for 15 minutes, then cut into 3-inch-thick slices. Arrange the slices on a warmed serving platter, garnish with parsley sprigs, and serve.

SERVES 4 TO 6

"PROPER" ROASTED POTATOES

An extremely common variety of baking potato in North America, the russet, russet Burbank, or Burbank potato is the principle potato crop in Idaho, hence the name "Idaho potato." In England, they favor potato names that sound distinctively royal, like Victoria, Royal Kidney, Majestic, White Lady, Duke of York, Ulster, King Edward, and, lest we forget, the Winston. I once overheard a very English gentleman talking to his friend at a London restaurant when their food arrived, and he reveled in the fact that they were being served "proper" roasted potatoes. Guess he'd had the "improper" kind somewhere else!

- 4   large baking potatoes, halved lengthwise
- 5   tablespoons extra-virgin olive oil
- 4   tablespoons butter, melted
- 4   teaspoons chopped fresh rosemary
- 3   cloves garlic, minced
- 2   tablespoons minced fresh parsley

Place the potatoes in a large saucepan, cover with cold water, and bring to a boil for 10 minutes.

Meanwhile, prepare a charcoal or gas grill for indirect grilling (it is not necessary to use a drip pan with this recipe). Preheat to 400°F. Make sure the grill rack is clean and oil it thoroughly with nonstick cooking spray.

Drain the potatoes well, then return them to the pan and add 4 tablespoons of the olive oil, butter, rosemary, and garlic, gently rolling the potatoes to coat each of them in the oil, butter, and aromatics.

Place the potatoes directly on the prepared grill rack over indirect heat and roast for about 40 minutes, turning them a couple of times during the cooking period, until they are golden brown and crisp on the outside, and tender when pierced with a fork.

Transfer the potatoes to a heated bowl, drizzle with the remaining olive oil, then sprinkle on the minced parsley, and serve.

SERVES 4

FRANCE

A Week in Patrick Payet's Provence

To paraphrase the first line of Peter Mayle's lovely book *A Year in Provence*, the week began with lunch.

My television crew and I met our gracious host M. Patrick Payet at the Marseilles airport. He bundled us into his car and drove us through a countryside still damp from torrential rains, on our way to Provence and its twenty-seven villages and two-hundred restaurants. Patrick was trained by famed French chef Roger Vergé, and his own restaurant, perched high on a hill, is the most popular in his tiny village of Goult. His cooking classes are, if anything, even more popular. We were lucky enough to have him

as our guide for the week, and we got a taste of how lucky we were going to be when we sat down for our first lunch with him. For hungry travelers whose only sustenance that day had been a miniscule offering of airline food, the meal Patrick had waiting for us—Danish salmon, green salad, olive oil–laced and salted cherry tomatoes, local cheeses, baguettes, honey, fresh strawberries, and red wine—was a banquet from heaven.

But barbecue was our quest—we wanted to see what a country and region, famed for food but not so well known for barbecue skills, had to offer. Our week in Provence featured more amazing local wine and cheese than we encountered elsewhere on our travels, but we also discovered that the French have a way of bringing the best out of the food they prepare on the grill. No surprise there, if you think about it.

On our first full day, we visited another Patrick, Patrick Haeseleer, who, with his wife Nadine, owns and staffs the restaurant Bleu de Toi in the village of Bonnieux. Patrick and Nadine's restaurant features an all-grilled menu. For our supposed "light lunch," we gorged on honey-marinated duck breast, pork shanks in mustard sauce, lamb shanks, beef rib-eye, grilled prawns, fried parsley, baked potato, cheese croquettes, and some luscious wines. It was decadent, to say the least.

And so it went. Our meals in Provence were as exquisite as the sights. After walking the charmingly narrow and winding streets of Avignon, we had a glorious lunch done entirely by our hosts, Regis and Chantal Sanglier, on a small barbecue: grilled bread with a tasty tapenade; grilled corn on the cob; grilled garlic and tomatoes; lamb kebabs, chops, and shanks; barbecued potatoes; eggplant with red peppers;

and grilled Camembert, pineapple, bananas, and strawberries. In the next few days, we visited the quintessentially French farmer's market in Coustellet, antique shops in l'Isle Sur la Sorgue, and France's "Grand Canyon" near Roussillon; we ate grilled monkfish with red pepper coulis, lavender ice cream, and cheeses right from the farm.

Back at Goult, Patrick and I worked apron to apron preparing a French-American home barbecue, grilling up sausages, lamb chops, and my signature beer-butt chicken done French style. Although Patrick tends to go heavy on the charcoal, the meal turned out perfect, and was lubricated with yet more local wines.

We left the hillside villages of Provence sated with visual and culinary experiences, not to mention the seven or eight bottles of wine each of us had consumed. Maybe I'll come back some day, stay a while, and write my own book, just like Peter Mayle. I'll call it *A Year* Eating *in Provence* and the first line will be: "The year began with breakfast, lunch, tea, dinner, cheese, and an aperitif."

GRILLED CRAB BURGERS

The most common edible crabs in the U.S. include the blue crab, king crab, peekytoe (or rock) crab, stone crabs, and the ubiquitous Dungeness crab. The Dungeness variety gets its name from the former small town in the state of Washington, where it was first commercially harvested. Although the French feature crab in their famed Marseilles bouillabaisse, they also use them in other ways like these crisp-outside tender-inside cakes. This recipe was inspired by a week I spent in the kitchen with chef Paul Bocuse.

1 tablespoon celery seeds

6 dried bay leaves

$1/2$ teaspoon ground cardamom

$1/2$ teaspoon ground mustard

$1/4$ teaspoon ground cloves

1 teaspoon freshly ground black pepper

1 teaspoon sweet Hungarian paprika

12 ounces fresh crabmeat or 2 (6-ounce) cans, drained

3 cups fresh white bread crumbs

$1/2$ cup chopped green onions, green and white parts

$4 1/2$ tablespoons mayonnaise
Pinch of saffron

1 egg, beaten

$1 1/2$ tablespoons Dijon mustard
Juice of 1 lemon

3 tablespoons olive oil

4 hamburger buns, split

In a spice grinder, grind the celery seeds and bay leaves until powdered; pour into a small bowl and add the cardamom, mustard, cloves, pepper, and paprika. Stir well and set aside.

In a small bowl, combine the crabmeat, $2 1/2$ cups of the bread crumbs, green onions, 2 tablespoons of the mayonnaise, saffron, and $1 1/2$ teaspoons of the ground spice mix. Stir in the beaten egg and, with your hands, shape the mixture into four 4- to $4 1/2$-inch-diameter patties.

Place the remaining bread crumbs in a shallow bowl and dredge the patties in the crumbs, coating each one completely.

In a small bowl, mix the remaining $2 1/2$ tablespoons of mayonnaise with the mustard and lemon juice, stirring until smooth. Set aside.

Preheat a charcoal or gas grill to 375°F.

Pour the oil into a nonstick or cast-iron skillet and add the crab patties, placing the pan directly over the coals or flames. Cook the burgers until golden brown, 4 to 5 minutes per side. Place the buns on the grill when you turn the burgers.

Spread the mayonnaise mixture on one side of each bun, top with a crab patty, and serve.

SERVES 4

STUFFED CHICKEN IN A SALT CRUST

A lot of production goes into this dish, but the reaction from your dinner guests will be well worth it. Presenting a chicken en croûte (in pastry) at the table, removing the crust to discover a steaming, moist bird with a luscious fruit stuffing, will satisfy the pickiest gourmet. Just don't let anyone eat the crust—the salt will ruin anyone's taste buds for a week. It's rumored that this dish was invented by poor people who didn't have enough money for fancy pots and pans, but had salt and flour available to fashion into a cooking container. It's similar to Chinese beggar's chicken, which uses a clay crust to steam the meat, but dough is much more palatable to many. I have seen this method used in Italy on fish as well, and by chef Alton Brown using beef tenderloin, but the French version avec le poulet won my heart after I ate it in a tiny bistro in Avignon five years ago.

STUFFING

- 2 1/2 cups chicken stock
- 1 cup small pasta like bumbola, cavatelli, fiori, orecchiette, or radiatoria
- 1/2 cup diced unpeeled tart apples (Pippin or Granny Smith)
- 1/4 cup raisins
- 1/2 cup diced peeled plums
- 1/4 cup fresh cranberries
- 1/4 cup minced rehydrated chipotle chiles (see Note)
- 1 teaspoon fresh minced sage, or 1/2 teaspoon dried
- 1 teaspoon minced fresh rosemary
- 1/2 teaspoon dried savory
- 1/2 teaspoon garlic salt
- 1/2 teaspoon freshly ground black pepper
- 1 cup diced fresh bread (1-inch dice)
- 1 tablespoon olive oil
- 1 (5- to 6-pound) roasting chicken

CRUST

- 12 cups (3 pounds) flour, plus more if dough is sticky
- 9 egg whites
- 2 to 2 1/2 cups water
- 3 1/4 cups table salt

BASTING

- 3 tablespoons soy sauce
- 1/4 cup (1/2 stick) butter, melted

  Freshly ground black pepper

- 6 (4-inch-long) rosemary sprigs
- 1 egg
- 1 tablespoon cream
- 1 lemon, for garnish
- 4 to 5 large parsley sprigs, for garnish

For the stuffing, in a large saucepan over high heat, bring the chicken stock to a boil, add the pasta, apples, raisins, plums, cranberries, and chiles, lower the heat, cover, and simmer for 15 minutes. Pasta should be just al dente and fruit nice and soft.

Remove the pan from the heat and add the sage, rosemary, savory, garlic salt, pepper, bread, and olive oil, mixing well. Loosely pack the stuffing into the cavity of the chicken. Spray a roasting pan with nonstick cooking spray. Place the chicken in the pan and set aside while you prepare the crust and the fire.

To make the crust, combine the flour, egg whites, 2 cups of water, and salt in a very large bowl and mix with an electric mixer on medium speed until a large ball forms, 1 to 2 minutes. Add more flour, 1 tablespoon at a time, to the dough if it's sticky; if it's dry, add more water, 2 tablespoons at a time, until it feels soft but not sticky. Remove the dough from the bowl, form it into a ball and set it on a lightly floured work surface. Cover with a moist cloth to keep it from drying out.

Prepare a charcoal or gas grill for indirect grilling (it is not necessary to use a drip pan with this recipe). Preheat to 325°F.

For the basting, in a small bowl, mix the soy sauce with the melted butter. Season it with pepper only (the chicken will pick up salt from the salt crust). Brush this mixture onto the chicken.

continued

On a lightly floured surface, roll out the salt dough to a 20- by 20-inch oblong about $^1/_3$ inch thick. It should be large enough to easily envelop the chicken. Place the rosemary sprigs in the center of the dough, and then place the chicken, breast-side down, on top of the herbs. In a small bowl, lightly beat together the egg and cream. Brush all around the edges of the dough with the egg wash, and fold the dough over the chicken, pinching together the edges and crimping with a fork to seal.

Turn the chicken over and place it in the prepared roasting pan, seam-side down, and transfer it the preheated grill over indirect heat. Cover and cook for $1^1/_2$ to $1^3/_4$ hours. After $1^1/_2$ hours, use a large nail to punch a small hole through the upper part of the crust and insert a meat thermometer into the breast. It should read 150 to 155°F if the chicken is done; the remaining 5 to 10 degrees will be reached by the time the chicken is carved. The crust may be starting to brown but shouldn't be very dark.

Place the chicken on a serving tray and take it to the table still in the crust. With a sharp knife or kitchen shears, cut around the base of the crust, being careful to avoid the steam that will be released when you lift the crust off. Remove the chicken from the crust, cover it with aluminum foil, and let it rest for 20 minutes.

Discard the salted crust and check the temperature of the stuffing; it should be at least 160°F (if it isn't, microwave it for 8 to 10 minutes until it is the right temperature). Transfer the fruit stuffing to a serving dish, carve the super-moist chicken, and serve.

SERVES 4 TO 6

NOTE: To rehydrate the chipotles, submerge them in warm water for 15 to 20 minutes, drain, and use.

When the chicken is removed from the salt-flour crust, it usually isn't a nice golden brown. It's basically been steamed, and although fully cooked, it may not look as appetizing as you'd like. The soy sauce baste helps; you can also brush the chicken with soy sauce or a browning sauce like Kitchen Bouquet after you remove the crust.

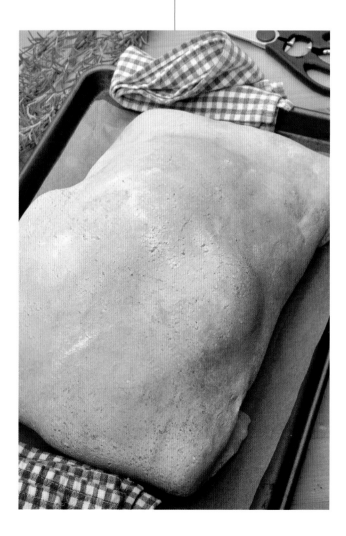

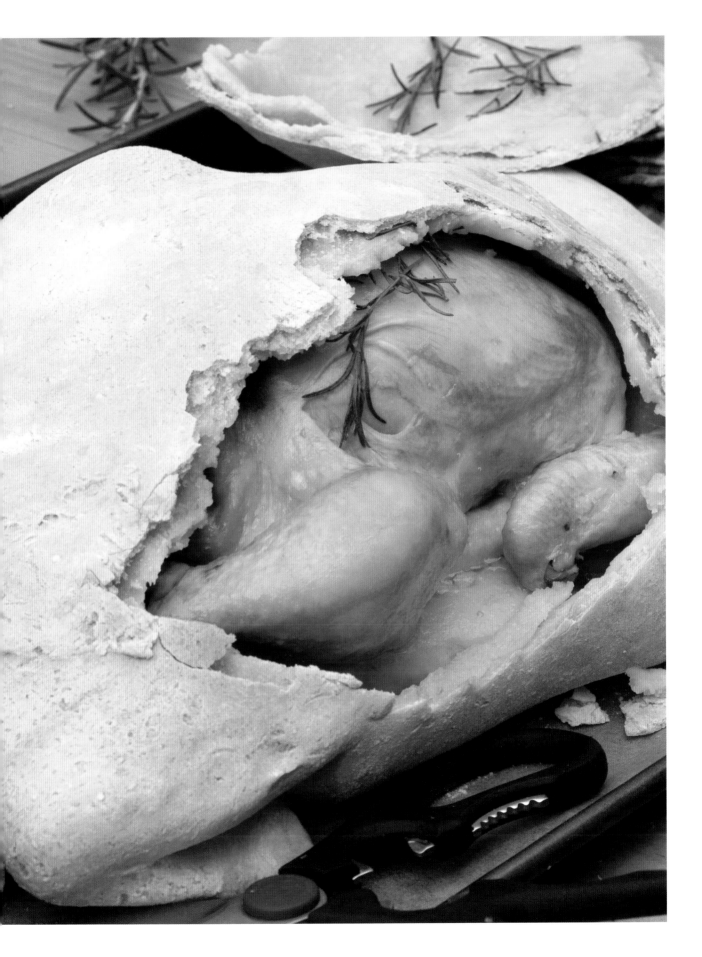

FLANK STEAK WITH GRILLED VEGETABLES

Flank steak is a lean, flavorful, boneless cut that comes from a well-exercised part of the animal, as evidenced by its striated muscle fibers and connective tissue. However, when marinated, broiled, and cut against the grain, flank steak becomes quite tender. When shopping, select a steak that is very red and without noticeable fat. While in Provence, I noted that many the restaurants offered up thin flank steaks as well as the ubiquitous filet mignon. "They are quick to cook, and very flavorful, and not too much meat" was the answer when I asked a chef why he serves them.

- 3 cups dry red wine
- 3 cups chopped onions (about 3 medium onions)
- 2^1/$_4$ cups soy sauce
- ^{3}/$_4$ cup plus 3 tablespoons olive oil
- 8 large cloves garlic, minced
- 1 tablespoon dry mustard
- 1 tablespoon ground ginger
- 1 tablespoon mayonnaise
- 1 teaspoon oregano

  Salt

  Freshly ground black pepper
- 1 (4^1/$_2$-pound) beef flank steak
- 6 large red, green, and yellow bell peppers (2 of each), stemmed, seeded, and cut lengthwise into ^{1}/$_2$-inch strips
- 8 green onions, green and white parts, cut into 4-inch lengths
- 4 large zucchini, cut lengthwise into quarters
- 1 large red onion, cut lengthwise into ^{1}/$_2$-inch strips
- ^{1}/$_2$ teaspoon garlic powder

  Pinch of cayenne pepper

In a large resealable plastic bag, combine the wine, onions, soy sauce, ^{3}/$_4$ cup oil, garlic, mustard, ginger, mayonnaise, and oregano. Season with salt and pepper. Shake to mix, then add the flank steak, seal, and refrigerate for 2 to 3 hours.

In another large resealable plastic bag, combine the peppers, green onions, zucchini, and red onion with the remaining 3 tablespoons olive oil, garlic powder, and cayenne. Season with salt and pepper and shake to mix. Refrigerate for 2 to 3 hours.

Preheat a charcoal or gas grill to 350°F. Make sure the grill rack is clean and oil it thoroughly with nonstick cooking spray.

Drain the steaks and vegetables, discarding both marinades. Let the steaks come to room temperature, transfer them to the prepared grill rack over direct heat, and grill them to your desired degree of doneness, about 4 to 5 minutes per side for rare; when juices rise to the top of the meat, turn it over. At the same time, grill the vegetables in a grill basket or on a grilling tray for 8 to 10 minutes total, turning the basket or the vegetables often, until they begin to get grill marks and to soften and crisp around the edges.

Transfer the vegetables to a heated platter, slice the steaks thinly across the grain, and arrange the meat on top of the vegetables.

SERVES 4 TO 6

GRATIN DAUPHINOIS

This dish is also called "dauphin potatoes" or pommes dauphinois and comes from the Dauphiné region near the Italian border. It consists of sliced potatoes that are drenched in heavy cream and cooked with various seasonings. For the diet conscious, you can substitute half-and-half or whole milk for the cream in this recipe. Try the cream once, though, and you won't want to change the recipe!

- 1^3/$_4$ pounds medium-starchy potatoes, such as long white or Yukon
- 2 tablespoons chopped fresh rosemary

  Salt

  Freshly ground black pepper
- 4 ounces mild Cheddar cheese, grated

1 egg

2 cups heavy cream

1/4 cup (1/2 stick) butter, cut into slices

Spray a baking pan with nonstick cooking spray and set aside.

Fill a large bowl with cold, salted water. Using a food processor fitted with a slicing blade, cut the potatoes into 1/8-inch-thick slices; transfer the potatoes to the water as you go.

Prepare a charcoal or gas grill for indirect grilling (it is not necessary to use a drip pan with this recipe). Preheat to 375°F.

Drain the potatoes and pat them very dry. Put one layer of potatoes in the bottom of the pan, but do not overlap. Season with 1/2 tablespoon of the rosemary and some salt and pepper, and sprinkle over 1/4 of the cheese. Repeat the layers two more times, including the seasonings, finishing with a potato layer. Set aside the last of the cheese and rosemary. In a small bowl, whisk together the egg and cream, then pour over the potatoes. Dot with the butter and the remaining cheese and rosemary.

Transfer to the barbecue over indirect heat, cover, and cook for 1 hour, or until the potatoes are soft, the sauce is bubbling, and the top of the dish is nicely browned.

Serve immediately.

SERVES 4 TO 6

WILD MUSHROOMS IN CREAM

Did you know there are more than 140,000 species of mushrooms? My favorites among the tiny number of edible fungi: shiitakes, which have a rich, full-bodied, almost steaklike flavor, with a meaty texture when cooked; oyster mushrooms, which are prized for their smooth texture and subtle, oysterlike flavor; and the bright yellow- to orange-hued chanterelles, beloved for their nutty and delicate flavor and texture. If you don't like basil, or don't have any in the kitchen, you can substitute oregano, thyme, tarragon, summer savory (my favorite), cilantro, mint, or equal parts parsley and celery leaves.

8 ounces shiitake mushrooms, stems discarded, and coarsely chopped

8 ounces oyster mushrooms, dry ends of stems removed, and coarsely chopped

8 ounces chanterelle mushrooms, dry ends of stems removed, and coarsely chopped

1/2 cup thinly sliced shallots

1 tablespoon fresh thyme, chopped, leaves only

1 tablespoon chopped fresh basil

1/4 cup heavy cream

2 teaspoons extra-virgin olive oil

2 large cloves garlic, minced

1/2 teaspoon salt

1/8 teaspoon freshly ground black pepper

Grated Parmesan or Emmentaler cheese, for garnish (optional)

Preheat a charcoal or gas grill to 375°F.

In a bowl, combine the mushrooms, shallots, thyme, basil, and cream, and toss to coat the mushrooms with the cream. Add the oil and garlic, season with salt and pepper, and stir to combine.

Arrange the mixture in the center of a 20- by 14-inch sheet of heavy-duty aluminum foil. Bring the long sides of the foil up and over the mixture and fold several times, while allowing enough room around the mushrooms for circulation and expansion. Fold the short ends up and crimp to seal the packet closed.

Place the foil packet on the grill rack over direct heat, cover the grill, and cook for 20 minutes. Open the packet carefully to allow steam to escape. The mushrooms should be tender.

Serve the mushrooms as a savory side dish, topped with grated Parmesan or Emmentaler cheese if desired.

SERVES 4 TO 6

PROVENÇAL BARBECUE SAUCE

Talleyrand—the French states-man, diplomat, and grand gour-met, who once was called "the first fork of France"—is quoted as say-ing: "England has three sauces and three hundred and sixty religions, whereas France has three reli-gions and three hundred and sixty sauces." Make that three hundred and sixty-one, monsieur: here's a barbecue sauce that borrows from both sides of the Channel, with south-of-France shallots, wine, mustard, and herbs and one of the UK's finest culinary inventions, Worcestershire sauce. This sauce is great with steaks, pork spare ribs, sausages, or chicken.

1/3   cup minced shallots

3   tablespoons olive oil

1/3   cup honey or 1/4 cup tightly packed brown sugar

1/3   cup white wine

1/4   cup Dijon mustard

2   tablespoons Worcestershire sauce

2   tablespoon chopped fresh parsley

1   clove garlic

1   teaspoon salt

1/8   teaspoon freshly ground black pepper

In a small skillet, sauté the shal-lots in olive oil over medium heat until translucent and soft, but not browned, about 10 min-utes. Add the brown sugar, wine, mustard, Worcestershire sauce, parsley, garlic, salt, and pepper, and simmer for 10 minutes.

Cool to room temperature and use, or store in an airtight container in the refrigerator for 1 to 2 weeks only.

MAKES ABOUT 1 1/2 CUPS

GERMANY

Ich bin eine Wurst

The Federal Republic of Germany's location—bordered by the Baltic and North Seas, the Netherlands, France, Poland, Belgium, the Czech Republic, Switzerland, and Austria—has a lot to do with its cuisine and culinary history, because at one time or another, Germany has occupied all or part of each of its neighbors.

According to the early Romans, German cuisine was simple, consisting mainly of mead (a malt beverage made from honey, water, and yeast) and meat. Christianity brought with it the cultivation of produce and livestock. Char-

lemagne's conquest, which also encompassed parts of Italy, Austria, France, and Switzerland, brought new culinary customs to Germany. And finally, Russian influences brought potatoes, rice, and sugar to German cuisine.

Today beer has replaced the mead—good riddance: have you ever tasted mead? Give me a pilsner any day. But the Germans do have a well-earned reputation for a protein-rich diet.

Germans grill pork, beef, game, poultry, fish, and shellfish. But the fact that they are also inclined to grill up sausages is due to 1,500 varieties they have to choose from, including *die*

Bratwurst (veal, pork, nutmeg, and ginger), *die Wienerwurst* (beef, pork, garlic, and coriander), *die Jagdwurst* (beef, pork, mustard seed, mace, and cardamom), *die Knackwurst* (pork, beef, fresh garlic), *die Bockwurst* (veal and pork), and, of course, *die Bierwurst* (pork, beef, garlic, juniper berries, and onion).

German immigrants should be credited with creating most of what many Americans—well, Texans, anyway—think of as the traditional barbecue meal: smoked sausage, potato salad, beer, and coleslaw.

German cuisine also boasts 310-plus varieties of bread (not including all of the regional variations). In fact, Germany claims to have the highest daily consumption of bread in the entire European Union. Pumpernickel is the most famous, but there are dozens of varieties of breads, including *das Weizenmischbrot* (wheat-rye), *das Roggenbrot* (rye-wheat), *das Mehrkornbrot* (multigrain), *das Sonnenblumenkernbrot* (sunflower seed), *das Kürbiskernbrot* (pumpkin seed), and *das Zwiebelbrot* (onion).

Other starchy staples would have to include the dozens of rich potato and noodle dishes the Germans are known for. German cooks routinely use juniper, caraway, cardamom, dill, marjoram, parsley, pepper, thyme, laurel, and dried chives. Favorite condiments include varieties of mustards, many of them hot (with all those sausages, of course!), and bottles of horseradish.

We will not discuss German desserts because you will gain two pounds just from reading about the tortes, brandy-soaked rai-sins, cookies, Black Forest cake, strud. . . . Sorry, I forgot we weren't going to talk about them.

The backyard barbecues of Dusseldorf, Hamburg, and Munich are fired up frequently, in the temperate summers anyway, for beef steaks, pork roasts and chops, chicken, duck, turkey, and goose. But they also grill up venison, wild boar, rabbit, and game birds. And the number of sausages on the grill at any one time would stretch the length of the autobahn. And thanks to nearly fifteen hundred miles of coastline, the Germanic diet also includes herring, sardines, tuna, mackerel, salmon, mussels, and shrimp; freshwater trout, perch, pike, and carp are also available locally.

German wines and liquors are justly famous, but the national beverage is beer—really great beer. And for that we need only one word to sum up: Oktoberfest. Actually beginning in September, Oktoberfest is the biggest drinking party on the planet. Held in Munich, this twelve-day affair features huge beer tents filled with oom-pah bands in lederhosen, waitresses in dirndls, 1-liter steins of beer, lots of great local food, and more fun than you can possibly imagine.

And for the dedicated grillers like us, Oktoberfest features lots and lots of food: 88 whole oxen, 460,000 chickens, thousands of pounds of roast duck, pork loin, pig knuckles, noodles, dumplings, sauerkraut, cheeses, giant pretzels, and potato pancakes.

And—you were waiting for this, weren't you?—440,000 sausages.

BAVARIAN BRUSCHETTAS

Bruschetta is toasted bread, often rubbed with garlic and drizzled with olive oil, and a delicious way to salvage bread that was going stale. Sausage, apples, and cheese take this Italian concept north to make a thoroughly Germanic appetizer.

- 1 baguette, sliced diagonally into $1/4$-inch-thick slices
- 2 tablespoons olive oil
- 2 medium bratwurst, cut crosswise into $1/2$-inch slices (see Note)
- $1/4$ cup apple butter
- 8 ounces Gruyère cheese, thinly sliced
- 2 Golden Delicious apples, peeled, cored, and thinly sliced

Preheat a charcoal or gas grill to 350°F. Make sure the grill rack is clean and oil it thoroughly with nonstick cooking spray.

Brush the baguette slices lightly with olive oil then place on a baking sheet. Cook over direct heat in the covered barbecue for 6 to 8 minutes, until lightly browned. Remove and let cool. Put the bratwurst on the prepared grill rack over the hottest part of the grill and heat for 30 seconds to 1 minute per side, until the sausage starts to brown. Remove and let cool.

Increase the grill temperature to 500°F.

Spread one side of each baguette slice very lightly with apple butter, then place a few thin slices of cheese over the butter, add 2 slices of apple and top with one slice of sausage.

Place the bruschetta on a baking sheet over direct heat and grill for 5 to 7 minutes, until the cheese is melted, watching carefully as the cheese burns easily. Serve warm.

SERVES 4 TO 6 AS AN APPETIZER

NOTE: Bratwurst is a classic German pork and veal sausage made with herbs and spices such as ginger, marjoram, nutmeg, caraway, or coriander.

GRILLED DUCK BREAST WITH APRICOT-BLACKBERRY COMPOTE

This is a very fruity recipe, but the marriage of the tangy vinegar and onion with the sweet preserves and jams and fresh fruit works well with the strong flavor of the duck breast. I had a dish similar to this on the Romantische Strasse *(Romantic Road) in the walled city of* Rothenburg ob der Tauber.

3	tablespoons apple cider vinegar
2	tablespoons minced red onion
5	tablespoons apricot preserves
3	tablespoons blackberry jam
1	cup chopped fresh apricots
$^3/_4$	cup fresh whole blackberries
2	teaspoons chopped fresh chives
$^1/_2$	teaspoon coarse sea salt
	Pinch freshly ground black pepper
$^1/_2$	teaspoon ground coriander
$^1/_2$	teaspoon ground cinnamon
$^1/_8$	teaspoon ground cloves
4	(3- to 4-pound) boneless Peking duck breasts

In a small saucepan over medium-high heat, make the compote by heating the vinegar, onion, 2 tablespoons of the preserves, and 1 tablespoon of the jam for 3 minutes, stirring often. Add the apricots and berries, crushing the fruit with a spoon as you stir, cooking for 3 to 4 more minutes. Stir in the chives, remove from the heat, and set aside to cool to room temperature. Combine the remaining 3 tablespoons preserves and 2 tablespoons jam in a small bowl and set aside.

Preheat a charcoal or gas grill to 375°F. Make sure the grill rack is clean and oil it thoroughly with nonstick cooking spray.

In a small bowl, make a rub by combining the salt, pepper, coriander, cinnamon, and cloves. Set aside.

Score the skin of each duck breast at $^1/_4$-inch intervals, being careful not to cut into the breast meat. Rotate breasts and score again, making a criss-cross pattern. Season each breast with the rub.

Transfer the duck breasts, skin side down, to the prepared grill rack over direct heat, cover the grill, and cook until the skin is browned and crispy, about 4 to 5 minutes. Turn the breasts over and grill for 1 to 2 minutes more. Turn again, then remove from the grill and put the breasts in a cast-iron skillet or Dutch oven and top with the jam mixture, spreading it all over the surface of the breasts; continue cooking until the internal temperature reaches 165°F, about another 8 to 10 minutes. Remove from the heat and let stand, covered, for 10 minutes before slicing.

Serve each duck breast topped with 1 to 2 tablespoons of the warm fruit compote.

SERVES 4

BRAISED RABBIT IN SPICED RED WINE SAUCE

Like pork, rabbit needs to be cooked to an internal temperature of 160°F. The flesh of young rabbits (those smaller than 3 pounds and usually no older than 12 weeks) is tender and bright pink. Have your butcher cut the rabbits into serving pieces for you if you don't want to do it yourself.

- 1/2 cup red wine vinegar
- 2 cloves garlic, minced
- 2 bay leaves
- 2 1/2 teaspoons salt
- 1 teaspoon freshly ground black pepper
- 4 tablespoons olive oil
- 2 (2 1/2- to 3-pound) young rabbits, cut into serving pieces
- 1/2 pound lean smoked bacon, finely chopped
- 1/2 cup flour
- 1/2 cup minced shallots
- 1/2 cup minced onion
- 1/2 teaspoon minced garlic
- 1 cup Spätburgunder (German pinot noir) or any other pinot noir
- 2 tablespoons grated dark chocolate
- 1 cup chicken stock
- 3 tablespoons brandy
- 1 tablespoon currant jelly
- 1/4 teaspoon dried rosemary
- 1 tablespoon dried parsley
- 1/4 teaspoon dried thyme
- 3 teaspoons freshly squeezed lemon juice

  Egg noodles or spaetzle, for serving

  Chopped fresh parsley, for garnish

In a large resealable plastic bag, combine the vinegar, garlic, 1 bay leaf, 2 teaspoons of the salt, 1/2 teaspoon of the pepper, and the olive oil. Add the rabbit to the bag, shaking to coat; marinate in the refrigerator for 4 to 8 hours.

Preheat a charcoal or gas grill to 350°F.

In a heavy, 5-quart Dutch oven, or cast-iron skillet with a lid, cook the bacon over medium heat, stirring frequently, until crisp, about 10 minutes. Transfer the bacon to paper towels to drain, setting the pan with the bacon grease aside.

Remove the meat from the marinade and discard the liquid. Put the flour in a shallow bowl. Sprinkle the meat with the remaining salt and pepper; dip each piece into the flour and shake off any excess.

Put the Dutch oven over direct heat on the barbecue, heating the bacon fat until it sputters.

Add the meat to the Dutch oven, a few pieces at a time, browning on all sides. Don't crowd the meat. Transfer the pieces to a paper towel–lined plate as they are done.

When all the meat is cooked, pour off all but 2 tablespoons of the bacon fat from the Dutch oven. Add the shallots, onion, and garlic, stirring frequently, until the onions are soft and translucent, 4 to 5 minutes. Add the red wine, chocolate, and stock, and bring to a boil, scraping up any brown bits clinging to the bottom and sides of the pan. Stir in the bacon, brandy, jelly, the remaining bay leaf, rosemary, dried parsley, and thyme, and return the rabbit and any juices collected around it to the Dutch oven. Cover tightly, and place over direct heat in the barbecue. Cover the grill and cook for 1 to 1 1/2 hours, turning the pieces often, until the rabbit is tender but not falling apart. Internal temperature of the meat should be 160°F.

Remove the bay leaf, stir in the lemon juice, and taste for seasoning. The sauce should be quite peppery. Transfer the rabbit to a platter of buttered noodles or German spaetzle; pour the sauce over the rabbit, and garnish with chopped fresh parsley.

SERVES 6 TO 8

GRILL-BAKED GINGERBREAD APPLES

In American cooking, there are two distinct families of gingerbread cookies, the honey-based gingerbreads (Lebkuchen) of German origin and the molasses shortbreads that were developed in England and Scotland.

1 (16-ounce) package gingerbread cookies

1/4 cup finely chopped crystallized ginger

1/4 teaspoon nutmeg

1/4 teaspoon cinnamon

1/3 cup chopped walnuts

1 tablespoon dark honey

2 tablespoons butter, plus additional melted butter for brushing

6 baking apples, such as Honeycrisp, Fuji, or Gala

1 cup heavy cream

1 tablespoon confectioners' sugar

Crystallized ginger, cut in slivers, for garnish

Prepare a charcoal or gas grill for indirect grilling (it is not necessary to use a drip pan with this recipe). Preheat to 375°F. Oil a cast-iron skillet.

Crumble the gingerbread cookies into small pieces and place into a bowl; add the crystallized ginger, nutmeg, cinnamon, and nuts, and stir to combine.

In a small microwave-safe bowl, melt the honey and the 2 tablespoons of butter, and add to the cookie mixture. Stir to mix completely and set aside.

Core the apples without cutting all the way through leaving a half-inch core at the bottom. With a bird's-beak knife or melon baller, remove some of the inside of each apple to make room for the filling.

Place the apples in the prepared skillet. Spoon the filling into the openings of the apples, packing it down lightly. Brush the apples with the melted butter. Transfer the skillet to the barbecue over indirect heat, lower the grill cover, and cook for about 40 minutes, or until the apples are tender.

Remove the apples from the barbecue and let them cool for 15 minutes. Meanwhile, whip the cream with an electric mixer on high speed until it forms soft peaks, adding the powdered sugar toward the end of the mixing.

Serve apples with a dollop of whipped cream and garnish with the crystallized ginger.

SERVES 6

SMOKED SAUER-BRATEN STEAK

In Germany, this recipe originated using horsemeat, which is actually a deliciously sweet and cholesterol-free meat. Today it's more often beef, usually a top round or chuck or pot roast at least two inches thick. The most essential parts of this dish are the cloves, vinegar, and gingersnap cookie crumbs. Take note that if you want to make this dish, you will need to start two to four days in advance (depending on how sauer you like your braten).

$1^{1}/_{2}$ cups cider vinegar

$^{1}/_{4}$ cup balsamic vinegar

1   cup cola

2   cups water

3   onions, thinly sliced

2   stalks celery, chopped

2   carrots, chopped

10   whole black peppercorns

10   whole cloves

1   bay leaf

3   tablespoons brown sugar

$1^{1}/_{2}$ teaspoons salt

1   teaspoon paprika

1   (4- to 5-pound) boneless sirloin steak, or a less expensive beef roast

1   cup (1 large handful) fruit-wood chips (such as peach, pear, apple, or cherry wood)

5   tablespoons flour

3   tablespoons vegetable oil

1   cup plus 5 tablespoons gingersnap crumbs

2   cups golden raisins

For the marinade, in a large resealable plastic bag, combine the vinegars, cola, water, onion, celery, carrots, peppercorns, cloves, bay leaf, sugar, salt, and paprika, and shake to combine well. Add the meat to the bag and seal the bag tightly, pressing out the air, and lay it in a large flat pan. Refrigerate, turning the bag each day. If you like a sour sauerbraten, let the meat soak in the bag for 4 days; if not, 2 days will suffice.

When you're ready to grill, place the wood chips in a bowl or can, cover with water, and soak for at least 2 hours.

Preheat a charcoal or gas barbecue to 375°F. Make sure the grill rack is clean and oil it thoroughly with nonstick cooking spray.

Remove the meat from the bag and pour the marinating liquid (with the vegetables) into a small saucepan. Pat the meat dry with paper towels and set it aside. Boil the marinade for 12 minutes and set aside.

Put a handful of soaked wood chips on a piece of heavy-duty aluminum foil and fold it over like an envelope to enclose the wood. Using a pencil, poke 3 or 4 holes in the top of the foil envelope (don't poke all the way through). Place the foil directly on the coals or gas jets and when the wood inside starts to smoke, place the meat on the prepared grill rack over direct heat. Cook for 5 minutes per side to sear

the meat and give it a nice grill marking. Remove the meat from the heat and immediately sprinkle it all over lightly with 2 tablespoons of flour.

Place a Dutch oven on the grill over direct heat, heat the oil, and add the meat, then cover the pot and lower the grill lid. Cook for 10 minutes, then add 1 cup of the marinade, the reserved vegetables, and 1 cup of the cookie crumbs. Move the Dutch oven to the indirect side of the grill, uncover, and lower the grill lid. Cook, uncovered, for 3 to 4 hours, until the meat is fork-tender and it has an internal temperature of 145°F.

Keep at least $^{1}/_{2}$ inch of liquid in the Dutch oven during cooking, adding more marinade as needed.

Remove the meat and keep warm until ready to slice. Into a small bowl, strain the drippings, then transfer to a gravy separator to remove the fat.

In the Dutch oven over medium heat (on the grill or a side burner), make the gravy by combining the strained drippings, 3 tablespoons of flour, 5 tablespoons of cookie crumbs, and raisins; cook, stirring, about 5 to 7 minutes, until the gravy is thickened and has picked up any bits stuck to the bottom of the Dutch oven. Makes 3 cups of gravy.

SERVES 6 TO 8

KAUFHAUS PORK LOIN IN BEER

Berlin has its own gourmet paradise in Kaufhaus des Westens or, as it is more commonly known, KaDeWe. On the sixth floor, they display hundreds of cheeses, cold meats, and 1,200 varieties of sausage (I'm not kidding), a huge variety of seafood, wondrous pastries, teas and coffees, wines, chocolates, and breads. A chef at one of their thirty gourmet bars prepared this dish. German light beers like Kolsch ale or either Helles or pilsner lagers are superb with this dish. Dark beers will discolor the meat.

- $^1/_2$ cup Dijon mustard
- 1 large onion, chopped
- $^1/_2$ cup honey
- 4 cups German beer
- 1 ($3^1/_2$-pound) boneless pork loin, tied
- 1 teaspoon garlic powder
- 1 teaspoon onion powder
- 1 teaspoon paprika
- 1 teaspoon kosher salt
- 3 Granny Smith or Pippin apples, cored and cut into $^1/_2$-inch vertical slices (not peeled)
- 2 tablespoons olive oil
- 1 tablespoon butter, at room temperature
- 1 tablespoon flour
- 2 tablespoons Jägermeister (see Note following page)

In a large saucepan over high heat, prepare a marinade by combining the mustard, onion, honey, and 3 cups of the beer. Bring the marinade just to a boil, stirring constantly, and remove the pan from the heat.

In 2 batches, pour the marinade into a blender and puree. Transfer to a large bowl. Let cool to room temperature and spoon off any foam.

Fold the smaller end of the pork loin back over the meat and tie it with kitchen string; it should be one long cylinder of approximate equal size end to end.

In a large, resealable plastic bag, pour the marinade over the pork loin. Seal the bag, and refrigerate for 8 to 12 hours, turning the bag several times.

Remove the pork from the marinade and let it come to room temperature (this will take about 30 minutes). Meanwhile, transfer the marinade to a saucepan and boil over high heat for 12 minutes. Set aside.

Preheat a charcoal or gas grill to 375°F for direct grilling. Make sure the grill rack is clean and oil it thoroughly with nonstick cooking spray.

In a small bowl, combine the garlic and onion powders, paprika, and salt, to make a rub. Pat the pork dry with paper towels and season it generously with the rub, patting it into all surfaces of the meat. Place it in a roasting pan.

Transfer the pork in its pan to the grill rack over direct heat. Close the grill cover and cook the pork, basting frequently with the reserved marinade, until the internal temperature reaches 155°F for slightly pink meat, 1 to $1^1/_2$ hours.

While the pork is roasting, brush the apple slices generously with the olive oil and place the slices on the prepared grill rack around the roasting pan. Grill for 1 to 2 minutes per side, until the apples start to brown and get grill marks. Remove them from the grill and set aside.

When the pork is done, transfer it to a cutting board, reserving the remaining juices in the pan. Remove the string and let the meat stand, loosely covered with aluminum foil, for 15 minutes.

Meanwhile, to make the sauce, skim and discard the fat from the roasting pan and add the remaining cup of beer. Deglaze the pan by stirring the sauce over moderately high heat, scraping up any brown bits.

Increase the heat to high, bringing the sauce just to a boil, then decrease the heat to low. While the sauce simmers, whisk in the butter and flour until slightly thickened. Stir in the Jägermeister and remove from the heat.

Slice the pork and transfer it to a heated platter over a bed of

continued

grilled apple slices, drizzled with the sauce. Serve any remaining sauce on the side.

SERVES 4 TO 6

NOTE: Jägermeister is an herb-flavored, bitter 70-proof German liqueur. Made from 56 roots, herbs, and spices, Jägermeister is German for "master hunter," hence the elk head on the label. The original purpose of this concoction was medicinal, used to cure everything from an incessant cough to digestive problems.

BARBECUED BRUSSELS SPROUTS

Developed in northern Europe, these little cabbages were also thought to have been grown by the Romans around the fifth century, or perhaps even later. The sprouts we know today were first cultivated in large quantities beginning in 1580 in Belgium, and were brought to the U.S. by French immigrants in the early 1800s. Germany and the Netherlands share the bragging rights for growing the most sprouts in Europe.

- 1 medium onion, diced
- 1 tablespoon butter
- $1/2$ cup beef or chicken stock
- $1^1/2$ pounds fresh or frozen Brussels sprouts, trimmed
- 2 tablespoons heavy cream
- 1 teaspoon cornstarch

- 5 ounces Emmental cheese, grated (about 1 cup) (see Note)

   Paprika, for garnish

   Finely chopped fresh parsley, for garnish

Preheat a charcoal or gas grill to 375°F.

In a Dutch oven or cast-iron skillet over medium heat, sauté the onion in butter, until tender and starting to brown, for about 10 minutes. Add the stock and Brussels sprouts. Transfer the Dutch oven to the barbecue over direct heat, cover and let simmer for 25 minutes for fresh Brussels sprouts, 15 minutes for frozen.

In a small bowl, whisk together the cream and corn starch and pour over the sprouts, stir, and bring to a boil. Remove the Dutch oven from the heat and keep covered.

Transfer the sprouts to a casserole, sprinkle with the grated cheese, and return to the barbecue until the cheese starts to brown, about 10 to 12 minutes. Remove from the heat, sprinkle with paprika and parsley, and serve.

SERVES 4 TO 6

NOTE: Algu Emmental has a rich, nutty-sweet, flavor and a light yellow-gold color, and is made from Bavarian milk. This style of cheese was brought to Germany from Switzerland in the 1700s and is one of the country's favorite cheeses.

GUADELOUPE AND SAINT BARTHÉLEMY

Chris C. World Tour Part 26

———-Forwarded Message———-
From: Chris Columbus <ccolumbus@ninapintasmaria.com>
Sent: Nov. 14, 1493 16:40 GMT
To: Queen Isabella I <hrmisabella@alcazarcastle.gov>

Your Royal Majesty,

I know you were pleased about our discovery of the big America place, but you should see where I'm standing right now. I just planted the flag on a chain of islands and I'm naming them after Santa Maria de Guadalupe de Extremadura. So you have some warm islands to visit on holiday.

Have cc'd the kids as I know they're all getting married soon and perhaps they would like to honeymoon here.

The beaches here are wonderful, and there are more fish in these waters than I've ever seen anywhere. Good news, the water is so warm the crew all smells as fresh as the sea, a big change from the trip over here.

The vegetables here are incredible, sweet fruits the size of a loaf of bread, green and yellow globes that are tangy and sweet at the same time, and—I think I heard my translator correctly—they even have a plant that grows henfruit, so they call it eggplant.

And that chocolate powder we got from the *conquistadores*, they have it here too, a nut that when you grind it produces a dark brown liquor that has all the ladies swooning. Maybe I can send you some.

Anyway, ta-ta, gotta go discover some more islands for you and His Majesty, but I may need your help, I'm running out of saint names.

With great respect,
Chris C.

Guadeloupe was indeed discovered and claimed for Spain by Columbus in November 1493; however, it has been a French possession since 1635. This Caribbean archipelago of nine inhabited islands is actually part of the European Union and its currency is the euro. Guadeloupe proper is made up of five of those islands: Basse-Terre, Grande-Terre, La Désirade, Les Saintes, and Chris's other local discovery, Marie-Galante. Although the islanders voted in 2003 to become an "overseas territorial collectivity," since I don't know what that means, I'll just call them an island.

Guadeloupian cuisine is a reflection of its many cultures. The local Creole style blends the artfulness of French cuisine, the fiery spices of African cookery, and the unique flavors of East Indian and Southeast Asian cooking. Fresh seafood, including shellfish, smoked fish, stuffed land crabs, and stewed conch are favorites.

Guadeloupe (with Saint Barthélemy) is considered one of the culinary capitals of the Caribbean, with some two hundred restaurants, some overlooking the sea and some on the front porches of cooks' homes. Local rum drinks and punches often precede a meal and, of course, imported French wines often accompany it.

Saint Barthélemy, usually called Saint Barts or Saint Barths, was until early 2007 part of Guadeloupe; now this smallest of the islands, at only eight square miles, is its own collectivity of France. St. Barthélemy is unlike many of the other islands in the Caribbean; it is rocky and hilly and the climate is extremely dry.

Most of the population here are Caucasians of European descent, having arrived mainly from France, with a smattering of Swedes, hence French being their official language—a dialect that French visitors, though, have difficulty understanding. But just about everyone also speaks English.

Island tourism centers around a cadre of millionaires, and due to this plethora of high rollers, the villas, hotels, and restaurants are as opulent and high class as any in the world. Many have incredible views of the harbor or the magnificent beaches that surround the island, which are, as far as I'm concerned, some of the finest in the world.

GRILLED SNAPPER WITH CAPERS

Since Guadeloupe is a French island, a lot of its cooking uses recipes and ingredients common to France. This dish combines a very popular local fish, local hot peppers, and a bit of the old country (the capers) thrown in. The fiery habañero, grown mainly in the Caribbean, is one of the hottest peppers used in cooking, with some varieties hitting 325,000 on the Scoville chart—just short of the heat of an F-16 jet engine.

MARINADE

- $1/4$ cup freshly squeezed lime juice
- 1 teaspoon salt
- $1/4$ teaspoon dried thyme
- 1 teaspoon freshly ground black pepper
- 3 cloves garlic, chopped
- 1 to 2 Scotch bonnet or habañero chiles, minced (to taste)
- 4 (6-ounce) red snapper fillets, or other firm white fish

SAUCE

- 2 tablespoons chopped fresh cilantro
- 2 tablespoons freshly squeezed lime juice
- 2 tablespoons water
- 2 tablespoons extra-virgin olive oil
- $1/2$ tablespoons capers
- 1 tablespoon red wine vinegar
- $1/2$ teaspoons minced Scotch bonnet or habañero chile
- $1/4$ teaspoon salt
- $1/4$ teaspoon freshly ground black pepper
- 1 clove garlic, chopped
- 1 large shallot, chopped

To prepare the marinade, place the lime juice, salt, thyme, black pepper, garlic, and chiles in a blender and process until smooth. Pour the marinade over the fish in a large resealable plastic bag, squeeze out the air, and seal. Marinate the fish in the refrigerator for 3 to 4 hours, turning the bag occasionally.

Preheat a charcoal or gas grill to 325°F to 350°F. Make sure the grill rack is clean and oil it thoroughly with nonstick cooking spray.

For the sauce, in the blender combine the cilantro, lime juice, water, olive oil, capers, vinegar, chiles, salt, black pepper, garlic, and shallot and process until smooth.

Remove the fish from the marinade and discard the marinade. Place the fish on the prepared grill rack over direct heat and cook for 3 minutes per side, or until the fish flakes easily when tested with a fork. Serve immediately with the caper sauce.

SERVES 4

PINEAPPLE CHICKEN RUNDOWN

"Rundown" is a very popular stew-like meal we sampled on several islands in the Caribbean that's made with coconut and fish, poultry, or meat. The rundown is really "boil down," where the coconut milk is cooked until it loses most of its liquid, then is mixed with spices, meat, and vegetables. Serve this with grilled or broiled sweet potatoes and steamed rice with peas.

1/2 cup chopped onion

2 tablespoons minced fresh garlic

1 large green bell pepper, seeded, and finely chopped

2 tablespoons vegetable or olive oil

1/2 teaspoon dried thyme

1 tablespoon vinegar

1 small jalapeño pepper, seeded, and minced

Salt

1/4 teaspoon plus a pinch of freshly ground black pepper

3/4 cup unsweetened coconut milk

6 tablespoons heavy cream

6 (6- to 8-ounce) boneless chicken breasts or turkey breast fillets

1 fresh pineapple, halved vertically

To make the sauce, in a skillet, sauté the onion, garlic, and bell pepper in the oil until softened and just beginning to brown, about 10 minutes. Add the thyme and vinegar, then add the jalapeño and season with a generous 1/2 teaspoon of salt and the pepper, and simmer for 2 minutes. Cover and set aside.

Pour the coconut milk into a saucepan and bring to a boil, then reduce heat to very low and simmer until the water evaporates and what is left is coconut oil and a custardlike mixture, 30 minutes or so. Add the cream, stir, and set aside.

Preheat a gas or charcoal grill to 375°F. Make sure the grill rack is clean and oil it thoroughly with nonstick cooking spray.

Scoop out the flesh from the pineapple halves and cut into small chunks; set aside both the shell and the fruit.

Place the chicken breasts on the prepared grill rack over direct heat. Cook until just browned on both sides, 8 to 10 minutes.

Add the coconut custard to the onion-jalapeño sauce and stir well. Dice the chicken breasts and drop the pieces into the sauce, heating over medium-high heat just until the sauce starts to bubble. Remove from heat, pour the chicken and sauce into both pineapple halves, garnish with the pineapple chunks, and serve, with a serving spoon for each pineapple half.

SERVES 6 TO 8

SALMON WITH RED ONION–MANGO RELISH

As with any extremely well-off tourist locale, Saint Barts' restaurants feature foods from all over the world. The clients demand it and readily pay for imported goods, so even though Atlantic salmon isn't caught locally, I wasn't surprised to see it on most of the menus at the restaurants I visited. The onion-mango relish was a wonderful accompaniment at a wedding reception where I was taken by a local couple.

1¹/₂ cups coarsely chopped papayas (about 2 medium)

1 cup coarsely chopped mangoes

1 cup coarsely chopped red bell pepper

1 cup coarsely chopped red onion

¹/₄ cup thinly sliced fresh basil

¹/₄ cup white wine vinegar

¹/₂ teaspoon grated orange zest

¹/₄ cup fresh orange juice

2 tablespoons minced, seeded jalapeño pepper

2 tablespoons freshly squeezed lime juice

2 teaspoons sugar

2 cloves garlic, minced

¹/₄ teaspoon salt

¹/₂ teaspoon freshly ground pepper

4 (6-ounce) salmon steaks (or tuna)

For the relish, combine the papaya, mango, bell pepper, onion, basil, vinegar, orange zest and juice, jalapeño pepper, lime juice, sugar, garlic, and ¹/₈ teaspoon of the salt in a bowl, and stir well. Let the mixture stand, covered, at room temperature for 4 to 5 hours, stirring occasionally.

Sprinkle pepper and the remaining salt over the swordfish steaks.

Preheat a charcoal or gas grill to 375°F. Make sure the grill rack is clean and oil it thoroughly with nonstick cooking spray.

Place the fish directly on the prepared grill rack over direct heat and cook 5 minutes per side, or until the fish flakes easily when tested with a fork.

Serve immediately with the relish.

SERVES 4

BASSE-TERRE LIME-GARLIC PORK LOIN

Caribbean cooks use limes the same way we use lemons. Limes are more acidic than other citrus fruits, but have less vitamin C than their cousin lemons. They are great in marinades, drinks, jams and jellies, salad dressing, sorbets, and of course, in the famous Key lime pie.

MARINADE

- ½ cup finely chopped onion
- ¼ cup water
- 3 tablespoons freshly squeezed lime juice (from Key limes, if possible)
- 2 large cloves garlic, minced
- 1 tablespoon olive oil
- 1 to 2 teaspoons finely chopped jalapeño, to taste
- ¼ teaspoon dried thyme, crushed
- ¼ teaspoon salt
- ⅛ teaspoon freshly ground black pepper
- 1½ pounds boneless pork loin roast

SAUCE

- ½ cup beef broth
- 2 teaspoons sugar
- ¼ teaspoon dried thyme, crushed
- 1 tablespoon cornstarch
- 2 tablespoons chopped fresh parsley

For the marinade, in a small bowl, combine the onion, water, lime juice, garlic, olive oil, jalapeño, thyme, salt, and pepper; stir well.

Place the pork loin in a resealable plastic bag and pour the marinade over the meat. Seal the bag, place it in a bowl, and refrigerate for 4 to 6 hours.

Preheat a charcoal or gas grill to 350°F.

Remove the meat from the bag and set aside the marinade. Place the meat in a roasting pan and transfer to the grill rack over direct heat. Cover the grill and roast the pork for 40 to 50 minutes, until it reaches an internal temperature of 155° to 160°F for medium. Remove the meat from the pan, cover with foil, and let stand for 10 minutes.

Meanwhile, to make the sauce, strain the reserved marinade into a small saucepan, add the beef broth, the sugar, and the ¼ teaspoon thyme. Cook, stirring, until the sauce is thickened and bubbles are just starting to form, then add the cornstarch and stir continuously for another 3 minutes. Remove the pan from the heat and stir the parsley into the sauce.

Slice the pork and serve on a heated platter with the sauce on the side.

SERVES 6 TO 8

SWEET POTATO CASSEROLE

Since Saint Barts is a desert island (yeah, with cactus and everything), it's hard to grow most vegetables. But one enterprising couple, the Monyards, grow sweet potatoes on their deck in old whiskey casks. Their housekeeper/cook made this dish for a meal they invited me to share. When asked if she wanted credit for the recipe, she said, "No, I stole it from somebody, just can't remember who," and laughed devilishly. Serve with roast pork, chicken, or grilled fish.

TOPPING

- 1 cup firmly packed brown sugar
- 1 cup chopped pecans
- ½ cup self-rising or all-purpose flour
- ¼ cup (½ stick) butter, melted

SWEET POTATOES

- 3 cups cooked, mashed sweet potatoes (about 1½ pounds or 4 to 5 potatoes)
- 1 cup granulated sugar
- 1 cup unsweetened coconut flakes
- ½ cup golden raisins
- 2 eggs, lightly beaten
- 1 teaspoon vanilla extract
- ¼ teaspoon salt
- ½ cup (1 stick) butter, melted
- ¼ cup heavy cream

To make the topping, in a large bowl combine the brown sugar, nuts, flour, and melted butter, and stir with a fork to thoroughly mix the ingredients, then set aside.

For the sweet potatoes, in a large bowl, combine the mashed sweet potatoes, sugar, coconut, raisins, eggs, vanilla, salt, and the butter. If the mixture seems too thick, stir in up to $^1/_4$ cup heavy cream.

Prepare a charcoal or gas grill for indirect cooking (it is not necessary to use a drip pan with this recipe). Preheat to 350°F.

Spoon the potato mixture into a large, greased casserole and spread the topping over the sweet potatoes. Transfer to the grill rack over indirect heat and bake, uncovered, for 20 to 30 minutes, until the topping is golden brown.

SERVES 6 TO 8

BARBECUED PLANTAIN AND PEANUT MASH

Did you know that, there are over 500 different types of bananas, or that, though it is generally regarded as a tree, this large tropical plant is really an herb? Plantains are a type of banana that is longer, thicker skinned, and starchier than the sweet, soft variety we all know so well. Plantains are used more like a vegetable than a fruit; the green ones especially must be cooked before they're eaten. Most supermarkets today carry plantains; if you can't find them there, go to an Asian or Latino market.

In this recipe, it's fine to use commercial peanut butter, but if you simply grind up $^1/_4$ cup of roasted peanuts or cashews this recipe will rock. Serve with grilled poultry, shellfish, or barbecued pork loin or ribs.

- 2 large green plantains
- 1 egg
- $^1/_2$ teaspoon salt
- $^1/_2$ cup milk
- 2 tablespoons crunchy peanut butter or $^1/_4$ cup roasted, unsalted peanuts, ground
- $^1/_2$ cup fresh bread crumbs or panko (Japanese bread crumbs)
- 1 onion, minced
- 1 stalk of celery, minced

Cut off the ends of the plantains and make a lengthwise slit on the skin of each; do not peel. Place the plantains in boiling salted water to cover by 2 inches and boil for 15 to 20 minutes. Test with a fork; they should be soft, but not mushy, on the edges and slightly hard at the center.

Meanwhile, prepare a charcoal or gas grill for indirect cooking (it is not necessary to use a drip pan with this recipe). Preheat to 375°F.

While they are still hot, remove the skins from the plantains, then crush them in a wide flat baking dish. Add the egg, salt, milk, peanut butter, bread crumbs, onion, and celery, stirring to incorporate.

Place baking pan on the grill rack over indirect heat, lower the lid, and cook for about 25 minutes, until plantains are lightly browned and can easily be pierced with a fork.

SERVES 4

HONG KONG

Cowardice in the Face of a Lobster

Having had the pleasure not only of visiting Hong Kong eighteen times, but also living there for six months, I can easily say it's one of my favorite places on earth. One reason: a dizzying variety of restaurants.

Because the average Hong Kong apartment is only seven hundred square feet and the average family size is 5.8, there's very little scope for "Hey, bring the missus and the kids over for dinner tonight" kinda invitations. So the Chinese are famous for their entertaining away from home, and Hong Kong's twenty thousand restaurants are usually filled to the brim every night.

That's right: twenty thousand restaurants, serving every stripe of Chinese regional cooking as well as just about any other kind of world cuisine you can imagine. I could write a whole book and talk for days about the culinary wonderland that is Hong Kong. Ask me sometime about Luk Yu, the restaurant that serves 200 kinds of dim sum. Or Jumbo, which claims to be the world's largest floating restaurant (they seat 2300 people at a time).

Right now, since we're talking grilling, I'm going to cut to the chase and tell you about a visit I made to Lei Yue Mun, where I had not only the best grilled seafood meal of my life, but the best

80

seafood meal of my life, period. This tiny fishing village sits at the point where the harbor narrows between Kowloon and the northeastern shore of Hong Kong Island. Thirty live-fish stalls line your route to about fourteen restaurants. You choose from a vast assortment of fish and shellfish, which you then take to the restaurant of your choice (or you can have them delivered). Within minutes—sometimes seconds—your dinner goes from the brine to the broiler, the pan, or the grill, and the freshness is impossible to describe.

I walked down the long aisle peering into small buckets of fish, large clear glass tanks, and huge wriggling bins, at what was soon to be my dinner. My host, having asked me what seafood I liked ("Me? Everything!"), picked "two of these, one large one of those, and how about a dozen of those." Soon, holding plastic bags filled with perky fish and shellfish, we headed to a restaurant, settled into an outside table with a spectacular view of Hong Kong's Central District, and handed our dinner to the waiter.

Not two minutes later, the first of our six-course seafood feast arrived still sizzling from the fire; grilled scallops in black bean sauce, as fresh and tender and succulent as possible. The scallops were followed within three minutes by awesome barbecued jumbo shrimp with spicy salt-pepper and grilled crispy soft-shell crabs, drizzled with fresh garlic in oil. Next up, a huge platter of "fisherman-style clams," grilled and spiked with a spicy soy-hoisin-Hunan sauce, which appeared perhaps three minutes after the previous two courses had vanished. Then came a whole grilled grouper (stuffed with fresh ginger, scallions, and macadamia nuts), so fresh it could have swum to the table by itself—perfectly moist, tender, and richly flavored.

By now my hand was poised, ready to raise the white flag (er, napkin), and surrender, when I saw our waiter approaching with a huge tray of grilled lobster (my host had sneaked these critters onto our menu without my knowing it). I resignedly undid my belt, sighed, and took a deep breath, inhaling the intoxicating scent of the 747-sized grilled crustaceans, fiery red and steaming, bathed in a sea of butter, lime, grapefruit, and orange, with sprinkles of tarragon.

I put the napkin back in my lap.

GRILLED CHINA SEA TUNA

Until recently, China exported most of the deep-sea tuna caught in its waters to Japan for consumption as sushi, but the government is making a big push to get the Chinese people to eat more tuna caught just off their own coast, touting the idea that tuna is "pollution free," cheap, and nutritious. I first had this dish in Guangzhou (Canton) at the White Swan Hotel's Jade River Restaurant. Serve it with stir-fried or steamed Chinese cabbage and steamed brown rice.

2 (8-ounce) tuna steaks

1¼ teaspoons sesame oil

2 tablespoons freshly squeezed lemon juice

⅓ cup soy sauce

⅓ cup hoisin sauce (see Note page 86)

3 tablespoons honey

3 cloves garlic, finely minced

1 teaspoon Chinese five-spice powder (see Note)

In a shallow dish or pan, marinate the tuna steaks in the sesame oil and lemon juice for 1 hour, turning frequently.

Preheat a charcoal or gas grill to 375°F. Make sure the grill rack is clean and oil it thoroughly with nonstick cooking spray.

Mix the soy sauce, hoisin sauce, honey, garlic, and five-spice powder in a small saucepan, and heat over medium-high heat until it just starts to boil; remove the pan from the heat and keep warm.

Place the tuna steaks directly on the prepared grill rack and grill for about 2 minutes per side, basting often with the sauce, until the fish just turns translucent on both sides and is very lightly brown on the bottom side. The tuna should be rare to medium-rare in the center.

Drizzle the fish steaks with the remaining sauce and serve immediately.

SERVES 4

NOTE: You can easily make your own Chinese five-spice powder by combining 6 star anise, 1 tablespoon whole black peppercorns, 3 cinnamon sticks, 16 whole cloves, and 1 tablespoon fennel seeds in a coffee grinder and grinding to a fine powder. Store in an airtight container for two to three years.

CHINATOWN DELI BBQ PORK

Chef Martin Yan was born and grew up in China with his widowed mother, whom he still credits as one of his greatest cooking teachers. Today he is one of the best-known and loved Chinese cooks on the planet. He was kind enough to share this recipe with me. Just about every Chinese deli or butcher shop on earth sells this unique Chinese-style preparation of pork. The pork can be served hot or cold, and is great with stir-fried vegetables like baby corn, green onions, zucchini, and Chinese long beans.

- 1/3 cup sugar
- 1/4 cup soy sauce
- 1/4 cup hoisin sauce (see Note page 86)
- 1/4 cup honey
- 2 tablespoons Shaoxing rice wine or dry sherry (see Note)
- 1 tablespoon sesame seed paste or mashed white fermented bean curd
- 2 teaspoons minced garlic
- 1 teaspoon minced ginger
- 1 teaspoon sesame oil
- 1 teaspoon salt
- 1 teaspoon black pepper
- 1 teaspoon Chinese five-spice powder (see Note page 82)
- 5 drops red food coloring (optional)
- 2 to 2 1/2 pounds boneless pork shoulder or butt, trimmed of excess fat

Stir the sugar, soy sauce, hoisin sauce, honey, rice wine, sesame seed paste, garlic, ginger, sesame oil, salt, black pepper, five-spice powder, and red food coloring together in a large bowl.

Cut the pork into pieces roughly 1 inch thick, 3 inches wide, and 8 inches long. Place the pork in a large resealable plastic bag; pour the marinade into the bag, seal the bag securely, and turn the bag to coat the meat. Refrigerate for at least 4 hours or up to 8 hours, turning occasionally.

Preheat a charcoal or gas grill to 350°F. Line a baking pan with foil.

Remove the pork from the marinade and pour the marinade into a saucepan. Boil for 12 minutes and set aside as a baste.

Place the pork on a rack set over the prepared pan. Transfer the pan to the grill rack over direct heat and cook, uncovered, brushing occasionally with the basting liquid, for 30 minutes. Turn the pieces of pork over and cook, brushing occasionally with the basting liquid, until the pork is cooked through and tender, about 45 minutes longer.

Remove the pork from the heat and transfer it to a cutting board. Let it rest for 10 minutes before cutting it into thin slices.

SERVES 4 TO 6

NOTE: Shaoxing, also known as Chinese rice wine, is made with millet and yeast in addition to rice and water, and has a flavor similar to dry sherry. Do not confuse this wine with Chinese rice vinegar. Rice wine is made by a yeast fermentation process that transforms the sugar in glutinous rice to alcohol. Rice vinegar is made by adding bacteria to take the fermentation process one step further, which turns the alcohol into an acid. Sesame seed paste is made from (you guessed it) sesame seeds and peanut oil, and is available in Asian grocery stores, or the Asian section of your supermarket, as is mashed fermented bean curd.

BARBECUED PEKING DUCK WITH HOISIN SAUCE

The 1977 publication The People's Republic of China Cookbook *opens its exhaustive treatise on Peking duck with an ominous warning. "The making of Peking duck is a demanding specialty for which no exact recipe exists. It is a dish that is exclusively limited to restaurant cooking. The process itself can be observed and described, but in practice the special judgment, materials, and equipment make the dish very difficult to produce in the home kitchen." Author's comment: "Phooey, here is a great recipe that I've done many times." You can buy Mandarin pancakes at many Asian grocery stores, or even make them if you have the time, and the green onion "brushes" are easy to make (see below).*

- 1 cup white wine
- 1 cup honey
- 1/2 cup hoisin sauce (see Note)
- 1 teaspoon garlic powder
- 1 tablespoon powdered ginger
- 1/4 teaspoon salt
- 1 (5- to 6-pound) Peking duck
- 1 bunch green onions, trimmed
- 2 to 3 dozen Mandarin pancakes

To make the marinade, in a small bowl, combine the wine, honey, hoisin sauce, garlic powder, ginger, and salt; mix well and set aside.

Wash and dry the duck, place it in a resealable plastic bag, and pour in the marinade. Seal the bag and refrigerate for at least 8 hours.

Remove the duck from the bag. Drain off the marinade and reserve it in a covered container in the freezer or refrigerator. Using twine or kitchen string, make a loop through both wings and hang the duck from a cabinet, ceiling fixture, or pot rack so the bird is suspended over a pan in the kitchen. Let dry for 24 hours. (The Chinese have been doing this quite successfully for 2,000 years, so please don't worry about bacteria. If you're really antsy, drape one layer of cheesecloth around the bird while it hangs.)

Prepare a charcoal or gas grill for indirect grilling, placing a drip pan under the cool side of the grill rack (see page 3). Preheat to 375°F.

Transfer the reserved marinade to a saucepan and boil for 12 minutes.

To cook the duck, if possible, suspend it in your barbecue grill so the bottom of the duck is above the grill rack directly over the water pan. If you can't do this, place the duck on an upright, opened juice or soda can filled halfway with water, and use the duck's legs to form a tripod, balancing it in a vertical position centered over the water pan. While the duck is cooking, the vertical position allows the fat to drip off the duck into the water, removing most of the fat under the skin and preventing flare-ups from the fat dripping onto the coals. The fat under the skin melts and drips away as the skin pulls away from the meat because the marinade dries and shrinks the skin surface.

Close the grill lid and cook the duck for 1 1/2 to 2 hours, until the internal temperature at the breast reaches 160°F, replenishing the water in the drip pan from time to time. Use the marinade to baste the duck once per hour during the cooking time.

Meanwhile, use the green onions to make the traditional "brushes." On a counter, hold 1 onion with the white part facing away from you. With a sharp knife, cut lengthwise about 1 inch into the bulb of the onion, leaving the root end intact; repeat so that you've made 4 evenly spaced sections, the onion is quartered, and looks like a "brush" with 4 segments. Now do twice more so you have eight sections.

Repeat with the rest of the onions, then place them in cold water for up to two hours to curl the cut ends.

continued

Remove the duck from the grill, keeping it on the can (if used), then baste once more with a thick coat of the basting sauce. Remove the duck from the can and wrap it tightly in foil. Let the duck sit for 20 minutes, then put on cutting board and remove the foil. Cut both the duck skin and the meat into bite-sized slices and serve with hoisin sauce, green onion brushes, and mandarin pancakes.

To eat Peking duck the traditional way, use the green onion brushes to spread hoisin sauce on a pancake, add a piece of duck skin and a piece of duck meat, add the green onion brush itself, then wrap or fold up the pancake and eat.

SERVES 4

NOTE: Hoisin sauce is a thick, reddish-brown sweet and spicy sauce, widely used in Chinese cooking. It's a mixture of soybeans, vinegar, sugar, garlic, chile peppers, and various spices. There are dozens of recipes on the Internet, but why bother? Go to an Asian grocery store and buy a bottle of Pearl River Bridge or Koon Chun hoisin sauce, made in China—where they've been making it for several centuries.

HOISIN-CASHEW LAMB RIBS

Surprise! China is the world's largest producer of sheep for meat, followed by Australia. The Chinese produce over 1.6 million tons of lamb per year while the Aussies produce less than half a million. Lamb dishes tend to be most common in Islamic parts of China, and are associated with the north of the country (Mongolian lamb is perhaps the most famous lamb dish in Chinese cuisine). They are usually cooked or prepared with the ubiquitous hoisin sauce (no mint jelly here).

2	cups chicken stock
$1/2$	cup dry red wine
8	tablespoons sweet Thai chile sauce
1	tablespoon sesame oil
1	cup hoisin sauce (see Note page 86)
1	cup vegetable oil
1	cup Shaoxing rice wine (see Note page 83)
10	cloves garlic, minced
6	shallots, minced
4	tablespoons minced fresh ginger
$1/2$	teaspoon freshly ground Szechuan peppercorns
3	(2-pound) racks of lamb
4	cups minced roasted cashews
	Fresh minced chives, for garnish

In a large saucepan, heat the stock and red wine to a boil over high heat, decrease the heat, and simmer until the liquid is reduced to $3/4$ of a cup, about 20 minutes.

Add 4 tablespoons of the chile sauce, sesame oil, and $1/4$ cup of the hoisin sauce, and bring back to a boil. Lower heat to a simmer until the sauce is reduced to $1/2$ cup, about 5 to 6 minutes. Remove from the heat.

In a skillet, combine $1/2$ cup of the hoisin sauce, vegetable oil, rice wine, garlic, shallots, ginger, and black pepper. Cook over low heat until warm, about 3 minutes. Remove from the heat and let cool.

Place lamb in a $2^{1}/_2$-gallon resealable plastic bag or shallow pan. Pour the marinade over the ribs and shake bag (or turn lamb in the pan) to coat well. Marinate in the refrigerator for at least 8 hours.

Preheat a charcoal or gas grill to 375°F. Make sure the grill rack is clean and oil it thoroughly with nonstick cooking spray.

Drain the lamb and pat dry, discarding the marinade. Transfer the lamb to the prepared grill rack over direct heat. Sear on both sides, 4 to 5 minutes only, until the lamb is just beginning to brown and the internal temperature at the thickest part of the loin reaches 115°F. Remove the lamb from the heat, cover, and let rest for 10 minutes.

Spray a roasting pan large enough for the lamb with nonstick cooking spray. Mix the remaining chile sauce and hoisin sauce in small bowl. Using a barbecue brush, cover the meaty part of the ribs with the sauce, letting the sauce partially dry for 2 minutes. Reserve the remaining sauce for serving.

Pour the cashews into a shallow dish; roll the meat in the nuts, pressing down to coat evenly. Place the lamb in the prepared pan and transfer to the grill over direct heat. Cook until the internal temperature in the thickest part of the meat reaches 135°F for medium-rare, about 20 minutes.

Transfer to a heated platter, drizzle with a small amount of the reserved sauce, sprinkle with chives, and serve.

SERVES 6

NOTE: To maintain its outstanding flavor, fresh lamb should be eaten within four days of purchase. Refrigerate lamb until ready for cooking. If the lamb is to be stored more than four days, it should be frozen. Defrost in the refrigerator where the meat can thaw slowly.

SPICY SWEET POTATOES

Surprise again! China produces 80 percent of the world's sweet potatoes, growing more than 115 million tons and over 100 varieties each year, half of which are used as animal feed. The tuber probably reached coastal China aboard Portuguese ships in the late sixteenth century. This recipe had its origins in Shandong Province, one of the principal sweet-potato growing regions.

1	cup water
4	tablespoons soy sauce
3	tablespoons Shaoxing rice wine (see Note page 83)
2	tablespoons rice vinegar
2	teaspoons regular or toasted sesame oil
$1/4$	teaspoon freshly ground black pepper
$1/2$	teaspoon Chinese five-spice powder (see Note page 82)
2	teaspoons brown sugar
2	pounds sweet potatoes, peeled and cut in $1/4$-inch slices
2	tablespoons vegetable oil
	Grated zest of 1 orange
	Grated zest of 1 large lemon
	Grated zest of 1 mandarin orange
2	cloves garlic, minced
$1^1/2$	teaspoons minced fresh ginger
$3/4$	teaspoon chile paste
$1/4$	teaspoon crushed red pepper flakes
2	teaspoons minced fresh parsley

Preheat a charcoal or gas grill to 400°F. Make sure the grill rack is clean and oil it thoroughly with nonstick cooking spray.

In a small saucepan, combine the water, soy sauce, rice wine, vinegar, $1^1/2$ teaspoons of the sesame oil, black pepper, five-spice powder, and brown sugar; and bring to a boil, stirring often for about 10 minutes. Remove from the heat and set aside.

Toss the sweet potatoes with the vegetable oil. Place the potatoes directly on the prepared grill rack for about 2 minutes a side, until they pick up grill marks and the outsides begin to get crisp. Set aside.

Place a large cast-iron skillet or Dutch oven on the grill over direct heat and heat the remaining $1/2$ teaspoon of sesame oil in the pan. Quickly add the orange, lemon, and mandarin zests, garlic, ginger, chile paste, and pepper flakes. Stir constantly until the spices are warmed and begin to get fragrant, about 3 minutes. Add the soy sauce mixture and stir. Add the grilled sweet potato slices to the skillet, bring the liquid to a boil, cover, and move the pan to the cool side of the barbecue. Leave the grill lid open, and cook for 12 to 15 minutes, until the potatoes are soft, but not mushy. Sprinkle the sweet potatoes with the parsley and serve.

SERVES 4 TO 6

IRELAND

The Smoky Emerald Isle

Ireland's culinary traditions began quite modestly. A three-legged metal pot was hung over a fire, water was added, and then if you lived on the coast (and there is a lot of coastline), you threw in whatever fish or shellfish you had gathered that day, added some vegetables and some herbs or spices (if you had them), and let dinner cook all day.

Sometimes the cauldron was turned upside down over heated flat rocks and bread was baked under it. Ovens, grills, and barbecues weren't available until much later. But ingenious cooks did grill, sort of. They heated flat rocks, put a joint of meat or a chicken on the rock, perhaps drizzled it with honey and sprinkled it with salt, and then covered it with other heated rocks. The juices and fat running off the cooking meat often ignited and kept the rocks hot enough to cook the food.

Today, not only is Ireland becoming a culinary superstar, with dozens of excellent restaurants in every major city, it also hosts the World Cup Barbecue Championship every year. Every September barbecue fans from all over the world flock to Lisdoonvarna, Ireland (not Memphis, Kansas City, Dallas, or Lexington, North Carolina), for this event, which has literally put the Irish on the "barbeculinary" map.

With one of the fastest growing economies in Europe, the Irish are putting aside those potatoes, grabbing barbecue tongs, spreading the charcoal, and grilling like fiends. It makes perfect sense: they have a long tradition of good, simple food made from fresh, often home-grown ingredients. Even Ballymaloe, one of the top culinary schools in all Europe, has classes that focus on grilling (I was lucky enough to sit in on some of them).

In nearby Cork, my television crew and I visited the historic English Market and were struck by the amazing variety of meats, poultry, fish, vegetables, pastries, cheeses, sausages, and condiments being sold in this small market. One shop in particular, Tim O'Sullivan's butcher shop, drew my eye, and our cameras, as I stood, mouth agape, at their "Barbecue and Grilling" display—a dozen or so prepared meats all ready to be popped on the grill, all in support of what Tim describes an intense new customer interest in grilling and barbecue.

By the way, I've asked them to open a shop down the street from us.

The only downside I can imagine to the growth of barbecue and grilling in Ireland is that the pastoral scenes of rolling hills of emerald green, the picture-perfect homes in the valleys, and the flowers dotting the landscape may soon be clouded over by all those grills churning fragrant smoke into the air. They might have to change the name of this place from the Emerald Isle to the Smoky Isle. But, hey, no matter, as long as they don't run out of lamb, salmon, and Guinness.

IRISH SMOKED SALMON

Irish whiskey runs the gamut of price from around $10 to upwards of $700. If you can't get alder wood chips, try oak, maple, or pecan, or fruitwoods, but stay away from mesquite and hickory as they're too strong for salmon. This can be served as an appetizer or an entrée—perhaps with wild rice and sautéed green beans sprinkled with toasted, slivered almonds.

3	(1-pound) salmon fillets, with skin
1	cup Irish whiskey
½	cup firmly packed brown sugar
1	teaspoon garlic powder
1	teaspoon dried dill
½	teaspoon dried thyme
1	teaspoon freshly ground black pepper
1	tablespoon coarse sea salt
	About 4 cups wood chips, preferably alder

Place the salmon in a large baking dish, skin side down. Pour whiskey over the fish. Turn the fish over (skin side up), cover with aluminum foil, and weigh down the fish with foil-wrapped bricks, stones, or anything heavy, covering the fillets beneath completely. Marinate for 4 to 6 hours, refrigerated.

In a small bowl combine the brown sugar, garlic powder, dill, thyme, black pepper, and salt, stirring to mix. Remove the salmon from the whiskey and rub the spice mixture on the flesh side of the fish. Gently place the fish, skin side down, back into the whiskey marinade, top with the weights, and marinate 1 hour longer.

Place a cooling rack over a rimmed baking sheet. Drain the salmon, discarding the marinade, and transfer to the rack, skin side down. Poke several toothpicks into the top of the fish and lightly drape the fish with a piece of muslin or cheesecloth—the idea is to protect the fish from dirt and disturbance while letting air circulate all around it. Let air-dry for 2 to 3 hours.

Place the wood chips in a bowl or can, cover with water, and soak for at least 2 hours.

Prepare a charcoal or gas grill for indirect cooking to 120°F to 150°, or use a smoker. The lower temperature is reachable in a smoker, the higher is about the lowest you can get from a carefully watched barbecue grill.

For a charcoal fire, pile 8 briquettes on one side of your grill, leaving the other side unheated. Add 2 briquettes per hour, but watch the temperature; if it rises too high add only 1 briquette per hour. For a gas grill, light one burner, turned to its lowest setting, and leave the other burners turned off. Do not exceed the temperature or your fish will be ruined. In either case, to maintain the low temperature you may need to crack open the lid slightly or open vents fully to let excess heat out of the barbecue. If using a smoker, just follow the manufacturer's instructions.

Cover the grill rack with a sheet of aluminum foil, shiny side down; spray with nonstick cooking spray.

Put a handful of soaked wood chips on a piece of heavy-duty aluminum foil and fold it over like an envelope to enclose the wood. Using a pencil, poke 3 or 4 holes in the top of the foil envelope (don't poke all the way through). When ready to cook, place the foil directly on the coals or gas jets. Replace the chips about every 1½ hours during cooking.

Carefully remove the salmon from the cooling rack and place it skin side down on the foil-covered grill over indirect heat. Cook for about 8 hours, or until the fish is firm but not hard. Cover the grill during cooking if you can; prop the lid open if needed to maintain a low temperature.

SERVES 10 TO 12 AS AN APPETIZER

NOTE: Once prepared, home-smoked salmon will keep quite well for a week under refrigeration; if frozen (wrapped tightly in plastic wrap, and in a freezer bag) it can be kept for up to 2 to 3 months.

ORANGE-GLAZED PHEASANT

In earlier times, birds would be hung by their heads until the body fell off, at which point they would be "ready for cooking." Those birds would be a little too strong for today's palate, but hanging for a short time is worthwhile. I suggest no more than 3 days at 40°F or cooler, in a refrigerator. Serve these pheasants with buttered noodles and honey-glazed Brussels sprouts.

3	mandarin oranges, zest coarsely chopped
2	cups water
1$^1/_2$	cups orange juice
1	cup Grand Marnier
3	tablespoons tightly packed brown sugar
2	tablespoons Dijon mustard
2	tablespoons red currant jelly
2	(2$^1/_2$- to 3-pound) pheasants
1	small orange
1	mandarin orange
2	tablespoons butter
	Salt
	Freshly ground black pepper
2	tablespoons Bailey's Irish Cream liqueur

Prepare a charcoal or gas grill for indirect grilling, placing a drip pan under the cool side of the grill rack (see page 3). Preheat to 450°F.

In a saucepan, cover the zest with 1 cup of the water; bring to a boil. Remove the pan from the heat and drain the zest. Set aside 2 tablespoons of the zest and return the rest to the pan. Add 1 cup of the orange juice, $^1/_2$ cup of the Grand Marnier, and the sugar. Boil, uncovered, 10 to 15 minutes, until the liquid is almost gone, being careful not to burn the thick mixture, stirring often. Add the remaining $^1/_2$ cup of orange juice, the mustard, jelly, and $^1/_4$ cup of the Grand Marnier, stirring over medium heat until the jelly melts, about another 5 to 6 minutes. Set aside.

Remove any giblets and necks from the pheasants and reserve for another use. Rinse the birds inside and out and pat dry.

Cut two oranges in half and put two halves in the body cavities of the birds. With small skewers, secure the skin over the body cavities, pinning the neck skin to the back.

Lay the pheasants, breast side down, in a roasting pan. Add the remaining 1 cup of water to the pan and brush the skin with the orange sauce. Transfer the pan to the grill rack over direct heat, lower the lid, and cook for 15 minutes. Turn the birds over and move the roasting pan to the cooler side of the grill (ideally around 350°F), brush them frequently with orange sauce, lower the lid, and roast about 30 minutes longer, or until in the internal temperature at the thickest part of the breast registers 135°F and the meat at the breastbone looks moist, but not soft and wet.

Remove the birds from the pan and drain the juices back into the pan, then set the birds on a platter, cover, and let stand at least 10 minutes before serving.

Skim and discard fat from the drippings, deglazing as you go, and add to the orange sauce. Boil, uncovered, over high heat, until reduced to 1 cup, about 10 to 15 minutes.

Melt the butter in a small skillet on the grill over high heat, and add the reserved orange zest, the remaining $^1/_4$ cup of Grand Marnier, and the Bailey's to the pan, cooking for 3 minutes. Combine this sauce with the orange-dripping sauce, stir a couple of times, then pour a third of it over the pheasants on a serving tray. Serve the remaining two-thirds in a sauceboat at the table.

SERVES 4 TO 6

SPRING LAMB WITH THREE SAUCES

Darina Allen is a true celebrity in Ireland. Her cooking shows have been televised and her books are a staple in most Irish homes. She is the founder of Ballymaloe, a successful cooking school in East Cork which she runs with her husband Tim Allen (no, not THAT Tim Allen; this Tim is a chef, not a home improvement guy). This recipe is lent to us from her massive and inclusive cookbook Darina Allen's Ballymaloe Cookery Course.

    4 racks (1 pound each) spring
       lamb

       Salt

       Freshly ground pepper

       Sprigs of fresh mint, for
       garnish

       Fresh Mint Chutney (recipe
       follows), Onion Sauce
       (recipe follows), and Red
       Currant Sauce (recipe
       follows)

Score the fat of the lamb with several shallow cuts. Refrigerate until ready to use.

Preheat a charcoal or gas grill to 425°F. Make sure the grill rack is clean and oil it thoroughly with nonstick cooking spray.

Sprinkle the lamb generously with salt and freshly ground pepper. Transfer the lamb to the prepared grill rack over direct heat, fat side up. Lower the grill lid and cook for 25 to 30 minutes, until the remaining thin layer of fat is nicely crisped and browned, and a meat thermometer inserted into the meaty section of the chop reads 130°F for medium-rare.

Transfer the lamb to a warm serving dish and let rest for 5 to 10 minutes before carving.

Carve the lamb and serve 2 to 3 chops per person, depending on size (of both the guest and the chop). Serve with the three sauces on the side.

SERVES 4 TO 6

FRESH MINT CHUTNEY

       Handful of fresh mint

    4 tablespoons minced onions

 2 to 3 tablespoons sugar

    1 large cooking apple, such
       as Jonathan, Gravenstein,
       or Jonagold, peeled, cored,
       and coarsely chopped

       Pinch of salt

       Pinch of cayenne pepper

Process the mint, onions, and sugar in a food processor to a paste, add the apples, pulse once or twice only, then season with salt and a little cayenne pepper. It will look like a thick, chunky jam.

ONION SAUCE

  1/2 stick unsalted butter

    3 pounds (3 to 4 large) yellow
       onions, finely chopped

    1 teaspoon salt

    1 teaspoon freshly ground
       black pepper

    1 tablespoon flour

 1 1/2 cups milk

Melt the butter in a saucepan over low heat, add the onions, and cook, covered, until very soft but not browned, about 10 to 15 minutes. Season with salt and pepper. Stir in the flour and add the milk, bring to a simmer and simmer gently, stirring, 5 minutes longer, until the sauce looks like a thick salsa.

RED CURRANT SAUCE

  2/3 cup sugar

  1/2 cup water

  3/4 cup fresh or frozen red
       currants

In a saucepan over medium heat, combine the sugar and water, stirring until the sugar dissolves. Bring to a boil and add the currants. Boil, uncovered, for 4 or 5 minutes, until the currants burst. Serve hot or cold.

IRISH OATMEAL RISOTTO

Steel-cut oats are groats (the inner portion of the oat kernel) that have been cut into pieces using steel discs. Golden in color and resembling little rice particles, they are 100 percent natural. Rolled oats have been steamed, rolled, resteamed, and toasted; they lose some of their natural taste, goodness, and texture in processing. If you can't find McCann's for this recipe, you can substitute other steel-cut brands. If you want to, you can cook this over direct heat in a 375°F grill. Otherwise, your grill side burner or stove top is the way to go.

6	cups unsalted chicken or beef broth
3	tablespoons olive oil or butter
1/4	cup minced shallots
2	cloves garlic, minced
2	cups McCann's steel-cut Irish oatmeal
	Pinch of saffron (optional) (see Note)
2	tablespoons chopped fresh parsley
1	tablespoon freshly squeezed lemon juice
1/2	cup grated Parmesan cheese
	Salt
	Freshly ground black pepper

Bring the broth to a simmer in a saucepan. In a heavy skillet over medium-high heat, heat the oil until a drop of water sprinkled in in the pan sizzles. Add the shallots and garlic and sauté for 3 minutes, until they wilt and just begin to brown. Stir in the oats and sauté, stirring frequently, for about 4 to 5 minutes or until the oats are beginning to puff up and soften with liquid. Stir in the saffron. Add the hot broth, 1/2 cup at a time, stirring continuously, until each addition has been absorbed and the mixture has a rich, creamy texture, about 20 minutes.

Remove the pan from the heat and stir in the parsley, lemon juice, and cheese, season with salt and pepper to taste and serve.

SERVES 6 TO 8

NOTE: If you prefer not to spend a month's mortgage money on saffron threads to color this dish (they run anywhere from $45 to $75 an ounce), you can substitute safflower seed powder, available at health food stores. Do not use turmeric; it's the same color, but has a very strong flavor that would not work well in this dish. But then again saffron is so powerful you can get by using only a pinch, and the flavor and color it adds is unmatched.

IRISH WHISKEY CAKE

For dessert recipes, I like to use Tullamore Dew Irish whiskey as it has a mellow, smooth, slightly sweet taste. You can also try Black Bush, Bushmills Original, or a soft whiskey like Paddy Old Irish whiskey.

- 1 cup golden raisins
  Zest of 1 lemon, finely minced
- 1 cup plus 4 tablespoons Irish whiskey
- 1 (18$\frac{1}{2}$-ounce) package of chocolate devil's food cake mix
- 1 (5.9 ounce) package instant chocolate pudding mix
- $\frac{1}{2}$ cup milk
- $\frac{1}{2}$ cup vegetable oil
- 4 large eggs
- $\frac{1}{2}$ cup chopped walnuts
  Juice of 1 lemon
- 1 cup confectioners' sugar
  Warm water
  Lemon and lime gumdrops, for garnish (optional)

In a small bowl, combine the raisins and zest with 1 cup of the whiskey; let stand for 8 hours.

Prepare a gas or charcoal grill for indirect grilling (it is not necessary to use a drip pan for this recipe). Preheat to 325°F. Grease a 9-inch metal cake pan and line the bottom with parchment paper.

In a large bowl, combine the cake and pudding mixes. In another bowl, combine the milk, oil, and raisin-whiskey mixture. Mix well and add to the dry ingredients, stirring to just combine. Using a hand mixer at medium speed, beat in the eggs one at a time and continue beating, occasionally scraping down the sides of the bowl, for 2 to 3 minutes, until the batter is smooth. Stir in the walnuts.

Pour the batter into the prepared pan and transfer to the barbecue over indirect heat. Lower the grill lid and bake until the cake is lightly browned and a skewer inserted in the center of the cake comes out clean, about 1 to 1$\frac{1}{2}$ hours. Transfer to a wire rack to cool.

For the icing, in a small saucepan, combine the lemon juice, 2 tablespoons of the whiskey, and the confectioners' sugar. Cook over low heat until the mixture is melted and smooth and coats the back of a spoon, about 5 to 7 minutes. Stir in the remaining whiskey to incorporate then remove from the heat. If the icing is too thick, add warm water 1 teaspoon at a time until desired consistency is reached.

Put 2 pieces of wax paper on a plate, side by side (not overlapping), with the seam in the middle of the plate. Transfer the cake to the center of the paper and pour the icing over the cake, 1 tablespoon at a time, allowing it to course down the sides. When complete, pull out the wax paper for a clean serving plate. Let the cake stand until the icing is set, about 30 minutes. When set, decorate the cake with the gumdrops.

SERVES 8 TO 10

NOTE: Store leftovers of this cake by putting it in the freezer for 20 minutes to harden the icing, then wrap it in plastic wrap, and put under a cake storing dish or large bowl. It should last a week at room temperature. If using a glass cake pan (not recommended), reduce the grilling heat by 25°F. You can also make this cake with lemon, white, yellow, or any other cake mix you desire, just match the pudding flavors with the cake mix.

JAMAICA

Don't Be a Jerk, Mon!

Jamaica is of great importance to readers of this book. Know why? Because Jamaica was once home to the Taino Indians, who occupied the island when Columbus landed. Unfortunately their days were numbered after the welcoming flag ceremony—in less than two hundred years they were completely wiped out. The Tainos, however, left one critically important legacy—a way of slowly cooking meat over smoky green wood, and a word for this way of cooking: "barbacoa."

Yes, this island paradise may well be the birthplace of barbecue in its classic sense: slow, smoky cooking over low heat. This style of cooking evolved over the centuries, and these days Jamaican restaurants are happily filled with jerks. And so too, are Jamaican home kitchens, roadside eateries, cafés, and pricey bistros. Jerks are everywhere. No, not those kind of jerks! Jerk chicken, jerk pork, jerk beef, jerk mutton, jerk goat, jerk fish, jerk vegetables, jerk soup, and even jerk chicken salad sandwiches. The word "jerk" is used as both a noun to describe the seasoning applied to food that is smoked for a long time, and as a verb to explain the process of slow cooking that is used.

There are literally thousands of different jerk spice recipes, but everyone agrees on two key ingredients: allspice (also known as Jamaican pimento) and Scotch bonnet chiles. You need both for a jerk. Then, depending on your recipe, you can add cinnamon, cloves, nutmeg, thyme, garlic, sugar, salt, and pepper, or any of a number of spices. Jerk foods are rubbed with the jerk seasoning, then cooked over a fire, or coals, at a low temperature, with lots of green or soaked wood added to make a lot of smoke.

The method was first conceived by the Maroons, slaves brought to Jamaica to replace the rapidly disappearing native Arawak Indians (wait a minute, I see a pattern here). The Maroons brought their African spices and cooking techniques to the island, and a wonderful cooking style—and a huge and profitable spice and cooking industry—was born.

Before I go, I have to share my favorite Jamaican jerk joint with you. Right down the coast from Ian Fleming's spectacular beachside hideaway home, Goldeneye—and about ten minutes from famed James Bond Beach—is the Ocho Rios Village Jerk Centre. It's a wonderful place to relax, and between sips of Jamaican Red Stripe beer and bites of tongue-tingling jerked chicken and jerked pork-on-a-stick, you can close your eyes and match wits with Dr. No, Rosa Klebb, or Auric Goldfinger—that other bunch of classic jerks.

Sorry, I had to do that!

GRILLED SPICY SHRIMP WITH LIME

The marinade for these succulent shrimps uses some classic Jamaican flavors like chile, allspice, lime, and (surprise!) soy sauce—a gift to Jamaican cooking from the many East Asian immigrants on the island. Fresh shrimp should be prepared on the same day they are purchased. To store them before cooking, rinse the shrimp in cold running water and pat dry. Wrap in two to three damp paper towels, place in a resealable plastic bag, and refrigerate.

1/2 cup chopped yellow onion

1 jalapeño, stemmed, seeded, and chopped

3 tablespoons white wine vinegar

2 tablespoons soy sauce

2 tablespoons canola oil

1/2 teaspoon Krista's Jamaican Hot Sauce (or your favorite hot sauce)

1/2 teaspoon ground allspice

1/4 teaspoon granulated garlic

1/4 teaspoon cinnamon

1/4 teaspoon kosher salt

1/4 teaspoon freshly ground black pepper

1/8 teaspoon nutmeg

40 large (21/25) shrimp (about 2 pounds), deveined but not shelled

2 limes, cut into quarters, for serving

In a food processor or blender, combine onion, jalapeño, vinegar, soy sauce, oil, hot sauce, allspice, garlic, cinnamon, salt, pepper, and nutmeg. Process until smooth.

Put the shrimp in a large resealable plastic bag. Pour in the marinade, press out the air, and seal the bag. Shake to coat. Transfer the bag to a large bowl and refrigerate for 1 to 2 hours.

Preheat a charcoal or gas grill to 375°F. Make sure the grill rack is clean and oil it thoroughly with nonstick cooking spray.

Remove the shrimp from the bag, discard the marinade, and thread the shrimp lengthwise on skewers.

Transfer the shrimp to the prepared grill rack and grill over direct heat, turning skewers only once, until the shrimp are firm to the touch, pink all over, and just opaque, 3 to 4 minutes total.

To serve, transfer to a warm serving platter, squeeze a little fresh lime juice over the shrimp, and serve immediately.

SERVES 6 TO 8 AS AN APPETIZER

JAMAICAN BARBECUE BANANA BIRDS

A honeymoon here a long time ago brought a young photojournal-ist/writer and his new bride to the Sign Great House, a former planta-tion just outside of Montego Bay, where we experienced exotic cot-tages, geckos on the wall, coconut-infused drinks, ackee and salt fish for breakfast, and this dish pre-pared by their cook. I recreated it ten years later, and it was almost as good as the dish we had on the island—almost. But back then I was on my honeymoon, not collect-ing recipes. . . .

1/2	teaspoon cinnamon
1/2	teaspoon white pepper
1/2	teaspoon garlic powder
1/4	teaspoon ground cloves
1	cup dark Jamaican rum
2	(1 1/2- to 2-pound) Cornish hens, or small chickens
3/4	cup olive oil
1/4	cup chopped onion
1 1/2	cups diced ripe banana
1/2	teaspoon poultry seasoning
1 1/2	teaspoons salt
1/4	teaspoon allspice
2 1/2	cups tightly packed fresh bread crumbs
1/2	cup butter, melted
	Juice of 2 fresh lemons (see Note)

In a saucepan, combine the cin-namon, white pepper, garlic pow-der, cloves, and rum. Cook over low heat until warmed through. Set aside to cool.

Wash and pat the birds dry. Transfer them to a large reseal-able plastic bag and pour in the marinade. Marinate for 8 hours in the refrigerator.

Prepare a charcoal or gas grill for indirect grilling, placing a drip pan under the cool side of the grill rack (see page 3). Pre-heat to 375°F. Make sure the grill rack is clean and oil it thoroughly with nonstick cooking spray.

Drain the Cornish hens and set them aside. Discard the mar-inade.

In a bowl, combine 1/2 cup of the olive oil, the onion, banana, poultry seasoning, 1/2 teaspoon of the salt, allspice, bread crumbs, and butter, mixing well. Lightly pack the mixture into each of the hens and secure the body cavities with toothpicks or by trussing with kitchen string.

For the basting liquid, in a small bowl combine the remain-ing 1/4 cup of olive oil, remain-ing 1 teaspoon of salt, and the lemon juice; set aside.

Transfer the hens to the pre-pared grill rack over indirect heat. Lower the grill lid and cook for 1 to 1 1/2 hours, until the temperature in the thickest part of the thigh reaches 170°F. Using a long-handled brush, baste the hens 2 or 3 times during cooking with the basting liquid.

Let the hens rest, covered, for 10 minutes (the internal temper-ature will rise to 180°F). Remove the stuffing and serve it along-side a half hen on each plate.

SERVES 4 TO 6

NOTE: To get the most juice from a lemon, heat it in a microwave for 15 seconds before cutting and juicing.

TAXI STAND JERK CHICKEN WITH PINEAPPLE-MANGO SALSA

This recipe for jerk sauce is courtesy of Ray's Hideaway Restaurant and Taxi Stand, Montego Bay, Jamaica. It's fiery, but not incendiary, full of flavor, and worth the effort to make it. There are as many Jamaican recipes for jerk as there are Jamaicans; I settled on this as the best of the best. Serve with big, iced bottles of Jamaican Red Stripe beer.

- $^1/_3$ cup coarsely chopped shallots
- 4 green onions, green and white parts, chopped
- $^1/_2$ cup olive oil
- $^1/_2$ cup water
- Juice of 2 limes
- $^1/_4$ cup soy sauce
- $^1/_2$ to 1 Scotch bonnet chile, stemmed, seeded, and chopped
- 3 large cloves garlic, coarsely chopped
- 1 cup ketchup
- 2 tablespoons allspice
- 1 teaspoon nutmeg
- 1 teaspoon cinnamon
- 2 tablespoons ground ginger
- 1 teaspoon dried thyme
- 4 (4- to 6-ounce) skinless bone-in chicken breasts
- 1 cup chopped fresh pineapple
- 1 cup chopped fresh mango
- 2 tablespoons chopped onion
- 1 tablespoon minced jalapeño
- $^1/_4$ cup chopped fresh cilantro
- $^1/_4$ cup freshly squeezed lime juice
- Salt
- Freshly ground black pepper

In a food processor or blender, combine the shallots, green onions, oil, water, lime juice, soy sauce, Scotch bonnet, garlic, ketchup, allspice, nutmeg, cinnamon, ginger, and thyme and process until a smooth paste forms. Set aside.

Wash the chicken breasts and pat dry. Using rubber gloves, cover each breast with the jerk paste. Place the chicken in a resealable plastic bag and refrigerate for 4 to 8 hours.

Prepare a charcoal or gas barbecue for indirect grilling, placing a drip pan under the cool side of the grill rack (see page 3). Preheat to 350°F. Make sure the grill rack is clean and oil it thoroughly with nonstick cooking spray.

Remove the chicken from the bag and transfer to the prepared grill rack over direct heat. Cook for 5 minutes per side, then move the chicken to the cool side of the grill and cook for 10 to 15 minutes longer per side, until the internal temperature reaches 160°F. Remove the chicken from the grill and let stand, covered, for 10 minutes.

Meanwhile, prepare the salsa by combining the pineapple, mango, onion, jalapeño, cilantro, and lime juice in a food processor and pulsing 3 or 4 times until the ingredients are chopped, but still chunky. Remove to a bowl, season with salt and pepper, and set aside.

Serve each breast topped with a generous portion of salsa.

SERVES 4

SPICY CITRUS-RUM GLAZED HAM

Pickapeppa sauce, called by some "Jamaican ketchup," is a delightful condiment that is only produced in Jamaica. As anyone who has tried it knows, it is unlike any other hot sauce on the market. Sugar, vinegar, mangoes, raisins, tamarinds, peppers, and spices are cooked with tomatoes and onions and then aged like wine in oak barrels for a year. It's tangy, hot, sweet, complex, and the perfect accompaniment to jerk barbecued anything. Serve this ham with grilled sweet potatoes or Yamaica Casserole (see page 104).

4	tablespoons Pickapeppa sauce
1/2	teaspoon allspice (see Note)
1/2	teaspoon coriander
1/2	teaspoon cinammon
1/4	teaspoon cloves
5	teaspoons molasses
1	(3- to 4-pound) boneless precooked ham
10	thin slices of shallot
2	cups orange juice
	Juice of 2 lemons
1/2	cup dark rum
2	tablespoons butter

Prepare a charcoal or gas grill for indirect grilling to 375°F, placing a drip pan under the cool side of the grill rack (see page 3). Line a roasting pan with heavy-duty aluminum foil.

In a small bowl, combine the Pickapeppa, allspice, coriander, cinnamon, cloves, and molasses and set aside.

Using a sharp knife, make 10 cuts in the ham and insert a shallot slice into each cut. Transfer the ham to the prepared pan. In a large bowl, combine the orange juice, lemon juice, and rum. Pour half of the juice mixture over the ham, reserving the rest.

Using a butter knife, spread the spice paste over the ham, working some of it into the holes where the shallots have been placed.

Place the pan on the grill rack over indirect heat, lower the lid, and cook, basting with the juices from the pan, for 1 1/2 to 2 hours until a thermometer, inserted in the middle, registers 160°F. Pour the reserved juice mixture over the ham. Using oven mitts to protect your hands, cover the ham with foil, sealing the edges around the pan. Cook for 20 minutes longer.

Remove the roasting pan from the barbecue. Transfer the ham to a platter, cover it with foil, and set aside for 10 minutes. Carefully pour the pan juices into a saucepan and set it over medium-high heat. Cook until the liquid is reduced by half, about 12 to 14 minutes. Whisk in the butter just before serving.

Slice and serve the ham with the sauce on the side.

SERVES 6 TO 8

NOTE: Allspice was discovered by the Western world in 1494 when Christopher Columbus thought a local plant was a pepper plant. He named it "pimiento," Spanish for pepper. Today many people think the spice is a blend of spices, but it's just one plant. If you can find whole allspice berries (from the evergreen pimiento), and are willing to grind them yourself in a mortar and pestle just before cooking, you will find an incredibly vibrant and more intense flavor than you'll get using ground allspice. It's well worth the extra effort and time.

OCHO RIOS JERK PORK CHOPS

Ocho Rios, along with Boston Beach and Montego Bay, is ground zero for jerk restaurants, shacks, and roadside or beachside stands. These pork chops have a fairly mellow kick by Jamaican standards, but this marinade gives a nice taste of how some of the classic jerk spices meet and mingle. You can also use it on vegetables to make some fine veggie skewers.

3/4	cup water
1/3	cup freshly squeezed lemon juice
1/3	cup chopped onion
1	tablespoon firmly packed brown sugar

- 1 tablespoon chopped green onion, white and green parts
- 1 tablespoon olive oil
- $^3/_4$ teaspoon salt
- $^3/_4$ teaspoon allspice
- $^3/_4$ teaspoon cinnamon
- $^3/_4$ teaspoon freshly ground black pepper
- $^1/_2$ teaspoon dried thyme
- $^1/_4$ teaspoon cayenne pepper
- 6 (8-ounce) bone-in pork chops, each 2 inches thick

In a food processor or blender, combine the water, lemon juice, onion, sugar, green onion, oil, salt, allspice, cinnamon, pepper, thyme, and cayenne, pureeing until smooth. Set aside $^1/_2$ cup of the mixture, covered, in the refrigerator.

Place the pork in a resealable plastic bag and pour in the remaining marinade. Cover and refrigerate for at least 12 hours and up to 24.

Preheat a charcoal or gas grill to 375°F. Make sure the grill rack is clean and oil it thoroughly with nonstick cooking spray.

Remove the pork from the refrigerator. Drain off the marinade and discard it. Transfer the chops to the prepared grill rack over direct heat. Cook, turning and basting frequently with the reserved marinade, until the chops' internal temperature is 160°F (just past medium), 8 to 11 minutes. The meat should be very slightly pink when a sharp knife is inserted near the bone.

Let rest, covered, on a warm platter for 5 minutes before serving.

SERVES 6

RICE AND PEAS

Sunday dinner in Ocho Rios wouldn't be the same without rice and peas (actually, beans, as in kidney beans). It's the national dish prepared, of course, with the ubiquitous Scotch bonnet pepper. At Christmastime, Jamaicans substitute pigeon peas for the red kidney beans.

- 2 tablespoons olive oil
- 2 cups rice
- 1 Scotch bonnet chile, stemmed, seeded, and chopped
- 6 cloves garlic, diced
- 1 large sweet onion (Walla Walla, Maui, or Vidalia), diced
- 1 (16-ounce) can red kidney beans, drained and liquid reserved
- 1 (15-ounce) can coconut milk
  Water
- 3 chicken bouillon cubes

Prepare a charcoal or gas grill for indirect grilling (it is not necessary to use a drip pan with this recipe). Preheat to 375°F.

Heat the oil in a cast-iron skillet on the hot side of the grill

until a drop of water sprinkled in the pan sizzles. Add the rice and cook until opaque and beginning to brown. Add the chile, garlic, and onion and sauté for 2 to 3 minutes, until the onion becomes translucent.

Add the beans and stir only once. In a 4-cup measure, combine the coconut milk and the reserved bean liquid, adding enough water to make 4 cups. Add the bouillon cubes, stir to dissolve, and pour over the rice. Bring to a boil, then immediately move the pot to the cool side of the grill, lower cover, and cook for 20 to 25 minutes, until all the liquid is absorbed and the rice is tender. Remove from heat, cover, and let stand for 20 minutes. Serve.

SERVES 4 TO 6

YAMAICA CASSEROLE

Yams are slowly becoming more common in U.S. markets, and are one of the most popular vegetables in Latin American and Caribbean markets; they are blander and starchier than sweet potatoes. Either tuber will work in this recipe, which goes beautifully with jerked chicken or pork and lots of steamed rice.

4 pounds yams or sweet potatoes, peeled and cut in 2-inch-thick slices

2 large bananas, sliced

³/₄ cup orange juice

¹/₄ cup freshly squeezed juice

1 teaspoon cinnamon

1 teaspoon nutmeg

¹/₂ teaspoon salt

¹/₄ teaspoon freshly ground black pepper

4 tablespoons chopped pecans

4 tablespoons fresh or unsweetened flaked coconut (see Note)

Prepare a charcoal or gas grill for indirect grilling (it is not necessary to use a drip pan with this recipe). Preheat to 375°F. Grease a 1-quart casserole or Dutch oven. Add the yams, cover with the banana slices, pour in the orange and lime juices, sprinkle with the cinnamon, nutmeg, salt, and pepper, and top with the pecans and coconut.

Cover the casserole and transfer to the grill rack over indirect heat. Lower the grill lid and cook for 30 minutes. Remove the lid from the casserole and cook another 10 minutes. Serve hot.

SERVES 4 TO 6

NOTE: To open a coconut, pierce one of the three "eyes" with a nail and bake the coconut for 20 minutes at 350°F. Hit the coconut with a hammer to crack it open. Drain the milk (actually water), then bake the shells another 30 minutes; the meat will come out easily with the aid of a spoon. If you need to, use an oyster knife (the perfect coconut tool) to dig out the meat, and remember to cut off any brown skin on the underside.

JAPAN

Food as Culture, Culture as Food:
A Field Producer's Journal by Reed Kawahara

(Author's note: *Reed Kawahara, who wrote this piece, and videographer Joel Schroeder traveled with me to Japan to film an episode of* Barbecue America: The World Tour. *Reed, who happens to be married to my daughter, is of Japanese ancestry but had never been to Japan.*)

MARCH 26, 10:00 p.m. YAMANAKA, ISHIKAWA PREFECTURE

We have finally arrived at our first destination here in Japan after 16 hours and two flights. It is nighttime, so we can't see much of our surroundings. Mr. Jiro Takeuchi and Mr. Yuichi Kano greet Rick, Joel, and me at the airport, help us with our bags, and drive us to our hotel. They ask if we would like something to eat after such a long day. After responding we would like only a "snack" before heading to bed, Jiro and

Yuichi treat us to a full meal in the hotel restaurant. What hospitality!

MARCH 27, 3:20 p.m. YAMANAKA

We have had a full and exciting first day already. After waking early and taking a walk around town, we share laughs at our early experiences. We all thoroughly enjoyed the automatic warming toilet seats and warm water bidets—how soothing! Rick woke early to try out the community hot spring baths but had to forego it because the large hotel robes (their version of large, anyway) wouldn't quite wrap all the way around his ample middle.

We had a wonderful visit with an artisan who hand paints the local lacquerware, and a tour of a wood lathe workshop that has been handed down through generations. This area of Japan is known for its fine lacquerware, its hot springs, and its beautiful natural surroundings.

We then sat down to a nine-course traditional Japanese meal with "Chairman" Masanori Kamiguchi, the most important man in town and chairman of the Yamanaka Chamber of Commerce and Industry and the Hot Springs Tourist Association. Rick told the chairman that he is a dead ringer for Richard Widmark;

Mr. Kamiguchi responded, "Yes, but I'm not that old yet!"

We are now driving north to our next destination, Kanazawa, the largest city in Ishikawa. With us are Mr. Shoji Yamade from the Ishikawa Prefecture government and Ms. Noriko Nakarai, our interpreter.

MARCH 28, 3:00 p.m. KANAZAWA

We have just finished the most amazing meal at the Zeniya Restaurant, prepared and served personally by the owner and chef, Shin-Ichiro Takagi. It is called Counter Kappo cuisine, which Chef Shin tells us is an old word meaning "cut and grill"—Rick was thrilled at the little heated stones that we each got to grill our clams on. We were treated to sashimi, calamari, eels, clams, and even abalone guts! Almost as impressive as the taste of the meal is the presentation—such attention to detail. Tomorrow morning at 5:30 a.m. sharp, Chef Shin will take us to the local fish market, which he goes to almost every morning to pick out fresh fish for the day's menu. He doesn't freeze anything!

Earlier in the day, we met the governor of Ishikawa, toured the gold leaf factory, and visited the historic geisha district. We are really packing it in.

MARCH 29, 1:15 p.m. OUTSIDE KANAZAWA

We are on the road again, this time to a small fishing town in the north called Noto. It is beautiful, hilly countryside. We initially drove north alongside the Sea of Japan, but soon cut inland to drive on small roads through miles of rice fields. This is what I have imagined the Japan of my ancestors to be like. It is an interesting feeling to be here for the first time—so foreign and yet at the same time somehow familiar. As we drive, I still have remnants of a unique taste on my tongue from our tour of the shoyu and miso factory a couple hours before–shoyu (soy sauce) ice cream. Oishee!

MARCH 30, 12:30 p.m. OUTSIDE NOTO

Last night we arrived at a beautiful hotel here on the coast called the Hyaku Raku So. It is a traditional Japanese hotel with mats and futons to sleep on, set on a hillside overlooking the fishing village on Tsukomo Bay. Just before going to bed late last night, we finally got a chance to enjoy the hot community baths here (men only, of course), which are dug underground and accessible by a long cave tunnel!

This morning we took a boat ride on the bay to see the fish farms and the squid boats, and we are once again off to our next destination, Hakusan, just south of Kanazawa, to take in a performance of Taiko drums from the all-female group Asano Taiko. It's funny being on the road and seeing all the tiny cars here in Japan—they're so small they look like toys. And they have so many funny names like "Enjoy," "Life," "Guppy," and "Space Gear." There certainly aren't any Hummers or Escalades, which is definitely a breath of fresh air!

MARCH 31, 8:00 a.m. KOMATSU AIRPORT

Our whirlwind trip in Japan is winding to a close. Here at the airport we have to say our good-byes to our new friends Jiro, Yuichi, Noriko, and Mr. Yamade. It has only been a few days and yet Rick, Joel, and I all feel sad when we realize that we might never see them again. We have been so struck by the hospitality and generosity that we have received everywhere we've gone.

To me, this experience has been a reassuring reminder that we live in a small, small world and that people from Ishikawa are no different really than people from my own hometown in California, or for that matter, from people in São Paulo, Calcutta, or Istanbul. (One thing is for sure, we all love to eat!)

Thank you, new friends and acquaintances in Ishikawa, it has been a wonderful trip that we will never forget.

YAKITORI

Yakitori, or skewered grilled chicken, chicken is one of the best-known and most popular Japanese dishes. Grilled over a charcoal or gas fire and served while it's hot, yakitori is a favorite menu item in Japan in izakaya restaurants (the cheap and very casual places for after-work drinking) and outdoor beer gardens open in summer. Some say yakitori is Japanese fast food, the equivalent of our American hot dogs.

¹/₄	cup soy sauce
¹/₄	cup mirin (rice wine) or rice vinegar
¹/₄	cup sugar
1¹/₂	pounds boneless, skinless chicken breast, cut into 1-inch cubes
¹/₂	pound shiitake mushrooms
2	red or yellow bell peppers, stemmed, seeded, and cut into 2-inch pieces
5	green onions, green and white parts, cut into 2-inch lengths

Preheat a charcoal or gas grill to 375°F. Make sure the grill rack is clean and oil it thoroughly with nonstick cooking spray.

In a large bowl, combine the soy sauce, mirin, and sugar. Add the chicken, mushrooms, and peppers; marinate for 5 minutes.

Reserving the marinade, remove the chicken and vegetables from the bowl. Thread the chicken onto skewers and, separately, thread the mushrooms, peppers, and green onions on skewers as well. (Keep the chicken and vegetables separate so you can control the cooking time better. See Note.)

Pour the marinade into a saucepan and boil for 12 minutes to use as a basting and serving sauce. Set aside.

Transfer the skewers to the prepared grill rack over direct heat. Cook, basting often with the sauce, 5 minutes per side, until the chicken is starting to brown on the edges and the vegetables are soft and charred at the edges.

Transfer the skewers to a heated platter, drizzle with sauce, and serve as an appetizer.

SERVES 4 TO 6 AS AN APPETIZER

NOTE: The secret to quick and even skewer cooking is to leave a little space on the skewer between each piece of chicken. This allows the chicken to cook through on all sides. If using wooden skewers, soak them in water for about 30 minutes first.

TERIYAKI STEAK AND ONION SPRING ROLLS

Teriyaki is a glaze applied to fish, meat, or fowl in the final stages of grilling or panfrying. This glaze is sweet and is based on a trio of classic Japanese ingredients: soy sauce, sake, and mirin. Teri means "gloss" or "luster" and yaki refers to "grilling" or "broiling." These spring rolls are a nice appetizer, or would work well for lunch or a light supper with fried rice and stir-fried asparagus, yellow string beans, and strips of red bell pepper. Like balsamic vinegar, there are many varieties of shoyu (soy sauce) from unsalted to expensive, hand-crafted artisanal varieties.

- $^1/_4$ cup Japanese soy sauce
- $^1/_4$ cup sake (see Note)
- 4 tablespoons sugar
- 2 tablespoons mirin (sweet rice wine)
- 8 tablespoons water
  Pinch of fresh grated ginger
  Pinch of minced garlic
- 2 (8-ounce) boneless sirloin or rib steaks
- 6 green onions, white and light green part only, halved lengthwise and cut in 3-inch pieces

To make the teriyaki sauce, in a small saucepan over medium heat, combine the soy sauce, sake, sugar, mirin, water, ginger, and garlic and heat, stirring, until the sugar has dissolved. Set aside.

Cut the steaks into 3-inch wide strips, each the length of the steak, then cut each piece in half across the grain so you have approximately 3- by 4-inch pieces.

Place the steak strips between sheets of wax paper and pound to a $^1/_8$-inch thickness. Arrange one green onion piece in the center of each piece of meat. Starting with the long end roll the steak into tight cylinders. Secure with toothpicks (you can soak these in water for 10 to 15 minutes, but they usually don't burn).

Preheat a charcoal or gas grill to 375°F. Make sure the grill rack is clean and oil it thoroughly with nonstick cooking spray.

Dip the rolls in the teriyaki sauce and, using tongs, transfer the rolled meat to the prepared grill rack. Grill for 3 minutes without turning. Remove the rolls from the grill, dip them in the sauce again, and grill on the other side for 3 minutes longer.

Transfer the rolls to a cutting board and remove the toothpicks. Cut meat rolls in half and stand each piece on end on a serving plate. Serve with remaining teriyaki sauce on the side.

SERVES 4 TO 6 AS AN APPETIZER

NOTE: Sake, which is often mistakenly called "rice wine," is actually a result of the alcoholic fermentation of a mixture of steamed rice, koji (fermented rice culture), and water.

YAKITORI-STYLE GRILLED VEGETABLES

Yakitori is Japanese "fast food"—usually small pieces of chicken skewered and grilled. There are three basic types of dashi (Japanese soup stock, made from flaked dried bonito fish). Ichiban-dashi has a fragrant aroma and a delicate flavor and is used in clear soups. Niban-dashi *is used as a simmering liquid.* Konbu-dashi, *made from kelp, is used with meat and fish dishes that call for a gentler, mild taste. Dashi can be found in Asian grocery stores.*

- $1/4$ cup dashi
- 3 tablespoons mirin (sweet rice wine)
- 2 tablespoons sugar
- 1 tablespoon soy sauce
- 2 tablespoons red miso
- 2 tablespoons vegetable oil
- 1 tablespoon sesame oil, regular cold-pressed (see Note)
- 2 sweet potatoes, peeled and cut in $1/2$-inch slices
- Salt
- 2 Japanese eggplants, each about 5 inches long
- 2 small zucchini, each about 5 inches long
- 2 onions
- 8 to 10 fresh shiitake mushrooms, stems removed
- 1 teaspoon white sesame seeds

In a small saucepan, combine the dashi, mirin, sugar, and soy sauce over medium heat, stirring, just until the sugar dissolves. Remove the pan from the heat and whisk in the miso until fully blended.

In a small bowl, combine the vegetable oil and the sesame oil and set aside.

In another saucepan, cook the sweet potatoes in salted boiling water to cover until easily pierced with a fork, about 8 minutes. Remove from the pan, drain, and set aside.

Cut the eggplant and zucchini diagonally to make ovals about $1/4$ inch thick and 3 inches long. Cut the onions in half lengthwise, then crosswise into $1/4$-inch-thick slices, about the same size as the other vegetables. Using a bamboo or wooden skewer, skewer each onion slice horizontally through all the rings, to keep them from separating during cooking.

Transfer all the vegetables, including the mushrooms, to a large bowl, add the three tablespoons of oil, tossing to coat.

Preheat a charcoal or gas grill to 375°F.

Set a small skillet on the grill and toast the sesame seeds, shaking the pan frequently, until lightly browned, 3 to 4 minutes. Quickly transfer the seeds to a plate to cool.

Oil a vegetable grill basket or grill plate with nonstick cooking spray. Transfer all the vegetables from the bowl to the basket. Grill for 3 minutes per side, until vegetables are tender but not mushy.

Move the basket to the cool side of the grill and sprinkle with half the miso mixture, stirring to coat. Sprinkle on the rest of the mixture and cook 30 seconds longer to warm the miso mixture slightly.

Transfer the vegetables to a warmed serving plate and sprinkle with the sesame seeds before serving.

SERVES 4 TO 6

NOTE: Sesame oil is obtained from sesame seeds by pressing. Cold-pressed sesame oil is light yellow, has a mild flavor and is odorless. Hot-pressed sesame oil is darker and has a more pungent taste.

BARBECUED SWIMMING FISH

Properly done, this dish makes the cooked fish look like it's swimming on the serving plate, as the body is curved like an "S" so it looks like it's still swimming along. The word "daikon" comes from two Japanese words: dai *(large) and* kon *(root). Daikon is an essential part of Japanese cuisine; simmered and served alone, used as garnish, grated with tempura and soy sauce, and even pickled.*

- 2 ounces fresh lotus root (about 4 inches long), peeled and thinly sliced
- 1 cup plus 2 tablespoons sweetened rice vinegar
- 1 hot red Thai chile pepper, seeded and chopped
- 2 cups water
- $2/3$ cup sugar
- 2 teaspoons salt
- 1 large fresh daikon
- 1 whole ($1^1/2$- to 2-pound) trout, salmon or mackerel, cleaned and scaled

  Salt

  Lemon wedges, for garnish
- $1/3$ cup ponzu sauce (see Note)

Boil the sliced lotus root in water for 30 seconds, drain, and combine with 1 cup of the vinegar in a bowl. Let stand for 2 to 3 hours.

To make kabayaki sauce, heat the chile pepper for a few seconds in a small skillet over medium heat, add the water and the remaining 2 tablespoons of the vinegar, and stir while simmering for 2 to 3 minutes. Add the sugar and salt and stir until dissolved. Remove from heat and refrigerate.

Peel the daikon and grate it very finely and put it in a bowl of cold water to keep it fresh. Set aside.

Preheat a charcoal or gas grill to 375°F. Make sure the grill rack is clean and oil it thoroughly with nonstick cooking spray.

Rinse the fish and pat it dry with paper towels. Make 2 deep crosswise cuts on each side. Push a long metal skewer at an angle through the side of the fish near the tail end, bending the skewer so that it emerges through the center of the fish's body. Bend the skewer back toward the fish's body and reinsert it again so it emerges near the fish's head. The fish should have an s-shaped sideways curve, sort of rippling around the axis of the skewer.

Sprinkle both sides of the fish lightly with salt, which helps make the skin crispy when it cooks. Press plenty of salt onto the tail and fins (this helps prevent the tail from burning).

Transfer the fish directly to the prepared grill rack and cook, turning it once carefully, using the skewer to avoid damaging the skin, until the fish is golden on both sides and cooked through, about 10 to 12 minutes.

Remove the fish to a serving platter. Drain the grated daikon. Garnish the fish with lemon wedges, grated daikon, and marinated lotus root. Serve with the cold ponzu and kabayaki dipping sauces on the side.

SERVES 4 TO 6

NOTE: Ponzu sauce is made with lemon juice, soy sauce, mirin, seaweed, and dried bonito flakes and is used for dipping with fish and sashimi dishes. You can find it in any Asian grocery store, along with the sweet vinegar sauce, lotus root, and daikon also used in this recipe.

MISO-BARBECUED BEEF SHORT RIBS WITH GINGER-TERIYAKI SAUCE

Have your butcher cut the short ribs in half lengthwise, then into pieces, each containing three rib bones. Miso, made from fermented soybeans, rice, or barley, gives this marinade a rich, salty-sweet, earthy flavor. Very popular in Japan (there are over 1,400 companies that manufacture it there), miso is catching on in the U.S. as a healthy, protein-rich addition to any diet.

1¹/₂	tablespoons red miso
3	tablespoons mirin (rice wine)
3	tablespoons good quality sake (see Note)
3	tablespoons soy sauce
1	tablespoon distilled white vinegar
1	tablespoons sugar
2	teaspoons sesame oil, toasted or regular
2¹/₂	pounds beef short ribs, well trimmed (see headnote)
1¹/₄	cups teriyaki sauce
¹/₂	teaspoon finely minced ginger
	Cooked noodles or steamed white rice, for serving

Prepare a charcoal or gas barbecue for indirect cooking, placing a drip pan under the cool side of the grill rack (see page 3). Preheat to 400°F. Make sure the grill rack is clean and oil it thoroughly with nonstick cooking spray.

In a small bowl, combine the miso, mirin, sake, soy sauce, vinegar, sugar, and sesame oil to make a marinade. Place the ribs in a resealable plastic bag, add the marinade, shake and massage each rib to coat. Refrigerate 4 to 6 hours.

Remove the ribs from the marinade and wipe off the excess.

Pour the remaining marinade into a small saucepan and boil over high heat for 12 minutes, then cool to use for baste. Or you can use a favorite teriyaki sauce.

Transfer the marinated ribs to the prepared grill rack over direct heat and cook for 1¹/₂ to 2 minutes per side to sear. Then move the ribs to the indirect side of the grill for 20 to 25 minutes, turning often, and basting often with the miso or teriyaki sauce.

Serve hot over the noodles or rice with the remaining miso or teriyaki sauce on the side

SERVES 6

NOTE: When the Japanese created the sake recipe in AD 300, only naturally occurring yeasts were used. There were no cultivated yeasts. Yet. Some clever Japanese then invented "chewing-in-the-mouth sake," sparking a ceremony during which a whole village would gather to chew up rice, chestnuts, and millet, and then would spit mouthfuls of chewed grains into vats. The enzymes in their saliva would kick-start the yeast fermentation.

OSAKA CHICKEN BURGERS

In Japan, McDonalds offers Teri-yaki McBurger, Chicken Tatsuta, Bulgogi Burger (Korean meat strips), and a Thai Spice Chicken Burger. Freshness Burger (a local chain) offers takeout mini-burgers such as Salsa Burger, Menchi Burger (breaded and deep-fried), Teriyaki Burger, Negimiso Burger (adding miso powder and green onions), Teriyaki Chicken Burgers, and a Spam Burger. Whew! These chicken burgers are great for a barbecue picnic—tasty, moist, loaded with flavor. They're also good enough to make that you forget about those other kinds of burgers. Serve with grilled sweet potatoes and stir-fried cabbage for an Asian twist on French fries and coleslaw.

- 1 onion, cut into 1/2-inch-thick rounds
- 1 teaspoon chopped fresh oregano
- 1 teaspoon chopped fresh chives
- 1/2 cup white wine
  Olive oil
- 1 tablespoon maple syrup
- 2 teaspoons freshly squeezed lemon juice
- 3 tablespoons minced shallots
- 1 clove garlic, minced
- 1 teaspoon chopped fresh parsley
- 1 teaspoon sesame oil, toasted or regular
- 5 slices white bread, crusts removed and cubed
- 3 tablespoons teriyaki sauce
- 1 pound ground chicken leg or thigh meat
- 2 teaspoons prepared mustard
- 1 egg, beaten
  Salt
  Freshly ground black pepper
- 1/4 teaspoon cinnamon
- 1 small fresh pineapple, peeled, cored and cut in rings
- 1 teaspoon sweetened rice vinegar
- 4 hamburger buns

Preheat a charcoal or gas grill to 375°F. Make sure the grill rack is clean and oil it thoroughly with nonstick cooking spray.

Place the onion in a shallow baking dish. In a small saucepan over medium heat, combine the oregano, chives, wine, 2 tablespoons of olive oil, maple syrup, and lemon juice and stir. Bring to a boil. Let cool slightly, then pour the mixture over the onion. Cover and refrigerate for 2 hours.

In a small skillet over medium-high heat, sauté the shallots, garlic, and parsley in the sesame oil until softened, 1 to 2 minutes. Set aside.

In a large bowl, combine the bread and teriyaki sauce; stir well. Fold in the ground chicken, add the shallot mixture, and stir to combine. Add the mustard, egg, 1/2 teaspoon of salt, 1/2 teaspoon of pepper, and cinnamon, and mix well. Mold the mixture into 4 patties and refrigerate, covered, for 1 to 2 hours.

Using paper towels, pat the pineapple slices dry. Brush lightly with olive oil, then drizzle with the vinegar, sprinkle with 1 teaspoon of pepper and 1/4 teaspoon of salt, and set aside.

Brush the burgers lightly with olive oil and transfer to the prepared grill rack over direct heat. Cook for 3 to 4 minutes per side, until the internal temperature registers 175°F (medium-well).

While the burgers are cooking, transfer the onion slices directly onto the grill and cook, 2 to 3 minutes per side. Grill the pineapple slices, about 1 minute per side. You can carefully turn the onion slices with a spatula or insert a soaked bamboo skewer sideways, through all the layers, to hold the layers together.

If you wish, you can split and grill the hamburger buns.

Place the burgers on the grilled buns, top with slices of pineapple and onion, and serve.

SERVES 4

KOREA
Twelve-Chop with Kimchi

The Korean peninsula is suspended (sometimes uneasily) between the nearby culinary superpowers China and Japan. But Korean cuisine is totally distinct from its neighbors'. For one thing, Koreans love strong flavors, using pungent condiments like *kimchi* (fermented spicy cabbage), *jeotgal* (seafood fermented in salt), and *doenjang* (fermented soy bean paste) with just about everything they eat.

As in many parts of Asia, Korean meals are family style, with all the dishes served at the same time for everyone at the table to share. An average family will serve up three to four dishes; a larger family, or a family having a celebration, can cover the table with as many as a dozen plates of food. These settings are referred to as "chop," so a banquet would be called "12-chop," seven dishes a "7-chop," and so on. And yes, like most Asians, Koreans eat with chopsticks.

It's in the condiment department (remember those fermented cabbages, fish, and soybeans) that the Koreans stand apart from the crowd. After eating some of them, you'll be glad to stand apart too. Now let me say this right up front: I'm not a *kimchi* fan. But for many people it's a culinary blessing, so here's a *kimchi* primer.

- Vegetables have been stored in brine by Koreans for more than 3,000 years. From late November to mid-December, the nation is occupied in a culinary ritual to make the spicy dish that accompanies every Korean meal.
- *Kimchi* supplies the Korean people vitamins, fiber, and calcium all year long, especially in the cold Korean winters when nothing is growing.
- *Kimchi* is either four-season *kimchi* or *kimchi* for winter, depending on how the vegetables were salted and seasoned. Four-season *kimchi* comes in many varieties, depending on what is used to make it.
- *Kimchi* is made by placing cabbage or other vegetables in water, then adding radishes, mustard leaf, onion, garlic, ginger, salted fish juice, salt, powdered red pepper, and, often, raw oysters, raw shrimp, raw fish, and seaweed. It is left to ferment for up to a week, and when it's ready, it has a strong, spicy, tangy flavor and odor.
- *Kimchi* comes in 187 delicious flavors including: Korean cabbage *kimchi*, sliced radish *kimchi*, ponytail radish *kimchi*, white watery *kimchi*, watery radish *kimchi*, bundle *kimchi*, Korean lettuce *kimchi*, cucumber *kimchi*, mustard leaf *kimchi*, young green onion *kimchi*, and on, and on, and on.
- In Seoul, there's a *kimchi* museum (the Kimchi Field Museum) where you can learn all about those 187 varieties of *kimchi*. Yum.

Beyond their penchant for pungent condiments, Koreans are also world-class grillers (Korean BBQ, anyone?). Meats are usually marinated, then grilled (*gui*) over a charcoal or open flame fire. Three of my favorite *gui* entrées are:

- *Galbi* are individual beef or pork ribs marinated in sugar, soy sauce, diced green onion, minced garlic, and sesame oil, then grilled.
- *Dakgalbi* is chicken prepared with red pepper paste, pear juice, molasses, sugar, minced garlic, and diced green onion. The chicken is then seasoned with various spices, and grilled.
- *Bulgogi* ("fire meat") is beef or pork sliced thinly then marinated in pear juice or sugar, soy sauce, minced garlic, diced green onion, and sesame oil. The slices are then quickly grilled over open flame or very hot coals.

Seoul, the capital of South Korea, has more than 10,000 restaurants. I thought about listing them all here, but my publisher thought it might take up too much space. So I'll limit myself to two of my favorites. If you ever find yourself in Seoul and want an unforgettable meal, check these out. Yeongyang Center is the oldest restaurant in Myeongdong, and has kept the same, simple menu for more than forty years: *tongdak* (roasted chicken) and *samgyetang* (chicken broth with ginseng). The skin on their roasted chickens is crispy, and the meat is always tender because they use only one-month-old, locally raised chickens.

Odaegam, in the Gangnam district, offers up squid dishes serving only freshly caught squid from the East Sea. The most popular dish on the menu is the *ojingeo bulgogi*, or squid seasoned with red pepper paste dressing and grilled like *bulgogi*. Fleshy squid in hot dressing fires up the palate, and nothing beats a lunch of grilled squid with fritters. And yes, I know what you're thinking. Both of these restaurants serve *kimchi*.

SCALLION PANCAKES

Green onions should have green crisp tops and white bottoms. The more slender bottoms have a sweeter taste. Rinse the green onions thoroughly, trim off any wilted parts and the tip of the root end. They wilt quickly, so it's best to use them within a day or so of purchase.

6 whole green onions, plus 1 tablespoon chopped green onion, for dipping sauce

1/2 cup light soy sauce

1 tablespoon minced carrot

2 tablespoons minced red bell pepper

1 teaspoon crushed red pepper flakes

1 tablespoon sugar

1 tablespoon plus 1 teaspoon pale sesame oil (see Note)

3/4 teaspoon minced garlic

1/2 cup all-purpose flour

1/4 cup potato starch or cornstarch

1/2 cup water

4 eggs

1/2 teaspoon sea salt

1/4 cup chopped cooked bay shrimp

1 tablespoon minced green bell pepper

Preheat a charcoal or gas grill to 375°F.

Cut the green onions into 4-inch lengths, then quarter each section lengthwise into strips.

For the dipping sauce, in a small bowl combine the soy sauce, 1 tablespoon chopped green onion, carrot, half of the red bell pepper, red pepper flakes, sugar, 1 tablespoon of the sesame oil, and 1/4 tablespoon of the garlic. Set aside.

In a large bowl combine the flour, potato starch, water, eggs, salt, the remaining 1/2 teaspoon of the garlic, and the remaining 1 teaspoon of the sesame oil and mix well. Add the shrimp, green pepper, and the remaining 1 tablespoon of red bell pepper and gently mix.

Spray a griddle plate or large skillet with nonstick cooking spray and place on the grill over direct heat. Heat until a drop of water dropped on the surface sizzles and bounces around. Pour the batter onto the griddle, making one large pancake (or 4 to 6 smaller ones). Cook the pancake until golden brown, about 3 to 5 minutes per side, turning carefully with a spatula.

Remove the pancake from the griddle to a warmed platter. Cut it into wedges and serve as an appetizer with the dipping sauce on the side.

SERVES 4 TO 6 AS AN APPETIZER

NOTE: Sesame oil comes in two varieties: one is light in color and flavor and has a deliciously nutty nuance. It's excellent for everything from salad dressings to sautéing. The dark sesame oil has a much stronger flavor and fragrance and is used as a flavor accent for some Asian dishes. It's best not to cook on high heat with this kind.

GRILLED SPICED FISH

It is not a good idea to marinate fish for more than one hour, as the delicate meat can turn mushy. Scoring both sides of a whole fish helps the marinade penetrate into the flesh and adds lots of flavor. Serve with rice and an assortment of stir-fried vegetables.

- 1 (2-pound) whole Pacific halibut, flounder, or mackerel, gutted but with head and tail
- 1 teaspoon salt
- 2 tablespoons olive or vegetable oil
- 1 tablespoon light soy sauce
- 1/2 teaspoon chile powder, preferably Korean (see Note)
- 1 clove garlic, finely chopped

  Pinch of freshly ground black pepper
- 1 teaspoon sesame seeds, toasted
- 2 green onions, white and green parts, chopped

Make 4 deep diagonal cuts on each side of the fish. Rub the entire fish with salt and let stand for 15 minutes.

In a resealable plastic bag, combine the oil, soy sauce, chile powder, garlic, pepper, sesame seeds, and green onions. Shake the bag to combine. Add the fish to the bag, seal, and shake again. Transfer the bag to a shallow dish and refrigerate for 30 minutes to 1 hour.

Preheat a charcoal or gas grill to 375°F. Make sure the grill rack is clean and oil it thoroughly with nonstick cooking spray.

Remove the fish from the marinade, wipe off excess marinade, then transfer to a platter, and cover. Let stand to come to room temperature, about 20 minutes. Pour the marinade into a saucepan, bring to a boil, and cook for 12 minutes. Set aside to use as a basting liquid.

Transfer the fish to the prepared grill rack over direct heat. Cook for 5 minutes on the first side, turn, and cook 2 to 4 minutes longer, basting 2 to 3 times per side with the basting liquid. Skin will be browned and crispy and a fork will flake the flesh. Remove the fish to a warmed platter and serve.

SERVES 4

NOTE: *Gochugaru* means chile powder in Korean. You can find Korean brands at Asian markets, or you can use any bright red U.S. or Asian variety.

BULGOGI

This is a version of the classic beef bulgogi, sliced thinly, marinated overnight, and grilled quickly. If you can find them (try Japanese or Korean grocery stores), wrap each serving in a perilla or sesame leaf. Perilla (also known as shiso) *smells like an apple-mint mixture, while sesame leaves have a minty or licorice (fennel) taste. If you can't find* shiso, *butter lettuce will do as well. To make slicing the beef easier, put the sirloin or rib-eye steaks in the freezer for 30 minutes to firm up the meat before you slice it, and always cut across the grain. If you don't want to eat this dish the traditional Korean way, you can serve the slices of beef over rice and steamed vegetables.*

1 1/2 pounds sirloin or rib-eye steak

6 tablespoons dark soy sauce, plus more for serving

1 tablespoon sugar

2 tablespoons honey

4 tablespoons mirin (rice wine)

3 tablespoons toasted sesame oil

5 tablespoons minced green onions, white and green parts

4 teaspoons minced garlic

2 teaspoons freshly ground black pepper

2 tablespoons sesame salt (see Note)

1 tablespoon sesame seeds, toasted

15 to 20 perilla, sesame, or butter lettuce leaves, for serving

Hot sauce, for serving

Preheat a charcoal or gas grill to 375°F. Make sure the grill rack is clean and oil it thoroughly with nonstick cooking spray.

Slice the beef across the grain into 1/8-inch-thick strips. In a large bowl, combine the soy sauce, sugar, honey, mirin, oil, the green onions, garlic, the black pepper, and the sesame salt. Pour the mixture into a resealable plastic bag, shaking to combine. Add the beef, seal the bag, shake again to coat the meat, and marinate for at least 4 hours and up to 12 hours.

Drain the meat, discarding the marinade. Transfer the meat, a few pieces at a time, to the prepared grill rack over direct heat, searing until cooked through and browned on both sides, 1 to 2 minutes per side at most. Continue grilling until all the meat is cooked, removing pieces as they are done. Keep the cooked meat warm on a warmed platter, and, when finished, sprinkle the meat with sesame seeds.

Serve the meat with the perilla leaves, a hot sauce, and soy sauce. To assemble, take a leaf in the palm of your hand, add a slice of meat and a sprinkle of hot pepper or soy sauce, then fold the leaf over the meat and enjoy.

SERVES 4

NOTE: Make your own sesame salt by taking 1/2 cup sesame seeds, toasting them dry in a small skillet until they turn golden, cool, then grind with 1/4 cup salt in a spice or coffee grinder. Store in the refrigerator in a covered glass jar for up to 6 months.

SESAME-SOY CHICKEN

Chile paste with garlic is a fiery hot Asian condiment, made of mashed chile peppers, salt, soybean oil, vinegar, and garlic. It will warm up the chilliest night. Chile paste is available in Asian grocery stores; I think both Lan Chi (made in China) brand and Huy Fong (made in the U.S.) brands have a special fire.

- 2 tablespoons chile garlic paste (see Note)
- 3 tablespoons dry sherry
- 1 tablespoon soy sauce
- 4 cloves garlic, crushed
- 1 1/2 tablespoons toasted sesame oil
- 1 tablespoon grated fresh ginger
- 2 green onions, green and white parts, minced
- 2 teaspoons black pepper
- 1 tablespoon sugar
- 2 pounds chicken thighs
- 1 tablespoon sesame seeds, for garnish

In a small bowl, combine the chile garlic paste, sherry, soy sauce, garlic, sesame oil, ginger, green onions, pepper, and sugar. Pour the marinade into a resealable plastic bag and add the chicken thighs, shaking to coat. Let stand in the refrigerator for 4 to 6 hours.

Preheat a charcoal or gas grill to 375°F. Make sure the grill rack is clean and oil it thoroughly with nonstick cooking spray.

Remove the chicken from the bag, wipe off excess marinade, and pour the marinade into a saucepan. Boil the marinade for 12 minutes and set aside to use as a basting liquid.

Transfer the chicken, skin side up, to the prepared grill rack over direct heat. Lower the grill lid and cook the chicken, basting two to three times, for 12 to 15 minutes, until skin on bottom is crispy and browned. Turn the chicken skin side down, this time over indirect heat, close the lid, and cook 7 to 9 minutes longer, basting several times, until the juices run clear when pierced to the bone and the internal temperature at the thickest part of the thigh reaches 180°F.

Garnish the chicken with sesame seeds and serve it on a warmed platter.

SERVE 4 TO 6

NOTE: If you can't find Korean chile garlic paste you can substitute Japanese, Thai, Chinese, or Indonesian (*sambal*) varieties. Or you can make your own by combining 3 large roasted garlic cloves, 3 small rehydrated dried chiles (seeded and stemmed), 1 small chopped onion, 2 tablespoons vegetable oil, generous pinches of salt, cumin, and black pepper, a 1/4 cup of a sweetener (honey or sugar), and 1/4 cup water. Pour into a blender and process until smooth. Then cook in small saucepan over medium high heat for 10 to 12 minutes, cool and use or store.

SWEET POTATO-TOFU RICE

The beauty of tofu is that it absorbs the flavors of the food it is cooked with. Firmer tofu is recommended for stir-fries and grilling, while soft tofu works well in soups. This dish is loaded with flavor and even "non-tofu" people will like it, as the flavors of the sweet vinegar and zesty ginger, the gentle bite of the grilled onions, and smooth sugary sweet grilled potatoes are absorbed by the rice and the tofu.

- 1/2 cup soy sauce
- 1/2 teaspoon grated fresh ginger
- 1 tablespoon sweetened rice vinegar
- 1 tablespoon vegetable oil
- 1 large sweet potato, peeled, cut into 1/2-inch-thick rounds
- 2 yellow onions, cut into 1/2-inch-thick rounds
- 3 cups water
- Salt
- 4 ounces firm tofu, cut into 1/2-inch-thick slices
- 3 cups hot cooked rice (see Note)
- Freshly ground black pepper

Soak 12 to 16 bamboo skewers in water to cover for 30 minutes.

In a large shallow dish, combine the soy sauce, ginger, rice vinegar, and oil, and set aside.

Transfer the sweet potato slices to a small saucepan and add the water and a pinch of salt. Bring to a boil, lower the heat, and simmer for 10 minutes, until the slices are just starting to become tender. Remove and pat dry.

Add the onion, potato, and tofu slices to the soy sauce mixture, carefully tossing to coat. Let stand for 10 to 12 minutes. Drain the vegetables and reserve the marinade.

Run 2 soaked skewers, 1 inch apart, through each slice of onion to hold the onion together on the grill. Set aside.

Preheat a charcoal or gas grill to 375°F. Make sure the grill rack is clean and oil it thoroughly with nonstick cooking spray.

Transfer the onion, potato, and tofu to the prepared grill rack and cook for 2 to 3 minutes per side, generously basting with the reserved marinade, until they are grill-marked and beginning to brown.

Transfer the tofu and vegetables to a serving plate, removing the skewers from the onions. Serve over the steamed rice and season with salt and freshly ground pepper.

SERVES 4 TO 6

NOTE: When steaming rice, add a tablespoon of oil to the water so the grains stay separate and don't stick together. Never stir rice while it cooks because it will crush the rice grains, releasing starch and making the rice gummy.

GREEN DRAGONS WITH SWEET BEAN SAUCE

Azuki beans are small, sweet, and red. They are widely used in Japanese, Chinese, and Korean cooking, often in the form of a paste. In this recipe, azuki paste and sesame oil add an East Asian twist to a simple side dish of grilled dragons (er, zucchini).

- 1   tablespoon red bean (azuki) paste
- 2   tablespoons sweetened rice vinegar
- 2   tablespoons light corn syrup
- 1   teaspoon toasted sesame oil
- 1   teaspoon sesame seeds
- 1/2 teaspoon chili powder (optional)
- 4   large zucchini
     Vegetable oil, for brushing

Preheat a charcoal or gas grill to 375°F. Make sure the grill rack is clean and oil it thoroughly with nonstick cooking spray.

In a small bowl, combine the bean paste, vinegar, corn syrup, sesame oil, seeds, and chili powder; set aside.

Slice the zucchini lengthwise into 1/4-inch-wide sticks and brush with vegetable oil. Transfer zucchini to the prepared grill rack over direct heat and cook just until they are nicely marked and a knife easily pierces them, about 5 minutes.

Serve drizzled with the bean sauce.

SERVES 4 TO 6

MEXICO

Chiles, Camarones, and
Chocolate Turkey

First, for those of you who haven't had the pleasure of visiting Mexico, let me say that comparing the food in some Americanized Mexican restaurants to real Mexican food is a hilarious travesty. Sure there are the familiar-sounding tacos and enchiladas and frijoles in Mexico, but they bear little resemblance to many of their northern cousins. And the use of fresh fish and seafood, beef, pork, and poultry in Mexico is totally unlike so much of the bland and characterless Mexican-style chow offered in many U.S. joints.

In Mexico, I ate delicious, and deliciously fresh-from-the-brine, shrimp the size of small lobsters; indecently inexpensive lobster tails (ten for $20); pork stews that were as mouth-watering, tender, and flavorful as you can imagine; sumptuous, creamy, and exquisite flans; whole fish grilled over mesquite on the beach; tons of fresh fruit; tamales that turned me into a tamale lover; and, oh yes, margaritas by the bucketful. It was all wonderful, but the one dish that fired me up the most, both emotionally and culinarily was the fabulous turkey cooked with mole—Mexico's revered, labor-intensive, deeply delicious, and chocolate-tinged sauce (to try it yourself, see page 128).

Mexico is paradise for cooks as well as eaters—the markets are mind-blowing. One whole block of downtown Mazatlan is home to vendors tending many dozens of tubs of fresh shrimp, calamari, lobster, octopus, and other sea creatures, all brought still wriggling to the market each morning, direct from the fishing boats that dot the harbor. The produce reflects Mexico's stature as an agricultural giant. I wandered markets brimming with huge limes, luscious pineapples, strawberries, and oranges, fresh tomatoes and avocados of many varieties, humongous papayas, bananas, and plantains, radishes, celery, jicama, melons, squash, tomatillos, onions, green beans, potatoes, garlic, dethorned cactus, huge bunches of cilantro, and chiles. And I do mean chiles.

I saw more varieties, sizes, shapes, and colors of chiles than I've ever seen. Dried chiles by the dozens, and just as many fresh, lined the market shelves. There were tiny green and red chiltepín, florescent orange habañero, rich green chile de árbol, mulato, ancho, pasilla, serrano, guero, jalapeño, bell (orange, yellow, red, and green), cayenne, and even the fiery tabasco.

But, and I must stress this to all the chile heads out there, at no time did my mouth catch on fire from super-hot, spiced dishes. Mexican cooks use chile peppers mostly for flavor, not flame—though of course there are always exceptions. Chef Gilberto del Toro Coello, the personable executive chef at the exquisite Pueblo Bonito Resort and Spa, told us that he likes to use chiles for smoky flavor, complexity, and gentle warmth. "If you go too far ,you can't taste the food," he confesses. "And we want people to taste our fresh fish, vegetables, fruits, and meats." But I think that's only for the guests. I tasted the hot sauce he put on his own plate and it was hot enough to light a jet engine. Gringos beware!

GRILLED FISH SINALOA STYLE

This recipe is from Chef Gilberto del Toro Coello. Because the odds of finding pargo in a U.S. market are slim, you can substitute tilapia, Pacific flounder, or sole. Serve this dish with fresh flour or corn tortillas and Mexican salsa. For this recipe, you will need a large fish-grilling basket.

1 whole (about 8-pound) pargo, tilapia, Pacific flounder, or sole, cleaned and butterflied

MARINADE

1 cup canola oil

3 cloves garlic, chopped

6 black peppercorns

1/4 cup white wine

2 bay leaves

1 tablespoon freshly squeezed lime juice

1/2 teaspoon salt

CHILE SAUCE

2 ancho chiles

1/2 yellow onion

3 Roma tomatoes

3 cloves garlic

1/8 teaspoon ground cumin

1/8 teaspoon dried oregano

6 black peppercorns

1/2 teaspoon coarse sea salt

3 tablespoons olive oil

Salt

Freshly ground black pepper

Juice of 2 limes

1 large red onion, thickly sliced

1 large tomato, sliced

1 green bell pepper, cored, seeded, and sliced

1 yellow bell pepper, cored, seeded, and sliced

1 red bell pepper, cored, seeded, and sliced

1/4 cup butter, melted

1 (12-ounce) bottle Mexican beer

Rinse the fish thoroughly with cold running water and pat dry with paper towels. Place it in a resealable bag or shallow pan.

For the marinade, in a food processor, combine the oil, garlic, peppercorns, wine, bay leaves, lime juice, and salt. Process until well blended. Pour the marinade over the fish and refrigerate for 1 hour.

Stem and seed the chiles, and let them soak in cold water for 1 hour. Drain and set aside.

Prepare a charcoal or gas grill for indirect grilling (it is not necessary to add a drip pan for this recipe). Preheat to 375°F. Make sure the grill rack is clean and oil it thoroughly with nonstick cooking spray.

For the chile sauce, roast the ancho chiles on the prepared grill rack over direct high heat until they begin to char, about 15 minutes, then remove them from the heat and let them cool enough to handle. Place the onion, tomatoes, and garlic in a skillet on the grill rack over indirect heat and cook, occasionally stirring until they become soft and fragrant, about 15 minutes.

In a large mortar, combine the cumin, oregano, peppercorns, and sea salt; using a pestle grind until pulverized. Gradually add the roasted chiles, tomatoes, onion, and garlic, grinding to a smooth paste. If you don't have a mortar and pestle, use a spice grinder for the spices and a food processor to combine spices and vegetables. Season with salt and pepper, stir in the olive oil, and set aside.

For the fish, line one side of a fish-grilling basket with aluminum foil. Remove the fish from the marinade, wipe off the excess marinade, and discard the marinade. Transfer the fish, skin side down, to the foil; season with salt, black pepper, and lime juice. Brush some of the chile sauce

onto the fish; top with the sliced onion, tomato, and bell peppers. Brush a third of the melted butter over the fish and vegetables. Line the other side of the basket with foil and close the basket.

Transfer the fish basket, skin side down, to the grill for direct cooking, making sure the grill has an even, moderate flame, to avoid overcooking. Grill the fish until it flakes and the edges are just starting to brown, 8 to 10 minutes per side, opening the basket halfway through cooking, to baste with more sauce, the remaining butter and the beer and to turn the basket over.

Remove the basket from the heat and let it stand for a few 5 minutes. Then open the basket, transfer the fish and vegetables to a serving tray, and serve immediately.

SERVES 6 TO 8

POLLO ASADO

Jalapeño is the most widely used fresh green chile in the U.S., and is so often used in Tex-Mex cooking that it's often referred to as the Texas sweet pickle. The heat mainly comes from the seed and the membrane of this 2-inch-long (average) pepper. When ripened it turns red, and when smoked, it becomes a chipotle chile. Pollo asado is a very spicy, grilled chicken that is popular all over Mexico—just how hot it is depends on the region and the

taste buds of the chef. This version is sorta fiery—call it medium hot. If you don't know how to butterfly a chicken, have your butcher do it for you.

1	(4- to 5-pound) chicken, butterflied
1/4	cup butter, melted
1	(12-ounce) bottle Pacifico beer (or other lager-type beer)
	Juice from 4 or 5 fresh limes (about 1/2 cup)
1/3	cup olive oil
4	cloves garlic, minced
1	tablespoon hot paprika
1	teaspoon ancho chile powder
1	medium jalapeño, chopped, seeded, and stemmed
2	teaspoons kosher salt
3	tablespoons chopped fresh cilantro
1	tablespoon minced lemon zest
2	limes, quartered
	Cilantro sprigs, for garnish

Place the chicken in a large resealable plastic bag.

In a bowl, combine the remaining ingredients, except the quartered limes and cilantro sprigs. Pour the marinade over the chicken, press out the excess air, and seal. Refrigerate for 8 to 10 hours.

Remove the chicken from the refrigerator 1 hour before cooking. Drain the marinade and discard it. Let the chicken come to

room temperature and wipe off excess marinade.

Preheat a charcoal or gas grill to 375°F. Make sure the grill rack is clean and oil it thoroughly with nonstick cooking spray.

Transfer the chicken to the prepared grill rack over direct heat and cook, turning often to avoid burning, for 10 to 12 minutes per side, or until the temperature at the thickest part of the thigh reaches 180°F.

Transfer to a platter, cover, and let stand for 5 minutes. Squeeze lime juice over the cooked chicken, garnish with the cilantro, and serve.

SERVES 6

NOTE: Yes, the old maxim that spicy food is addictive is true. When you eat something hot, your nerves actually feel pain. This pain is sent to your brain where endorphins are released to dull the pain, but at the same time create a brief euphoric feeling. Those who like spicy food learn to crave this feeling and become hooked on hot!

TURKEY MOLE

Now, three cautions about making your own mole sauce: 1) it is a long and involved process that can take several hours; 2) once you've made it, you'll never again avail yourself of canned, bottled, or otherwise premade mole sauces; and 3) you must use genuine Mexican chocolate—there is nothing made in the U.S. that can substitute for the real stuff.

The traditional red mole contains chiles, garlic, nuts, tomato, spices, and chocolate. Please note that the amount of chocolate used is actually very small and should not overpower the sauce, merely flavor it. Mexican chocolate is made from dark, bitter chocolate mixed with sugar, cinnamon, and sometimes nuts. You can make the mole sauce ahead; it keeps for several weeks in the refrigerator. Note that your turkey will need to be halved; you may want to have your butcher do it for you.

- 4 pasilla chiles, stemmed and chopped
- 4 mulato chiles, stemmed and chopped
- 6 ancho chiles, stemmed and chopped
- 1 onion, chopped
- 2 cloves garlic, chopped
- 3 tomatoes, peeled, seeded, and chopped
- 2 tablespoons sesame seeds
- 1/2 cup chopped almonds
- 1/2 cup raisins
- 1/2 teaspoon anise seeds
- 1/4 teaspoon cloves
- 1/4 teaspoon cinnamon
- 1/4 teaspoon ground coriander
- 1/4 teaspoon freshly ground black pepper
- 7 tablespoons lard or vegetable shortening
- 2 cups chicken broth
- 2 (3.72-ounce) disks Ibarra Mexican chocolate, chopped
- 1 (8- to 9-pound) turkey Olive oil, for brushing
- 1 teaspoon salt

Combine chiles, onion, garlic, tomatoes, 1 tablespoon of the sesame seeds, almonds, raisins, anise, cloves, cinnamon, coriander, and black pepper in a blender or food processor. Pulse 8 or 10 times until smooth.

Melt 2 tablespoons of the lard in a skillet over medium-high heat. Add the chile purée and sauté for 10 minutes, stirring frequently. Add the chicken broth and chocolate and cook over very low heat for 45 minutes. The sauce should be very thick.

Prepare a charcoal or gas grill for indirect grilling, placing a drip pan under the cool side of the grill rack (see page 3). Preheat to 375°F. Make sure the grill rack is clean and oil it thoroughly with nonstick cooking spray.

With a cleaver or heavy sharp knife, cut right alongside the turkey's breastbone. Pull the turkey open, then cut down the middle of the back so you have two half turkeys. Brush the turkey halves with olive oil, sprinkle with the salt, and transfer them, cut side down, to the prepared grill rack over indirect heat. Lower the grill lid and cook for about 20 minutes a pound. When the internal temperature at the thigh reaches 160°F, remove the turkey halves from the grill and cut the meat into serving pieces.

In a large saucepan over low heat, melt the remaining lard. Add the turkey pieces and cook over medium-high heat until browned on all sides, about 10 to 15 minutes.

With a slotted spoon, remove the turkey pieces from the pan. Drain off the lard, then return the turkey to the pan. Pour the mole sauce over the turkey, turning to evenly coat each piece.

Bring the mixture to a simmer over low heat, cover the pan, and simmer for about 20 minutes, occasionally spooning the sauce over the turkey pieces.

Remove the turkey pieces to a warmed platter. Drizzle some of the mole sauce over the turkey, sprinkle with the remaining sesame seeds, and serve the rest of the mole sauce on the side.

SERVES 6 TO 8

GRILLED STEAK WITH SWEET PLANTAINS AND CHIPOTLE SALSA

This recipe is courtesy of award-winning chef, restaurateur, cookbook author, and television personality Rick Bayless, who has done more than any other culinary star to introduce Americans to authentic Mexican cuisine.

- 4 cloves garlic, finely chopped or crushed with a garlic press
- 1/3 cup ancho chile powder
- 4 teaspoons brown sugar
- 1 teaspoon dried oregano, preferably Mexican
- 1/2 teaspoon ground cumin
- 4 teaspoons ground black pepper
- 5 teaspoons salt
- 1 (1 1/2-pound) flank steak (or substitute strip steak, rib-eye, or chuck steak)
- 2 black-ripe plantains
- 1 red onion, cut into 1-inch-thick rounds
  Oil, for brushing
- 1 cup Smoky Chipotle Salsa (recipe follows)

Prepare a gas or charcoal grill for indirect grilling, placing a drip pan under the cool side of the grill rack (see page 3). Preheat to 375°F. Make sure the grill rack is clean and oil it thoroughly with nonstick cooking spray.

For the rub, combine the garlic, chile powder, brown sugar, oregano, cumin, pepper, and salt. Spread a heavy coating over the meat—you'll need 1 to 2 tablespoons for a 1 1/2-pound flank steak. Set aside. (Refrigerate the leftover rub for another use.)

Cut off the ends of both plantains and cut them in half lengthwise, keeping the peel on. Lightly oil the plantains and the onion. Transfer the onion and plantains, cut side down, to the prepared grill rack over direct heat. Cook until well-browned, 2 to 3 minutes, then turn and brown the other side. Once they are tender and slightly browned, move the plantains and onion to the cooler side of the grill.

Transfer the meat to the grill rack over direct heat. Grill for 3 to 4 minutes per side, until deeply browned on both sides. Move the meat to the cooler side of the grill and cook until it reaches your desired doneness, about 10 to 15 minutes for medium-rare.

Transfer the plantains, onion, and meat to a cutting board. Slip the plantains from their skins, chop the plantains and onion into 1/2-inch pieces and transfer to a bowl; stir to combine. Season with salt to taste.

Slice the steak and divide it among 4 dinner plates. Serve with plantains and salsa on the side.

SERVES 4

SMOKY CHIPOTLE SALSA WITH PAN-ROASTED TOMATILLOS

- 3 cloves garlic, peeled
- 4 medium tomatillos (about 8 ounces total), husked, rinsed, and halved (see Note)
- 2 canned chipotle chiles en adobo (or more, if you like really spicy salsa), stemmed
- 1/4 cup water
  Salt

In a large nonstick skillet (or other skillet lined with aluminum foil) over medium-high heat, combine the garlic and tomatillos (cut side down). Cook, without stirring, until the tomatillos are well browned, 3 or 4 minutes. Turn everything over and cook until the other side is browned and the tomatillos are completely soft, about 5 minutes longer.

Transfer the garlic and tomatillos to a blender or food processor and add the chiles and the water. Process to a coarse puree. Transfer to a small dish and let cool. Thin with a little water if necessary to give the salsa an easily spoonable consistency. Taste and season with salt, usually a generous 1/2 teaspoon.

MAKES 1 CUP

NOTE: The husks of fresh tomatillos should be intact, and the fruits inside should be firm and without blemish.

SPICY STUFFED POTATOES

This stuffed potato is practically a meal in itself; just add a salad, and you're all set. You can also add cooked chopped beef, turkey, chicken, or Mexican sausage to fill even the biggest appetite. Potatoes are an important part of the Mexican diet—though they'll never supplant tortillas or beans—and are grown just about everywhere in the country.

- 4 large russet potatoes, scrubbed
- $1/2$ cup milk
- 1 cup grated Cheddar cheese (about 4 ounces)
- $1/3$ cup crushed tortilla chips
- $1/3$ cup chopped fresh cilantro
- $1/4$ cup chopped green onions
- 1 tablespoon minced garlic
- 1 teaspoon chipotle chile powder
- Salt
- Freshly ground black pepper
- Salsa, for serving
- Sour cream, for serving

Prepare a charcoal or gas grill for indirect cooking (it is not necessary to use a drip pan with this recipe). Preheat to 425°F.

Pierce each potato several times with a toothpick. Transfer to the grill and cook until tender, over indirect heat, about 1 hour 10 minutes.

Transfer the potatoes to a work surface, let them cool just enough to handle, and cut one-quarter, lengthwise, off the top of each potato. Scoop the potato flesh from the skin into a large bowl, leaving a $1/4$-inch-thick shell. Add the milk to the potato and mash. Add the cheese, chips, cilantro, onion, garlic, and chile powder, and season with salt and pepper. Fill the shells with the potato mixture.

Transfer the stuffed potatoes to a cast-iron skillet or baking pan and place that on the barbecue over direct heat, and cook until heated through, about 20 minutes.

Top the potatoes with salsa and sour cream and serve.

SERVES 4

SOUTH OF THE BORDER BEANS

Ancho chiles are poblano chiles that have been dried and have, as a result, become somewhat sweeter. They are the most popular dried chile in both Mexico and the U.S. Anchos have are a rich, black-red color and a smoky and somewhat fruity taste. You can find these peppers, or a powdered version of them, in the spice department at most grocery stores. These beans are a great side dish with steak, chicken, or ribs.

2 cups dried pinto beans (see Note)

$1/2$ pound smoked bacon, diced

1 large Spanish onion, minced

1 tablespoon dried Mexican or regular oregano

1 clove garlic, minced

1 tablespoon brown sugar

1 teaspoon ancho chile powder

6 cups water, plus additional if necessary

$1/2$ cup sliced jalapeño chiles (about 4 or 5)

1 (12-ounce) bottle Mexican beer

2 teaspoons salt

1 teaspoon freshly ground black pepper

In a large pot, soak the dried beans in cold water to cover for at least 4 hours, then drain. Or you can put them in boiling water, cover, and allow them to sit for 2 hours to accomplish a faster soak.

Prepare a charcoal or gas grill for indirect grilling (it is not necessary to use a drip pan for this recipe). Preheat to 300°F.

In a 6- to 7-quart Dutch oven on the grill or a side burner over medium-high, combine the bacon, onion, oregano, garlic, brown sugar, and chile powder and cook, stirring, until the onions begin to brown, about 5 to 6 minutes. Add the beans, water, jalapeños, and beer, and bring to a boil. Move the pot to the cool (indirect) side of the grill, and cook, covered, until the beans just begin to soften, $1^{1}/2$ to 2 hours. Add more water or beer if the beans begin to dry out. The mixture should be soupy, with beans that are soft but not mushy.

Stir in 2 teaspoons of salt and 1 teaspoon of pepper and cook for 10 minutes longer. Taste, adding more salt or pepper if desired.

Remove the pot from the grill and keep covered until ready to serve.

SERVES 4 TO 6

NOTE: The beans can be cooked a day or so ahead and reheated with no loss of flavor. Mash leftover beans, heat, and serve as *frijoles refritos* **(refried beans).**

CACAXTLA CHOCOLATE SOUFFLÉ

Called "food of the gods" by the Aztecs, chocolate is very important in Mexican culture. The Mayans used cacao beverages in religious ceremonies, and passed the rituals on to the Aztecs for whom cacao symbolized power and glory. Cacaxtla, in the state of Puebla, was one of the main centers for the cacao trade in Mexico. The invention of what we now know as "Mexican chocolate" has been attributed by some to Spanish nuns in Puebla.

1/2 cup (1 stick) unsalted butter, plus 2 tablespoons to butter soufflé dishes

3 tablespoons white sugar

5 (3.72-ounce) disks Mexican chocolate, chopped (see Note)

8 large eggs, separated, at room temperature

1/2 teaspoon ancho chile powder

1/4 teaspoon ground cinnamon

Sweetened whipped cream, for serving

Cinnamon, for garnish

Unsweetened chocolate curls, for garnish

Prepare a charcoal or gas grill for indirect grilling (it is not necessary to use a drip pan with this recipe). Preheat to 375°F. Butter eight 6-ounce soufflé dishes or custard cups with the 2 table-spoons butter and sprinkle them with the sugar.

Heat the chocolate and the 1/2 cup butter in a heavy sauce-pan over low heat, stirring constantly, until melted. The chocolate mixture will be grainy, not smooth.

Whisk the egg yolks in a large bowl to blend, then gradually whisk in the hot chocolate mixture, chile powder, and cinnamon. In another large bowl with an electric mixer on medium speed, beat the egg whites until they stand in soft peaks. Using a rubber spatula, fold one-quarter of the egg whites into the chocolate mixture; then gently fold in the remaining egg whites, making sure there are no streaks of white. Divide the mixture among the prepared dishes.

Place the dishes on a rimmed baking sheet and transfer to the grill rack over indirect heat. Lower the grill lid and bake until the tops have risen about 1/2 inch above the rim of each dish, are light brown, appear dry, and the centers are softly set, about 18 minutes.

Serve the soufflés with sweetened whipped cream, sprinkled with cinnamon and unsweetened chocolate curls.

SERVES 8

NOTE: In this century, most people simply buy chocolate. But in some Mexican villages, chocolate is still made by hand. The cocoa beans are roasted, then ground using a *metate y mano*, a Mayan stone version of a mortar and pestle that has been heated over coals. The crushed, heated beans melt, and sugar, spices, and sometimes nuts are added.

MOROCCO
Take-Away Lamb's Head from the Souk

Morocco lies barely nine miles from Spain across the Strait of Gibraltar, and while many people think of it as a Mediterranean country, most of its coastline fronts the Atlantic Ocean. Many of its best-known cities—Tangier, Casablanca, Rabat, and Agadir—are located south along the "African" coast rather than north along the "European" coast.

Marrakesh, the former capital, is situated inland at the base of the snow-tipped Atlas Mountains. Founded more than a thousand

years ago, Marrakesh began as an oasis where water and sustenance were readily available for the camel and donkey caravans of old. Today the red-walled city is the second largest in the country with a population of 1 to 2 million, the uncertainty due to the number of Berber tribesmen who live just outside the city in the surrounding mountains. In the city center is Djemaa el-Fna, where the grand "souk," or market, is located beside the soaring Koutoubia Mosque. The square is a beehive of jugglers, storytellers, fortune-tellers, snake charmers, orange juice salesmen, magicians, souvenir shops, and dozens of tiny food stalls.

At night, Djemaa el-Fna is dominated by larger food concessions with picnic tables seating hundreds. A haze of fragrant smoke hovers over the square from dozens of fires cooking up tagines, kebabs, stews, and soups. Vendors with pushcarts sell fresh orange juice (perhaps the best I've ever tasted), dried fruits, pastries, and ice cream.

Due to the previous landlords, it is often assumed that Moroccan cuisine must be heavily influenced by French and Spanish cooking. Some of these culinary influences are certainly evident; however, Moroccan food is based firmly on the cooking of the native Berbers and the Arabs, who arrived in the seventh century. A fusion of meat (especially lamb), fruit (mainly dates, raisins, figs), nuts (walnuts and almonds), grains (couscous, of course), with clever blends of spices that enhance rather than mask the ingredients, makes Moroccan cuisine one of the most varied in the world.

Just outside the ancient imperial city of Dar Liqama, you will find a grove of over 150,000 palm trees surrounding a luxurious villa, also called Dar Liqama, that houses an internation-

ally renowned cooking school where I spent three very special days.

The villa, built in a traditional Moroccan architectural style, is replete with incredible antique doors, a columned entrance, graceful arches surrounding a peaceful domed courtyard, and a delightful indoor bubbling fountain filled with roses. There are four stunning guest rooms for cooking school students.

From Dar Liqama's chef, I learned that the tagine (both the name of the distinctively shaped cooking vessel as well as the food prepared in it) serves as the framework for a collage of ingredients, spices, and styles. Dishes I learned how to prepare included chicken with olives and preserved lemons; minced meat kebabs; sweet mint tea; and my favorite, *b'steeya* (a mix of diced chicken, nuts, cinnamon, and sugar, enclosed in a golden pillow of flaky puff pastry).

Rafik Kilardi, the former director of the Dar Liqama cooking school, had mentioned a particular delicacy throughout my visit: boiled lamb's head. So on a nighttime trip to the Djemaa el-Fna, I decided to give it a try and ordered it as a "take-away, without bones" and watched as the skin and skull were removed and the meaty flesh placed in a brown paper bag.

We returned to the villa where we sat down to a wonderful farewell dinner of tomato, beet, and cucumber salad; a golden chicken *b'steeya*; minced lamb skewers cooked on a small barbecue right in the kitchen; flat bread; and a creamy-crunchy milk *b'steeya* for dessert. I had asked the cook to serve the lamb's head as an appetizer. The salad, *b'steeya*, lamb skewers, bread, and dessert, were perfectly delicious. The appetizer was perhaps best left atop the sheep.

B'STEEYA

Moroccan tradition has this dish made with pigeon, but I've opted for chicken, as I looked far and wide in my local supermarkets and the only pigeons I found were in the parking lot. You can also use game hens or other small birds.

- ¹/₂ pound slivered almonds (about 3 cups)
- 1 tablespoon olive oil
- 1 cup confectioners' sugar, plus additional for garnish
- 1¹/₂ teaspoons cinnamon, plus additional for garnish
- 2 tablespoons honey
- ¹/₃ cup (about ³/₄ stick) butter, plus ¹/₂ cup (1 stick) butter, melted
- 1 onion, minced
- 2 large boneless, skinless, chicken breasts, cut into ¹/₂-inch pieces
- ¹/₂ teaspoon freshly ground black pepper
- 1 teaspoon ground ginger
- ¹/₈ teaspoon powdered saffron
- ¹/₂ teaspoon marjoram
- ¹/₂ teaspoon paprika
- ³/₄ cup minced fresh parsley
- ¹/₄ cup minced cilantro
- ¹/₄ teaspoon salt
- 2 eggs, beaten
- 1 (1-pound) package phyllo dough, thawed (see Note)

In a large skillet, heat the almonds and oil over medium-high heat until golden, about 8 minutes, stirring or shaking the skillet almost constantly after the first 4 minutes. Let cool completely. Transfer to a food processor and add the sugar, 1 teaspoon of the cinnamon, and the honey. Pulse 3 or 4 times, until the almonds are finely chopped. Remove to a bowl and set aside.

In a skillet over medium-high heat, combine ¹/₃ cup of the butter and the onion; sauté until the onion becomes translucent, about 3 minutes. Add the chicken, pepper, ginger, saffron, marjoram, the remaining ¹/₂ teaspoon of cinnamon, paprika, parsley, cilantro, and salt. Simmer until the chicken is cooked through, about 5 minutes.

Slowly stir the eggs into the chicken mixture until combined. Remove the pan from the heat and let it cool for 10 minutes.

On a work surface, lay out the phyllo dough. Cut in half lengthwise to make long rectangles about the half the width of a 9- or 10-inch cast-iron skillet, and twice as long. Brush one sheet with the melted butter, and transfer it, butter side up, to the skillet with the excess dangling over the sides. Add another sheet, brushed with butter, at an angle to the first. Repeat with 4 more sheets so that you have phyllo entirely covering the bottom of the pan and dangling all around the edges. Repeat the process, forming another 6-sheet layer. Top the phyllo with half of the almond mixture and the chicken mixture. Top the chicken with the remaining nut mixture. Arrange 4 or 5 more buttered phyllo sheets on top of the filling. Fold the dangling ends of the phyllo up over the top of the pie. Brush the top with butter.

At this point, the *b'steeya* can be refrigerated for a couple of hours if desired, but you should bring it to room temperature before you cook it.

Preheat a charcoal or gas grill to 375°F.

When ready to cook, transfer the pan to the grill rack over direct heat, cooking until the crust is golden, 15 to 20 minutes. Remove from the grill and cover the skillet with a large plate. Invert the pastry onto the plate, then slide it back into the skillet, bottom up, and return to the barbecue to brown on the other side, 15 to 20 minutes longer.

Transfer the pastry to a platter and let it rest for 5 minutes. Sprinkle with powdered sugar and cinnamon before serving.

SERVES 8 TO 10 AS AN APPETIZER

NOTE: As the phyllo sheets you buy in the supermarket are usually frozen, you must let them come to room temperature before using. While they sit on your cutting board, cover them with a slightly damp towel to keep them moist.

MARRAKESH FISH STEAKS

This spicy, pungent marinade is commonly called sharmula. *It can be used with any fish that's suitable for grilling or broiling, and can also be used to marinate fish before baking. Despite its proximity to the Sahara, much of Morocco is fertile, arable land, while the extensive coastline offers a protein-rich bounty from the sea.*

12	cloves garlic
1/2	teaspoon kosher salt (see Note)
1	bunch cilantro
1/4	cup chopped fresh parsley
1	tablespoon paprika
1	teaspoon ground cumin
1/2	teaspoon cinnamon
	Pinch of cayenne pepper
1/4	teaspoon powdered saffron
	Juice of 2 large lemons
1	teaspoon olive oil
6	(6-ounce) halibut steaks, or striped bass, bream, or flounder
	Chopped cilantro, for garnish

In a food processor, combine the garlic, salt, cilantro, parsley, paprika, cumin, cinnamon, cayenne, saffron, lemon juice, and olive oil. Process until smooth. Place the fish steaks in a wide, flat pan and add the marinade. Refrigerate for several hours, turning occasionally.

Preheat a charcoal or gas grill to 375°F. Make sure the grill rack is clean and oil it thoroughly with nonstick cooking spray.

Remove the fish from the marinade and drain, wiping away the excess marinade. Transfer to a large plate and let it stand to come to room temperature, about 20 minutes. Pour the marinade into a small saucepan and boil for 12 minutes.

Transfer the fish to the prepared grill rack over direct heat. For each 1/2-inch thickness of the steak, cook 4 minutes, turning the fish halfway through, until it's just beginning to brown on the edges and flake. Baste with the marinade several times as it cooks, and when done serve immediately, garnished with additional cilantro.

SERVES 6

Note: Kosher salt is not really, in itself, kosher, but is used in preparing meat to make it kosher for eating. Kosher salt has larger grains than table or canning salt, and is most often flattened to make the grains dissolve more easily.

DATE-STUFFED GAME HENS

"Hen" is often used as a generic term in the world of poultry, meaning that the Cornish game hen you might be cooking could just as well be male. These birds are actually miniature chickens, hybrids of two distinct breeds, the White Rock and the Cornish varieties of chicken.

- $1/2$ cup loosely packed chopped cilantro leaves
- 10 cloves garlic, minced
- 1 tablespoon ground cumin
- 1 tablespoon paprika
- $1/2$ teaspoon dried marjoram
- 4 Cornish game hens
- 1 cup tawny port wine
- $1/2$ cup olive oil
- $1/4$ cup balsamic vinegar or red wine vinegar
- 4 tablespoons honey
- 2 oranges, thinly sliced
- 2 lemons, thinly sliced
- 40 whole dates (approximately 1 pound, or 2 cups), pitted
- 3 tablespoons minced green olives
- Salt
- Freshly ground black pepper

In a small bowl, combine 6 tablespoons of the cilantro, the garlic, cumin, paprika, and marjoram. Rub the mixture generously on both hens and transfer them to a large resealable plastic bag.

In another small bowl, whisk the port, oil, vinegar, and honey and pour over the birds and into the cavities. Seal the bag and refrigerate for 8 to 10 hours.

When ready to cook, drain the hens, wipe away excess marinade, and pour the marinade into a saucepan to boil for 12 minutes.

Prepare a charcoal or gas grill for indirect cooking (it is not necessary to use a drip pan for this recipe). Preheat to 375°F.

Arrange the orange and lemon slices in the bottom of a Dutch oven. Add the game hens, breast side up, sprinkle with the dates and olives, and season with salt and pepper.

Transfer the pot, uncovered, to the grill rack over indirect heat. Lower the grill lid and cook, basting occasionally, until the hens are cooked through, or when the internal temperature in the thickest part of the thigh reaches 170°F, about 40 minutes.

Transfer the hens to a warmed platter and cover with aluminum foil until ready to serve. Pour the juices from the pan into a small saucepan, straining out and discarding the lemon and orange slices. Boil, whisking often, until the liquid has reduced to $1/2$ cup, about 5 minutes.

Garnish the hens with the remaining cilantro and serve with the sauce on the side.

SERVES 4

CHICKEN WITH PRESERVED LEMONS

One note for future visitors: because Moroccan chefs take great pride in spicing their food according to recipes passed down from their ancestors, and are precise in what seasonings they add and when they add them, it is considered vulgar to put a salt shaker on the table. There's no need to add any salt to this recipe, as the preserved lemons will add a unique salty-lemony flavor that is absolutely delicious. Preserved lemons can be purchased online or in the ethnic foods section of your grocery store, or you may wish to make your own, following the recipe on page 141.

You may use water instead of the wine used here, but the wine adds a nice tang that you'd otherwise miss.

1	(4- to 5-pound) chicken, butterflied (see Note)
2	tablespoons olive oil
1	large onion, chopped
2	teaspoons paprika
1	teaspoon ground ginger
1/2	teaspoon ground turmeric
1/2	teaspoon freshly ground black pepper
1	cup dry white wine
1/4	cup chopped picholine olives
10	preserved lemon quarters
2	tablespoons preserved lemon brine
1/4	cup chopped cilantro, for garnish

Preheat a charcoal or gas grill to 375°F. Make sure the grill rack is clean and oil it thoroughly with nonstick cooking spray.

Brush the chicken halves with 1 tablespoon of the olive oil. Transfer to the prepared grill rack over direct heat. Cook, turning often, until well-browned on all sides, about 15 to 20 minutes. Remove the chicken, cover, and set aside.

Pour the remaining olive oil into a skillet over medium-high heat. Add the onion and cook, stirring often, until it begins to brown, about 5 minutes. Stir in the paprika, ginger, turmeric, and pepper. Add the wine, chicken, olives, lemon quarters, and lemon brine. Cover and simmer for 5 minutes.

Spray 2 large pieces of heavy-duty aluminum foil with nonstick cooking spray. Transfer each chicken half to a piece of foil. Pour half the lemon mixture over each chicken, making sure each has 5 lemon quarters, and fold the foil around the chicken halves, securely sealing the foil packages by double folding the edges.

Transfer the foil packages to the barbecue over direct heat and cook until the internal temperature at the thickest part of the thigh reads 180°F, which will take approximately 25 to 30 minutes.

Open the foil packages carefully to avoid a steam burn, cut the chickens in half again, garnish with cilantro, and serve.

SERVES 4

NOTE: Rather than waste lots of precious recipe space, I want to direct anyone who doesn't know how to butterfly a chicken (or duck or turkey, etc.) to a wonderful, instructional website hosted by the fine folks at Weber. Go here and get a quick, concise course in Butterflying 101: www.virtualweber-bullet.com/butterflychicken.html#backbone.

MOROCCAN PRESERVED LEMONS

A classic Moroccan ingredient, preserved lemons lend an almost indescribable flavor to dishes such as tagines and salads. The strong lemony-ness you'd expect is softened, and sour and salty elements combine with a hint of sweetness for an entirely new flavor experience. Preserved lemons are usually sold in bottles or cans and packed in a mild brine solution, which transforms the once bitter lemon rind into an enticing and indispensable ingredient. Here's how you can make your own.

12 lemons with unblemished skin

Kosher salt

Scrub the lemons under running water and pat them dry. Cut a thin slice from both ends of each lemon. Set a lemon on end and make a lengthwise cut three-quarters of the way through, leaving the halves attached. Turn the lemon upside down and rotate it 90 degrees, and make a second lengthwise cut, again three-quarters of the way through the fruit. Pack as much salt inside the lemon as it will hold. Place the lemon in a sterilized wide-mouth 1-quart canning jar. Repeat the process for the remaining lemons. Press as many lemons into the jar as possible, leaving some air space ($1/4$ to $1/2$ inch) before sealing the jar.

Seal the jar and let it stand in a warm place for 30 days, shaking it each day to distribute the salt and juice. As the lemons pickle they shrink, so if you like you can start adding additional lemons as the rinds of the first lemons soften and the juices in the jar rise to cover them. If the juice released from the fruit does not cover any additional lemons you add, cover with freshly squeezed lemon juice, not processed lemon juice or water. This will prevent the top lemons from darkening.

To use, remove the lemons from the jar as needed and rinse them under running water to rid the lemons of excess salt. Remove and discard the pulp, if desired. There is no need to refrigerate after opening. Preserved lemons will keep up to a year, and the pickling juice can be used two or three times over the course of the year to start new batches of lemons.

MAKES 1 QUART

NOTE: There is nothing on earth like the taste of Moroccan preserved lemons, and although the process of making them at home takes a while, it's well worth if for the intense lemony flavor you get using them in your cooking.

RICK'S CAFÉ LAMB BARBECUE

Couscous is a variety of granular pasta that originated in North Africa. The word "couscous" refers not only to the finished dish but also to the grain it comes from. While some like it steamed so that it retains its granular texture, I prefer it cooked in liquid for a smoother dish. I had this dish in Casablanca; though I wasn't at the famed "Rick's" of Casablanca, I still kept looking for Rick or Sam or Louis or Major Strasser to walk in. The waiter did look like Ferrari, though.

1	cup loosely packed chopped fresh cilantro
1	cup firmly packed chopped fresh mint
1	cup olive oil
1/4	cup chopped peeled fresh ginger
8	large cloves garlic, chopped
4	teaspoons ground cumin
2	teaspoons freshly ground black pepper
2	teaspoons cardamom
1 1/2	teaspoons ground allspice
1 1/2	teaspoons dried marjoram
1 1/4	teaspoons salt
1 1/2	teaspoons turmeric
1	teaspoon ground coriander
3	large yellow summer squash, trimmed and quartered lengthwise
2	red onions, peeled and cut lengthwise (through the stem end) into 6 wedges, peeled
3	large russet potatoes, scrubbed and quartered lengthwise
1	(5- to 6-pound) leg of lamb, boned
3 1/2	cups chicken broth
1	(10-ounce) box couscous (about 1 1/3 cups dry) (see Note)

In a food processor, combine the cilantro, mint, olive oil, ginger, garlic, cumin, pepper, cardamom, allspice, marjoram, salt, turmeric, and coriander and process until pureed. Remove this spice paste to a bowl and set aside.

In a large resealable plastic bag, mix the squash, onion, and potatoes with 1/4 cup of the spice paste. Seal the bag and refrigerate for 1 to 2 hours.

Tuck the boned sections of the lamb leg together like a roast and tie with kitchen twine so that none of the smaller sections of the meat can become overcooked.

Place the lamb in a shallow roasting pan and rub 1/2 cup of the remaining spice paste all over the lamb, under the string, in crevices, everywhere you can reach, reserving 3 tablespoons of the paste in a covered container in the refrigerator. Refrigerate the lamb for 2 to 3 hours.

Prepare a charcoal or gas grill for indirect cooking (it is not necessary to use a drip pan for this recipe). Preheat to 450°F.

Take the meat and vegetables out of the refrigerator and let them come to room temperature, then pour the vegetables around the lamb in the uncovered roasting pan.

Transfer the roasting pan to the grill rack over direct heat and cook for 15 minutes, with lid down, then move to the cooler side of the grill, lower the lid again, and roast until the internal temperature at the center of the lamb reaches 130°F, about 1 hour 10 minutes. Transfer the lamb and vegetables to a warmed platter and cover with foil.

Return the roasting pan to the grill over direct heat, add 2 cups of the broth, and bring to a boil, scraping up the browned bits on the bottom of the pan. Boil until the liquid is reduced to $1^1/2$ cups, about 8 minutes, spooning off the fat as you go. Transfer the sauce to a gravy boat and stir in 2 tablespoons of the reserved spice paste. Place the roasting pan back on the grill over direct heat and add the remaining $1^1/2$ cups of broth and the remaining 1 tablespoon of the spice paste, bringing to boil. Add the couscous, stir, and remove from the heat. Cover the pan tightly with foil and let stand until all of the liquid has been absorbed, about 8 to 10 minutes.

Fluff the couscous with a fork and spoon it around the lamb and vegetables. Serve with the sauce on the side.

SERVES 8 TO 10

NOTE: Made from durum wheat, and sometimes called African pasta, couscous is an important side dish that usually accompanies meat stews or vegetarian meals in North Africa. You can buy it dried, and often pre-steamed, at many grocery stores or, as always, get it online. There are also varieties that use black-eyed peas, corn, or even rice as a substitute for the wheat.

LOVERS' SPICED CARROTS

The combination of cumin, black pepper, and honey is thought to be an aphrodisiac in some African countries. This dish was served to Kate and me in the candlelit dining room at Dar Liqama, with an incredible tagine, some Moroccan white wine, and the music of Vivaldi. After that, I couldn't dispute the name. I can't guarantee that this potion (er, recipe) will help aim Cupid's arrows, but it is delicious. I recommend you serve it alongside grilled game hens or barbecue-roasted chicken. If you can find Moroccan baldi picholine olives, I recommend using them in this dish.

3	tablespoons pine nuts
$1^1/2$	teaspoons cumin seeds
16	carrots ($1^1/2$ pounds), peeled and cut into $1/4$-inch julienne
2	tablespoons sesame seeds
$1/4$	cup honey
4	tablespoons freshly squeezed lemon juice
12	black olives, chopped
1	teaspoon freshly ground black pepper
2	tablespoons chopped fresh cilantro
2	tablespoon chopped fresh mint
$1/2$	teaspoon kosher salt
$1/4$	cup olive oil

Prepare a charcoal or gas grill for indirect grilling (it is not necessary to use a drip pan with this recipe). Preheat to 350°F.

Scatter the pine nuts in a lightly greased skillet and toast, stirring often, in the covered barbecue for 9 to 10 minutes, over indirect heat, until golden brown. Remove and set aside

Pour the cumin seeds into the same skillet set over direct heat and toast, stirring, until they are brown and fragrant, 3 to 4 minutes. Transfer the seeds to a coffee or spice grinder and grind into a powder.

In a large bowl, combine the pine nuts, ground cumin, carrots, sesame seeds, honey, lemon juice, olives, pepper, 1 tablespoon of the cilantro, mint, and salt, and mix well.

Pour the olive oil into a wide shallow baking pan, large enough to hold the carrots in one layer, add the carrot mixture, and turn to coat them in oil. Then transfer the baking pan to the grill rack over direct heat. Lower the grill lid and cook for about 15 minutes, or until the carrots are tender and golden brown, gently shaking the pan several times for even heating.

Transfer the carrots and their sauce to a wide, flat serving dish and garnish with the remaining cilantro.

SERVES 4 TO 6

FEZ DATE CAKE

There are six varieties of dates available in most U.S. markets, all hailing originally from the Middle East. In addition to the "king" of dates—the glorious Medjool, which was brought to California from Morocco in 1927—look for the Deglet Noor, Halaway, Khadrawy, Zahidi, and Thoory varieties. A white powdery film will sometimes form on the skins of Medjool dates as natural sugars come to the surface. This does not affect the flavor. Put them on a baking tray, cover with a wet towel, and place in a warm (200°F) oven for about 15 minutes. This will allow the sugars to be absorbed back into the dates.

½ cup (1 stick) butter, at room temperature

½ cup loosely packed brown sugar

4 eggs

1 cup flour

1 teaspoon baking powder

1½ teaspoons cinnamon

1 teaspoon nutmeg

½ teaspoon ground cloves

½ cup heavy cream

½ teaspoon vanilla extract

1 cup pitted, chopped Medjool dates

¼ cup dried apricots, soaked in water and drained, then chopped

½ cup chopped walnuts

Freshly whipped cream, for serving

Confectioners' sugar, for garnish

Prepare a charcoal or gas grill for indirect cooking (it is not necessary to use a drip pan for this recipe). Preheat to 325°F. Butter and flour a 9-inch cake pan.

In a large bowl, beat the butter and sugar with an electric mixer on medium-high speed until pale and fluffy, 3 to 5 minutes. Beat in the eggs, 1 at a time, until completely incorporated.

In a small bowl, combine the flour, baking powder, 1 teaspoon of the cinnamon, nutmeg, and cloves. Add the dry ingredients to the wet ingredients, beating for 1 minute, until just combined. Add the ½ cup heavy cream and vanilla, and continue beating for another minute or two until cream is thoroughly mixed with the dry ingredients.

Add the dates, apricots, and walnuts, and stir well with a spatula to combine.

Pour the batter into the prepared pan and transfer to the grill rack over indirect heat. Lower the lid and cook for about 30 minutes, until a knife inserted into the center of the cake comes out clean.

Serve with lots of fresh whipped cream dusted with the remaining cinnamon and some confectioners' sugar.

SERVES 6 TO 8

PORTUGAL

Cod and Custard

Bordered on one side by Spain and on the other by 1,793 miles of North Atlantic Ocean coastline, Portugal has always relied on the sea for its sustenance. Both seafood and foods from abroad have shaped the cuisine of this oceangoing nation, whose influence once reached all corners of the globe. In the south, African and Moorish cuisines formed the basis for contemporary cooking, but the Spanish moved across the northern borders to set up shop. Garlic, pasta, and a heavy use of pork came from the pantries of these folks.

The Arabs who occupied the southern parts of Portugal from the early eighth century AD influenced not only the types of foods grown and eaten, but also their preparation. They brought irrigation methods that turned the desert into viable agricultural land, allowing them to grow almond, fig, and even citrus trees. And they introduced rice, ginger, coriander, cloves, cardamom, and saffron to the region. Further driven by a desire to find more exotic spices, it was the Portuguese explorer Vasco da Gama who sailed to India and the Far East and brought back samples of the treasure trove of spices waiting there. Even the voyage itself led to an important discovery—salt cod (*bacalhau*), which was an important staple on the long sailing trips and became, and is still, the quintessential Portuguese dish.

Seafood, spiced or not, rules the roost here: the Portuguese love their sole, red mullet, swordfish, and conger eel. But *bacalhau*, that dried, salted codfish, is still king of Portuguese seafood cooking and appears at least several times a week on most tables. It's said to be the basis for some 365 recipes, one for each day of the year. Two dishes are particularly notable. *Bacalhau à Gomes de Sá*, which is a tasty casserole of cod, white potatoes, and sliced onion, is thought by many Portuguese to be THE *bacalhau* recipe. *Bacalhau à brasa*, which features scrambled eggs with the salted fish, and the same potatoes and onions, also is very popular.

At the Restaurante O Fuso, owner Antonio Coucello barbecues his salted cod the old-fashioned way over a roaring wood fire and very hot coals. "Not many restaurants serve *bacalhau* these days. It's so inexpensive that many people cook it in their homes, but it's our specialty, and we're always filled," he said. Indeed as I watched the grill men sweating in front of a blazing fire, 90 percent of the orders I saw were for the strong-tasting fish. "We cook it partway, then take it off the grill and let it sit," he told me. "When we get orders, the fish is put on a hot part of the grill and browned up

nicely, then it's served with plain boiled potatoes, and lots of garlic."

The other national seafood is the common ordinary sardine. But not the diminutive version, crammed into a small tin can. These sardines are 6 to 8 inches long and are grilled whole (meaning guts, head, tail, bones, and all). One of the less expensive but tastier fish, the sardine is an essential component of outdoor celebrations throughout the country. Grilled fresh sardines are as popular in Portugal as hot dogs and hamburgers are in North America. People devour them in large quantities from street vendors, in informal seaside fish houses, in both budget and upscale restaurants, and at backyard cookouts.

If your experience with sardines is limited to the canned variety, you're in for a revelation—that is, if you can find fresh sardines. If you live in an area with a large Iberian or Italian population, you may be able to find them at a fishmonger, especially in the warmer months. The best time of year to eat sardines is between May and October, when the fish fatten for spawning. Alternatively you may have to settle for frozen sardines. To barbecue them, simply salt them, drizzle with olive oil, grill quickly over a hot fire, and serve whole. (Remove the head, tail, and innards if you prefer.)

Barbecued chicken seasoned with *piri piri*, garlic, and olive oil, is one of the other local dishes that has made its mark outside Portugal, where it can be found in cities with a large Portuguese population. The highly aromatic *piri piri* chicken is so popular that there are more than a few restaurants in a couple of regions of Portugal that serve only this dish.

Another favorite is roasted piglet, golden and crunchy outside, moist and tender inside, which is often served at picnics, family gatherings, and even business meetings.

And let us not forget dessert, at least not here. You see, the Portuguese people are sweet-toothed. Their specialties include at least two-hundred different types of pastries, dozens and dozens of them based on eggs. For the Portuguese, nothing compares to an egg pastry or egg candies piled into a little blue and white cone. This national addiction to sweet desserts began with the Moors, then blossomed in the fifteenth century when sugarcane was introduced from the New World. Two centuries later, pastries became the exclusive purview of the monasteries and convents. The nuns raised vast numbers of chickens and, as they formed one of the richer levels of Portugese society, they had money enough to buy sugar and almonds, which they combined with all those eggs to bring vast varieties of sweet temptations to the upper crust of society: "monk's bellies," "angel's breasts," "fat of heaven," and delicacies with many other names that seemed to have come from above, but which settled distinctly below (the waist, that is). (For your information, that "fat of heaven" dessert is indeed heavenly, but is made with—I shudder to share—lard, butter, sugar, egg yolks, ground almonds, and cinnamon.)

Portuguese cooking is simple, straightforward, and delicious. The fish taste like fish, the suckling pigs are crisp outside and tender

inside, the codfish are loaded with flavor (and a bit of garlic), and the steaks not over-seasoned. So I laughed when I heard Chef Jean Paul Copitaine (he runs the kitchens at the luxury seaside Praia Del Ray Resort) respond to a question about the latest trend in cooking—the fusion of Portuguese with other cooking styles. In regal tones, he jutted out his chin, stared at the person who asked the question, and loudly declared: "Fusion equals confusion," then marched back to the kitchen to grill up some sardines.

GRILLED FRESH SARDINES

Portuguese sardines are not the familiar cute, tiny fish jammed in a tin can. They're big (averaging 3 ounces each), cooked whole on a grill, and delicious. In Portugal, the sardines are served on a piece of bread and you eat the whole fish—tails, head, bones, innards, and all. For those of you who prefer to not ingest fish guts, the sardines may be cleaned and the guts served to your favorite pussycat.

- 24 fresh sardines (6 to 8 inches long), heads and tails left on (see Note)
- 1 cup flaked or coarse sea salt
- 1/4 cup minced garlic
- 2 tablespoons extra-virgin olive oil

  Freshly ground black pepper
- 1/4 cup loosely packed chopped fresh parsley

  Lemon wedges, for serving

Rinse the sardines under cold running water; drain and pat dry with paper towels. Scatter 1/3 of the salt across the bottom of a roasting pan, then 1/3 of the garlic. Transfer half the sardines to the pan and top with half of the remaining salt and garlic. Add another layer of sardines, topping with the remaining salt and garlic. Cover and let stand for 1 hour in the refrigerator.

Preheat a charcoal or gas grill to 400°F. Make sure the grill rack is clean and oil it thoroughly with nonstick cooking spray.

Rinse the salt off the sardines and pat dry with paper towels. Brush the sardines with the oil and season with pepper.

Transfer the fish to the prepared grill rack over direct heat (or use a fish grilling basket). Cook the sardines until the skins are lightly charred and the meat is flaky when tested with a fork, 3 to 4 minutes per side.

Using a wide spatula, carefully transfer the fish to a platter, being careful not to break them. Garnish with parsley and serve the fish whole with lemon wedges on the side.

SERVES 6 TO 8 AS AN APPETIZER

NOTE: Unless you're lucky enough to have them at your local fish market, whole Portuguese sardines can be ordered online from several sources including: www.prawnco.com or www.vitalchoice.com or www.allfreshseafood.com.

GRILLED SALT COD WITH POTATOES

This is a favorite dish every day in Portugal but especially on holidays and for celebrations. You can usually find salt cod (bacalhau) at Portuguese or Italian markets, although a number of people say they've also found it in their local grocery stores. It comes dried, of course. You must soak the salty dried fish in cold water, changing it often, for at least 24 hours to get rid of the salt and rehydrate it.

- 1 (1¹/₂- to 2-pound) piece dried, salted codfish, with bones (see Note)
- 2 pounds (about 10 to 12) red potatoes
- ¹/₄ teaspoon salt
- ¹/₂ cup plus 1 tablespoon extra-virgin olive oil
- 1 large onion, sliced in ¹/₄-inch-thick slices, for garnish
- ¹/₄ cup sliced black olives, for garnish
- 4 large garlic cloves, minced
- 3 hard-cooked eggs, chopped, for garnish
- 2 tablespoons chopped fresh parsley, for garnish

Soak the codfish in cold water for 24 hours, changing to fresh water every 6 hours, discarding the old water. Drain, cover, and set fish aside.

Preheat a charcoal or gas grill to 350°F. Make sure the grill rack is clean and oil it thoroughly with nonstick cooking spray.

Put the potatoes in a large pan, cover with water, and add the salt. Place on the stove top or barbecue side burner over medium-high heat and boil until the potatoes just begin to get soft, about 15 minutes. Drain, and when they are cool enough to handle, cut them in half. Set aside.

Remove the codfish from the water, wipe dry, and brush lightly with 1 tablespoon of olive oil. Transfer to the prepared grill rack over direct heat and cook until the fish flakes easily and is just starting to lightly brown, about 5 minutes per side.

Remove the fish from the barbecue and place in a large bowl. Remove the bones, and flake the cod into 2-inch chunks. Place the fish on a large platter, surrounded by the potatoes, the sliced onions, and the olives.

In a saucepan, add the remaining ¹/₂ cup olive oil and cook over medium-high heat until a drop of water sizzles on contact, then add the minced garlic and heat for about 1 minute until garlic just starts to sizzle and turn light golden brown. Immediately remove the pan from the heat and pour the garlic-oil over the fish, potatoes, onions, and olives.

Sprinkle the platter with the chopped eggs and fresh parsley and serve with very cold white wine or beer.

SERVES 4 TO 6

NOTE: The dried, salted cod that is so enjoyed by the Portuguese used to come from local waters, but the fish almost disappeared from the coast in the mid-1980s. Even though the fishing industry has rebounded somewhat, still today more than 25 percent of the *bacalhau* eaten in the country is imported from Norway or Canada's Newfoundland.

CRIMSON PORK CHOPS

Called colorau, *paprika is a favorite seasoning in Portuguese cooking, especially in sausages and with salt cod. It deteriorates quickly so it should only be purchased in small quantities and kept in airtight containers away from light. The generous use of paprika in this dish turns the meat a crimson red, which should certainly get the attention of your guests.*

- 6   red or green jalapeños
- 4   red bell peppers
- 1   tablespoon sweet or hot paprika
- 4   (¹/₂-pound) bone-in pork loin chops
- 4   teaspoons olive oil
- 1   onion, minced
- 1   teaspoon minced fresh ginger
- 2   cloves garlic, minced
- ³/₄   cup Portuguese red wine
-     Salt
-     Freshly ground black pepper
- 1   tablespoon chopped parsley

Prepare a charcoal or gas grill for indirect cooking (it is not necessary to use a drip pan for this recipe). Preheat to 375°F. Make sure the grill rack is clean and oil it thoroughly with nonstick cooking spray.

Place the jalapeños and bell peppers on the grill rack over direct heat, turning until charred all over, about 10 to 12 minutes. Transfer to a brown paper bag, fold closed, and let stand 20 minutes. Remove the peppers from the bag and peel off their skins. Cut each in half and remove the stems, seeds, and membranes.

In a blender, puree the jalapeños and bell peppers until smooth. Add the paprika and pulse to combine. Transfer to a resealable plastic bag.

Rinse the pork chops and pat dry thoroughly. Transfer to the plastic bag, shaking to coat with the pepper puree. Seal the bag and refrigerate for 30 minutes to 1 hour.

Place a 12-inch cast-iron skillet on the grill rack over direct heat. Add the oil and the onion and sauté until lightly browned, 8 to 10 minutes. Add the ginger and garlic and sauté for another minute, until fragrant. Transfer to a small bowl and set aside.

Remove the chops from the marinade and wipe off the excess. For the sauce, pour the remaining marinade into the skillet and boil for 12 minutes. Add the onion mixture and the wine, returning just to a boil and stirring to blend. Remove the skillet from the heat and set aside.

Transfer the meat to the prepared grill rack over direct heat and cook, 2 minutes per side, to sear with grill marks. Transfer to the skillet with the sauce. Cover the skillet, transfer to the cool side of the grill, lower the grill lid, and cook until the meat is very tender when pierced and pulls easily from the bone, about 1¹/₂ hours.

Transfer the chops to a platter and pour the sauce over them. Season with salt and pepper, sprinkle with parsley, and serve.

SERVES 4

PORTUGUESE STEAK AND EGGS

I had this dish in a restaurant in Macao, once a Portuguese colony, and never saw it anywhere else until I came to Lisbon, where it was on several breakfast menus. It's not a breakfast for the weak-kneed and it's certainly not on any diet regimen but, man, does it fill you up for the day. Crème fraîche has a nutty, slightly sour taste produced by culturing pasteurized cream with a special bacteria. It's available in most grocery stores in the dairy section.

- 1 (1½- to 2-pound) aged sirloin steak

  Salt

  Freshly ground black pepper

- 4 tablespoons clarified butter or 2 tablespoons butter plus 1 tablespoon olive oil

- 1 tablespoon minced garlic

- 4 tablespoons Cognac

- 4 tablespoons red wine

- 4 tablespoons low-sodium beef broth

- 4 tablespoons crème fraîche

- 2 thin slices Spanish or Italian-style ham about ¼-inch or 6 ounces each

- 4 eggs

Preheat a charcoal or gas grill to 400°F.

Season the steak with salt and pepper. Place a cast-iron skillet over the hottest part of the grill; add the clarified butter, then the steak, and sear it on both sides. Add the garlic, remove the pan from the grill, pour the Cognac into the pan, and flambé by lighting the Cognac with a long match or long lighter (see Note). Transfer the steak to a plate, cover, and set aside. Return the skillet to the grill and pour in the red wine, bringing it to a boil and scraping up the browned bits. Add the beef stock, return to a boil, and reduce the liquid by one-quarter, about 15 minutes. Add the crème fraîche and reduce by another quarter, about 15 minutes. Pour the sauce into a bowl and set aside.

Return the steak to the pan, along with any of its juices, and cook over direct heat until a meat thermometer inserted sideways into the center of the steak reaches 145°F for medium-rare, about 6 to 8 minutes.

Place the ham slices on the grill rack over direct heat and cook until crisp and brown, about 1 minute per side. Remove from the heat, cut in half, and set aside.

Meanwhile, if there's room on the grill for a large cast-iron skillet, quickly fry the eggs in a little butter or oil, keeping the yolk runny. (If there's no room on the grill, fry the eggs on a side burner or on the stove top.)

Transfer the steak to a cutting board and cut into 4 equal portions. Put one portion on each of 4 serving plates, top with a slice of ham and a fried egg, and drizzle with the gravy. Serve immediately.

SERVES 4

NOTE: When you flambé, never pour liquor from a bottle into a pan that is near an open flame (the open flame can follow the stream of alcohol into the bottle and cause it to explode). With a long fireplace match or a long barbecue lighter, immediately ignite the fumes at the edge of the pan and not the liquid itself. Never lean over the dish or pan as you do this.

CHICKEN PIRI PIRI

Piri piri *chiles (also known as African bird's eye chiles) are world champion travelers. They began in Brazil, were taken to Africa—Angola and Mozambique in particular—and then to Portugal and Macao by Portuguese adventurers. Now they are common in all five counties, and indeed all over the world. In fact they are so popular in Portugal that many Porguguese at home use* piri piri *sauce like ketchup to flavor just about everything they eat. You can find the sauce and the peppers online and in specialty stores.*

- 1   cup plus 1 teaspoon freshly squeezed lemon juice
- ³/₄ cup olive oil
- ¹/₄ cup minced garlic, about 8 large cloves
- 4   tablespoons piri piri sauce
      Generous pinch of piri piri chile powder
- 2   teaspoons dried oregano
- 1   teaspoon dried thyme
- 1   teaspoon ground cumin
- 1   teaspoon salt
- 1   (3¹/₂- to 4-pound) chicken, butterflied
- 2   cups (1 stick) butter
- 2   tablespoons chopped fresh parsley
      Lemon wedges, for garnish

In a bowl, combine 1 cup of the lemon juice, oil, garlic, *piri piri* sauce, chile powder, oregano, thyme, cumin, and salt, and stir. Set aside.

Rinse the chicken, pat dry, and transfer to a large resealable plastic bag. Pour the marinade over the chicken, seal the bag, and shake to distribute the marinade. Refrigerate for 2 to 3 hours, turning occasionally.

Preheat a charcoal or gas grill to 375°F. Make sure the grill rack is clean and oil it thoroughly with nonstick cooking spray.

Using tongs, remove the chicken from the marinade and drain well. Pour the marinade into a saucepan and boil for 12 minutes to use for basting.

Transfer the chicken to the prepared grill rack over direct heat. Lower the grill lid and cook the chicken, turning occasionally and brushing with the marinade, until the skin is well browned and the internal temperature at the thickest part of the thigh reaches 180°F, 35 to 40 minutes.

Transfer the chicken to a platter and cover with foil to keep warm.

Place the saucepan of basting liquid over low heat and bring to a simmer. Add the butter, the remaining 1 teaspoon of lemon juice, and parsley, and stir until melted and incorporated. Transfer to a small gravy boat.

Carve the chicken, garnish with the lemon wedges, and serve with the remaining sauce on the side.

SERVES 4

NOTE: To prevent flare-ups, have a spray bottle of water handy. Spray with a medium mist to douse flames; a strong steady stream blows ashes up onto the food you're cooking.

PORTUGUESE BEANS

Cooks in Portugal use beans in many "old family recipes" as side dishes for pork, chicken, grilled fish, and beef. Most often they use black beans, but they also make use of navy, kidney, or pinto beans. This recipe is written for the stove top, but if you like, you can cook these beans on the cool side of a grill heated to 375°F.

1 pound dried beans (pinto, navy, or kidney)

1 tablespoon olive oil

6 strips bacon, chopped in $^1/_2$-inch pieces

1 large onion, chopped

2 cloves garlic, chopped

2 tablespoons tomato paste

1 teaspoon cinnamon

$^1/_2$ teaspoon ground allspice

$^1/_2$ teaspoon ground cloves

$^1/_2$ teaspoon ground cumin

Freshly ground black pepper

In a large pot, soak the dried beans in cold water to cover for at least 4 hours, then drain. Or you can put them in boiling water, cover, remove from heat, and allow them to sit for 2 hours to accomplish a faster soak. Drain and return to the pot.

In a skillet, heat the oil over medium-high heat. Add the bacon, onion, and garlic, and sauté for 5 minutes, stirring often. Add the tomato paste, cinnamon, allspice, cloves, and cumin; season with pepper, mix well, and simmer for 5 minutes. Stir the tomato paste mixture into the beans and add enough fresh water to just cover. Bring to a boil over high heat, reduce the heat to low, and simmer, stirring often, until beans are tender but not mushy, about 50 minutes. During cooking, the beans should remain covered with liquid. If they are not, add more water, $^1/_2$ cup at a time.

SERVES 4 TO 6

LISBON-STYLE CREAM TARTLETS

Selling for about seventy-five cents apiece, these tempting custard tartlets are the rage of Lisbon, indeed all of Portugal. Elsewhere in the country, they are called pastéis de nata, *but only in Lisbon, and only at the Pastéis de Belém Café, are they called* pastéis de Belém. *They must be special as they sell as many as 48,000 per day! This recipe is an attempt to duplicate these wonderful* pastéis *served since 1837. They are an amazing taste sensation, especially served warm from the oven, sprinkled with powdered sugar and cinnamon. I've written this recipe so you can bake it either in the barbecue over indirect heat or in your oven—your choice.*

1	(10-ounce) package puff pastry, defrosted
8	tablespoons superfine sugar
1	teaspoon ground nutmeg
1	teaspoon ground cinnamon, plus additional for garnish
3	tablespoons flour
1$\frac{1}{4}$	cups milk
1$\frac{1}{3}$	cups granulated sugar
1	cinnamon stick
$\frac{2}{3}$	cup water
$\frac{1}{2}$	teaspoon vanilla extract
6	egg yolks, beaten

Prepare a charcoal or gas grill for indirect grilling (it is not necessary to use a drip pan for this recipe). Preheat to 550˚F. Or preheat your oven to 550˚F (500˚F if that's as high as it goes). Grease the cups of a standard muffin pan.

Fill a small bowl with water and place it near a work surface that you've lightly dusted with flour. Using a rolling pin, roll out the puff pastry into one large sheet, about 12 by 12 inches; sprinkle with 4 tablespoons of the superfine sugar, nutmeg, and the 1 teaspoon of cinnamon. Fold the pastry in quarters (folding in half and half again) and, with the rolling pin, roll out to the same size as the original sheet. Using your hands, roll the pastry into a log. With a sharp knife, slice into 10 equal rounds.

Place the rounds in prepared muffin pan. Dip your thumbs into the bowl of water, then push straight down into the middle of each dough spiral, flattening the pastry against the bottom of the muffin cup to a thickness of about $\frac{1}{8}$ inch, then smooth the dough up the sides and create a raised lip about $\frac{1}{8}$ inch above the pan. The pastry sides should be thinner than the bottom.

In a bowl, whisk the flour and $\frac{1}{4}$ cup of the milk until smooth. Set aside.

In a small saucepan, combine the granulated sugar, cinnamon stick, and water, and bring to a boil. Cook, without stirring, until an instant-read thermometer registers 220°F, about 10 minutes. Remove from the heat and discard the cinnamon stick.

In another small saucepan, scald the remaining 1 cup milk. Whisk the hot milk into the flour mixture. Add the sugar mixture in a thin stream to the flour mixture, whisking briskly. Add the vanilla and stir the mixture for another minute or so, until it's cooled down to just warm. Whisk in the egg yolks until the liquid is completely mixed and smooth. Strain the custard mixture into a bowl.

Fill each pastry shell three-quarters full with the custard. Transfer to the grill rack over indirect heat, or to the oven, and bake until the edges of the dough are frilled and brown, about 8 to 9 minutes.

Remove the tarts from the barbecue or oven and let cool for a few minutes in the pan, then transfer the tarts to a wire rack to cool until just warm, about 20 minutes. Sprinkle generously with the remaining superfine sugar and cinnamon, and serve.

SERVES 4 TO 6 (MAYBE)

SCOTLAND
A Wee Bit o' This, and a Wee Bit o' That

"Peace and plenty; and no killing;
Beef at a groat, and meat at a shilling.
Whisky for nothing, beer at the same.
A bonnie wee wife; and a cozy wee hame."

—The Laird of Logan

Perched atop the British Isles, Scotland is divided into three regions: the famously mountainous highlands, graced with lakes, lochs, and fast-flowing streams; the central lowlands, a belt of fertile valleys bordered by hills and rivers; and the southern uplands, which alternate between moorland and green rolling valleys.

Through the centuries, Scottish cuisine has been influenced by Celtic, Scandinavian, and French cultures. In fact, many believe that today's Aberdeen Angus cattle are descended from cows brought by the Vikings, as were food preservation techniques like smoking and brining. The French influences came from the marriage of King James V to Marie de Guise

Lorraine, who brought French cooks and culinary customs with her to the Scottish court.

Historically Scottish staples for the masses were oats and barley, which meant one thing: boiling. Oatmeal cooked in water or milk (porridge) was daily fare, and for a treat, it was left to cool, then sliced and cooked quickly over a fire. (Some grilling, eh?) Wealthy Scots, however, enjoyed spit-roasted meat and fowl and oven-baked bread made with imported wheat flour.

Today Angus beef, Scottish venison, and game birds, such as pheasant and grouse, are among the best and most sought-after in the world. And I'd be boiled in my own porridge if I didn't talk about salmon. The Scots are famous for their smoked salmon and hot-smoked haddock.

And then there's the Scottish national dish: haggis, which many believe has Scandinavian roots. *Hoot mon*, haggis from Sweden? For those who are blissfully ignorant, the main ingredients are sheep's heart, sheep's liver, fresh suet (the white fat found around animal kidneys), a wee dram of whisky, and oatmeal. This awful—sorry, offal—collection is then chopped, placed in a sheep's stomach, and boiled for three hours. I'll just have the wee dram of whisky please. And oh yes, it's served with *neeps* and *tatties*, aka: turnips (rutabagas) and potatoes, that are, you guessed it, boiled.

And since we're onto quaint Scottish culinary terms, I'll share a few others with you:

Arbroath smokies: smoke-cured fish

Bree: soup

Bridie: pastry casing for meat filling, traditionally flavored with beef dripping

Chappit tattles: mashed potatoes

Clapshot: potatoes and turnips

Cock-a-leekie: chicken and leek soup

Collops: thin slices of meat, usually from the leg

Crowdie: cottage cheese

Hough: shin of beef

Mealy pudding: puddings made from animal intestines

Porridge: oatmeal boiled in water or milk

Rumbledethumps: potatoes, onion, and cabbage, topped with cheese and grilled

Skink: a soup of vegetables boiled in a beef stock

Skirlie: onion and oatmeal fried with dripping

Stovies: potatoes cooked au gratin

On my regrettably short trip to Edinburgh, I was delighted to visit wonderful farmers' markets, fantastic fish shops (Simon Clark's Fish Mongers), and a world-class smokehouse (Belhaven Smoke House). But I was most pleasantly surprised by an invitation to a Sunday barbecue at a nearby sheep farm.

After a leisurely drive with my guide and culinary/whisky expert Gordon Elphinstone, we arrived at Cairns Farm, home to the Hamilton family: Caroline, Graham, and their two children, Bobby and Molly. During summer the Hamiltons grill just about every day—lamb and mutton, chicken, game hens, pheasant, Angus beef, and, of course—this *is* Scotland—fresh salmon, often smoking it over apple and other fruit woods.

When we arrived, the grill was already covered with lamb chops, lamb sausages, lamb leg roasts, mutton, and lamb steaks. Get the picture? It's a sheep farm. And, like the Irish, English, and Welsh, the *Scots* have a fondness for lamb that is legendary.

After a gentle walk through emerald green pastures populated by lambs cavorting through the grass, bleating and gamboling like, well, lambs, we headed back to the house for a lunch of very fresh, slaughtered that morning . . . lamb! Yikes, I had to put those cute black and white faces out of my mind while cutting into my chop.

Curiously many Americans seem to have a disdain for—or maybe it's a distrust of, or maybe just an aversion to—lamb. But let me tell you, a medium-rare lamb chop served up with a freshly made mint gravy or jelly is as good a meat as there is. And the sausages and steaks and leg roast were just as flavorful and tender and juicy.

I could write about my tour of Edinburgh, the wondrous castle, the incredible gardens, the cobbled streets, the pubs, a tour of the royal yacht *Britannia*, the Glenkinchie whisky distillery, and the Witchery Murder and Mystery Tour, but I'd rather leave those for you to discover on your own when you visit.

Me, I'm going to sit down, put on my DVD of the George Watson College pipe band, sip a neat glass of Glenkinchie, nibble on David Pate's smoked salmon and smoked Gouda, close my eyes, and drift back to the moors of Scotland.

SALMON WITH SCOTCH WHISKY SAUCE

The biggest difference between Irish and Scotch whiskies is the method each country uses to dry the barley after it's been malted. Malting is accomplished by soaking the barley in water for a couple of days, allowing the grains to germinate, then letting the natural chemical reaction change starches into sugars. The Scottish brewers heat their barley over smoldering peat fires, which results in their famed peat-smoky flavor. In Ireland, they use sealed ovens to dry the barley, which intensifies the malt flavors. Irish whiskeys are distilled three times, while Scotch whisky is distilled only twice. As with most liquor used for cooking, it is best to use blended whisky rather than more expensive malt. Save the good stuff to sip by the fireside after dinner. Serve this dish with buttered potatoes and grilled vegetables.

- 4 (8-ounce) salmon fillets, preferably sockeye or King salmon
- 2 tablespoons salt
- 4 tablespoons brown sugar
- 2 tablespoons grated orange zest
- 1 teaspoon freshly ground black pepper
- 3 egg yolks
- 1 tablespoon freshly squeezed lemon juice
- ½ cup (1 stick) butter, cut into pieces
- 3 tablespoons Scotch whisky
- 3 tablespoons very hot tap water
-    Olive oil

Wash the salmon well, then pat dry. Combine the salt, sugar, zest, and pepper. Rub all over the salmon and refrigerate for about 2 hours.

Preheat a gas or charcoal grill to 350°F. Make sure the grill rack is clean and oil it thoroughly with nonstick cooking spray.

For the sauce, combine the egg yolks and lemon juice, whisking to blend. Transfer to a heatproof bowl set over a saucepan of hot (but not boiling) water over low heat. Whisk until the mixture begins to thicken. Gradually stir in the butter, a little at a time. If any lumps appear in the mixture, remove the bowl from the heat, add a teaspoon of cold water, then return to the heat. Continue cooking until the sauce is smooth and thick enough to coat the back of a spoon, about 8 to 10 minutes. Remove the bowl from the heat and add the whisky and water and whisk until just smooth. Keep this sauce warm while the salmon is cooking.

Brush the salmon with olive oil and transfer it to the prepared grill rack over direct heat. Grill until just cooked through, about 2 to 3 minutes per side. Transfer the fillets to serving plates and serve with the whisky sauce on the side.

SERVES 4 TO 6

BARBECUE-BAKED BROWN TROUT

Vermouth is made from a neutral, dry, white wine that is blended with an infusion created with a special selection of herbs, flowers, fruit peels, seeds, and plants. Serve this dish with freshly grilled asparagus and jasmine rice.

4   (1- to 1½-pound) trout
    Kosher salt
    Freshly ground black pepper
    Sprigs of fresh herbs (dill, fennel, chives, and/or parsley)
2   tablespoons olive oil
½   cup dry vermouth

4   pinches fleur de sel (French sea salt, see Note) (optional)
1   lemon, sliced, for garnish

Preheat a charcoal or gas grill to 450°F.

Clean the trout if required, removing the scales and fins, and wipe with paper towels. Season the inside of each trout with salt and pepper and insert the herbs into each body cavity, dividing them evenly among the 4 trout.

Cut 4 pieces of aluminum foil long enough to enclose the fish, with about 3 inches extra at each end. Brush the foil with some of the olive oil and transfer each trout to the center of the foil.

Brush the fish with more olive oil, season with salt and pepper, and pour 2 tablespoons of vermouth over each fish. Pull the foil up around the fish, folding over 2 times at the top and sides, to enclose the fish completely. Transfer to a baking sheet and cook on the barbecue over direct heat until the fish is white and just beginning to flake when tested with a fork, 8 to 10 minutes, depending on the size of the fish. (You'll need to open the foil package to check for doneness.)

Remove the fish from the foil, sprinkle each with a generous pinch of *fleur de sel* (or use kosher salt), and serve garnished with slices of lemon.

SERVES 4

NOTE: In July and August, when the sea is calm and the weather conditions are just right, *fleur de sel* is harvested by hand off the Brittany coast. It is too elegant to use for cooking, but merely a pinch sprinkled over food brings the French sea coast to your table.

STEAK BALMORAL AND STEAK AULD REEKIE

Here are a pair of straightforward steak preparations with whisky-touched sauces: choose either one; you can't go wrong. The Witchery restaurant in Edinburgh is located in a building where The Old Hell Fire Club held their meetings. The restaurant serves steak Balmoral, kissed gently with a whisky-cream sauce. Auld Reekie was the name given to Edinburgh in the days when open coal fires filled the skies with smoke and smog. Steak Auld Reekie gets its smoke from your grill and from a bit of smoky Gouda or Cheddar. Roast potatoes and turnips make a great accompaniment to either of these steaks.

- 4   (8-ounce) Aberdeen Angus rib-eye or sirloin steaks (see Note)

BALMORAL SAUCE

- 6   tablespoons Scotch whisky
- 1   cup heavy cream
- $1/2$ cup beef stock
- $1/2$ cup sliced crimini or button mushrooms, caps only
- 1   teaspoon coarse-grain mustard
- 1   tablespoon butter

AULD REEKIE SAUCE

- 4   tablespoons Scotch whisky
- $1^1/2$ cups heavy cream
- $1/2$ cup grated smoked cheese (like Cheddar or Gouda)

- 2   tablespoons ($1/4$ stick) butter

    Salt

    Freshly ground black pepper

Preheat a charcoal or gas grill to 500° to 600°F. Make sure the grill rack is clean and oil it thoroughly with nonstick cooking spray.

Transfer the steaks to the grill and cook over direct heat until the internal temperature reaches 145°F for medium-rare, about 4 minutes per side. Transfer to a warmed plate, cover, and let stand.

To make Balmoral sauce, add the whisky to a cast-iron skillet set over high heat on the stove or barbecue side burner, and heat it until it's hot. Remove the skillet from the flame and, using an extra long barbecue match or lighter, quickly but carefully ignite the whisky (always ignite the alcohol fumes at the edge of the pan, not the liquid itself). Add the cream, stock, and mushrooms, return the pan to the flame and bring to a boil. Decrease the heat and simmer gently until the sauce has reduced by half, stirring from time to time, about 10 to 12 minutes. Whisk in the mustard and butter and remove from the heat.

Alternatively, to make Auld Reekie sauce, add the whisky to a cast-iron skillet set over high heat on the stove or barbecue side burner, and heat it until it's hot. Remove the skillet from the flame and, using an extra long barbecue match or lighter, quickly but carefully ignite the whisky (always ignite the alcohol fumes at the edge of the pan, not the liquid itself). Add the cream and cheese, return the pan to the flame and bring to a boil. Decrease the heat and simmer gently until the sauce has reduced by half, stirring from time to time, about 10 to 12 minutes. Whisk in the butter and remove from the heat.

To serve, transfer the steaks to 4 serving plates. Season the steaks with salt and pepper, and pour a generous amount of the sauce over them.

SERVES 4

NOTE: The Aberdeen Angus breed originated in Scotland in the Aberdeenshire and Angus regions. Two animals began the long history of the breed: Old Jock, a bull, who was born in 1842, and was given the number "1" in the *Scotch Herd Book* when it was first written; and Old Granny, born in 1824, the matriarch cow, who is said to have lived to be 35 years old. Most of the Angus cattle in the world that are alive today can trace their pedigrees all the way back to their Scottish ancestors, Jock and Granny.

DUNDEE LAMB CHOPS

World-famous Keiller's Marmalade was created by chance in the year 1700, when a Spanish ship carrying a cargo of Seville oranges, sought refuge from a winter storm in Dundee's harbor. A local grocer, James Keiller, bought a large quantity very cheaply but found them so bitter he couldn't sell any! His wife, Janet, added sugar and used them to make tangy preserves. Mrs. Keiller's marmalade was an instant hit.

8   (4-ounce) lamb chops, rib, or sirloin chops

1   tablespoon olive oil

1/2 cup (1 stick) butter

1   teaspoon ground ginger

1   teaspoon paprika

1/4 cup white wine vinegar

1/2 cup water plus more for simmering

Salt

Freshly ground black pepper

1/2 cup orange marmalade

Thinly sliced orange, for garnish

Prepare a charcoal or gas grill for indirect cooking (it is not necessary to use a drip pan for this recipe). Preheat to 400°F. Make sure the grill rack is clean and oil it thoroughly with nonstick cooking spray.

Brush the lamb chops with olive oil. Transfer them to the prepared grill rack and grill over direct heat for 2 minutes per side, until browned and nicely marked. Remove the chops from the grill, cover, and set aside.

Set a heavy Dutch oven over on the cool side of the barbecue and melt the butter in it. Add the chops, ginger, paprika, vinegar, and water and season with salt and pepper. Place a generous tablespoon of marmalade on top of each chop. Bring the pot to a slow simmer, cover it, and cook for 45 minutes, or until the chops can easily be pierced with a fork. Add additional water 1/4 cup at a time if the pan looks dry.

Transfer the chops to a warmed platter, garnish with orange slices, and serve.

SERVES 4

NOTE: Never cook lamb chops in their own fat, which becomes bitter when cooked. Instead, brush each chop on both sides with olive oil to keep the meat from sticking on the grill, and cook on a clean, well-oiled grill.

TOAD-IN-THE-HOLE

Nowadays this dish usually consists of small-link sausages cooked in a Yorkshire pudding batter, then baked. The batter puffs up around the sausages, and I suppose someone thought it looked like, well, a toad in a hole. In its eighteenth-century versions, a variety of meats were used, including steak and kidneys, fillet steak, and even lamb chops: this dish was a way to use any leftover bits of meat that were too big to throw away but too small to make into a meal.

1/2	pound pork link sausages
3/4	cup flour
	Salt
1/2	cup grated extra-sharp Cheddar cheese
1 1/4	cups milk
2	large eggs
2	tablespoons chopped parsley
	Freshly ground pepper
	Chutney (see Note)

Prepare a charcoal or gas grill for indirect cooking, placing a drip pan under the cool side of the grill rack (see page 3). Preheat to 425°F. Make sure the grill rack is clean and oil it thoroughly with nonstick cooking spray.

Grill the sausages over indirect heat, turning often, until browned on all sides and beginning to char, about 12 to 15 minutes.

In a mixing bowl, sift together the flour and a pinch of salt; stir in the cheese. In another bowl, beat together the milk, eggs, and parsley, and season generously with salt and pepper. Stir a small amount of the milk mixture into the flour to make a smooth, very heavy batter. Let it stand for 5 minutes. Add the remaining liquid, stirring to combine.

In a cast-iron skillet, arrange the sausages in a circle like the spokes of a bicycle wheel. Pour in the batter and place the skillet on the cooler side of the grill. Lower the grill lid and bake until the batter is puffed and browned, about 25 to 30 minutes.

Remove the pan from the grill and cut the toad-in-the-hole into wedges. Serve with chutney.

SERVES 4 TO 6

NOTE: The term chutney comes from the East Indian *chatni*, meaning "strongly spiced," and is described as a condiment that consists of chopped fruits, vinegars, spices, and sugar cooked into a thick, chunky jamlike consistency. Most chutneys are on the sweet-spicy-hot side, emphasize hot, and are often served with curries. They are very popular in India, which was once part of the British Empire—hence the emigration of curries and chutneys back to the UK, through the soldiers and diplomats that saw duty there. Busha Browne or Stonewall Kitchen chutneys would be good choices for this dish.

RUMBLEDETHUMP

Often called the Scottish version of England's "bubble and squeak," this dish can be eaten on its own as a quick and easy meatless supper. Author John Ayto, in his book An A to Z of Food and Drink, *suggests that the derivation of "rumbledethump may be onomatopoeic, suggesting the effect (of this food) on digestion." For variations, add crispy chunks of bacon, grilled chicken or fish, spring onions, leeks, or nutmeg grated on top. Like goulash in Hungary, there are as many recipes for this as there are Scot.*

4 to 6	large baking potatoes (2 pounds), coarsely diced
1/2	cup (1 stick) butter
1 1/2	pounds cabbage, finely shredded
2	large onions, thinly sliced
1/2	cup grated white Cheddar cheese
1/2	teaspoon salt
1/2	teaspoon freshly ground black pepper

Prepare a charcoal or gas grill for indirect grilling (it is not necessary to use a drip pan for this recipe). Preheat to 400°F.

In a saucepan, boil the potatoes for about 25 to 30 minutes, until they are soft enough that a sharp knife can be easily inserted. Drain the potatoes and return them to the pan, mashing them to a smooth consistency.

In a cast-iron skillet set on the hot side of the grill, melt the butter. Add the cabbage and onion, stirring to evenly coat with butter, and cook until the cabbage and onion wilt, making sure that they do not brown.

Add the potatoes and half of the cheese. Move the pan to the cool side of the grill and stir until the cheese has melted; season with the salt and pepper. Add the remaining cheese and move back to the hot side of the grill, cover, and cook about 10 minutes, or until the cheese has melted and the top is golden.

SERVES 4 TO 6

CHEESE AND WHISKY CAULIFLOWER

Adding a few ounces of Scotch whisky adds extra flavor to this popular side dish. There are dozens of great Scotch whiskies, but I favor three malts in particular: Laphroaig (mouth-cooling, pleasantly dry, and tastes like foggy peat fields), Cragganmore (sweet, then astringent, with a bitter herbal and light sherrylike finish), and Lagavulin (starts like a sweet candy, with a touch of salt, then dissolves in a clover-infused smoke).

  1 medium cauliflower, cut into bite-size florets

 ³/₄ cup chopped button or crimini mushroom caps

 ¹/₂ cup chopped green bell pepper

1¹/₄ cups heavy cream

 ¹/₂ cup grated sharp Cheddar cheese

  6 tablespoons Scotch whisky

  2 tablespoons finely ground oatmeal or oat flour

     Pinch of nutmeg

     Salt

     Freshly ground black pepper

Prepare a charcoal or gas grill for indirect grilling (it is not necessary to use a drip pan with this recipe). Preheat to 350°F. Grease a baking dish.

In a saucepan over high heat, cook the cauliflower in boiling water to cover for 5 minutes, until just soft enough to be pierced with a fork. Drain the cauliflower and transfer to the prepared baking dish. Add the mushrooms and bell peppers, stirring to combine.

In a small saucepan over low heat, heat the cream (do not bring to a boil), add the cheese and cook, stirring frequently, until the cheese has melted. Remove the pan from the heat and whisk in the whisky and the oatmeal. Stir in the nutmeg and season with salt and pepper. Pour the mixture over the cauliflower, and cook on the grill over indirect heat, with the lid closed, until the vegetables are just beginning to soften, about 30 minutes.

Serve immediately.

SERVES 4

SINGAPORE

Hawker Centers and
Satay Superstars

Every city on earth has small stands that sell food. In New York, they sell hot dogs and pretzels. In London, they fry up fish and chips. In Mexico City, it's charcoal-toasted tacos; in Hong Kong, steamed pork buns.

But nowhere on earth have they perfected food-stand cuisine like the independent city-state of Singapore. They get the grand prize for number, variety, and popularity of their street-, road-, and park-side eateries.

Singapore was founded as a British trading colony in 1819, was briefly part of the Malaysian Federation, and then became independent, subsequently becoming one of the world's most prosperous countries. But this giant of economic growth and world trading is only slightly more than three and a half times the size of Washington, D.C., and has a population of fewer than five million. Those five million absolutely love to eat, making Singapore a world-class superpower of cuisine as well as of international trading.

Without a doubt, a visit to Singapore isn't complete without a visit to a hawker (food-stand) center. These are groupings of individual stalls, usually on a street corner, roadside, or esplanade, and there are over a hundred to choose from, offering a staggering variety of food—all subject to stringent government health inspection. This no-frills dining experience is probably the best way to sample some of Singapore's most delicious, traditional foods. (Unfortunately many of the city's 113 hawker centers are being absorbed into indoor shopping mall food courts. Mall food is also more expensive than the street variety. My advice: avoid the malls and dine al fresco, under the stars.) A full meal, with dessert and drink, can cost as little as $5 to $7. Eating a meal amid the din of banging trays, shouted food orders, steaming heat, smoke of dozens of fired-up grills, smells of fermented fish paste, grilled satays, and bubbling curry, is an incomparable gastronomic and cultural dining experience.

My most recent trip to Singapore involved a scrumptious late-night visit to the famous hawker center, Makansutra Gluttons Bay, on the waterfront at the Esplanade Mall. Serving up dishes like barbecued stingray (skate wing), fried oyster omelet, chile crabs, grilled chicken wings, the ubiquitous satays, fried carrot cake, and bananas tempura, the stalls are packed from 6 p.m. until 3 a.m. when they close.

For the first-timer, who has never participated in the experience, I wanted to share a few hawker dining tips:

- Choose a table nearest to the stall you're buying from—both for convenience and to get your food delivered as hot as possible.
- Take note of the number on the table and inform the stall owner when you place your order, unless it's a self-service stall.
- You can order from as many food stalls as you like, everybody mixes and matches. It's like you're getting a burger from McDonald's, walking next door to get fries at Burger King, then hopping across the street for a cola from Wendy's.
- Avoid peak hours if possible; noon is a no-no.
- For popular food stalls, which are easy to spot because of their long lines, ask for the waiting time, especially if it is not self-service.

Oh, and by the way, keep an eye out for any stands that feature chile or black pepper crab. No trip to Singapore is complete without trying Singapore's unofficial national dish at least once. Mud or soft-shelled crabs are stir-fried with freshly ground black pepper or a mixture of hot red chiles, garlic, lime, lemon grass, and cilantro. Messy as all get-out but wonderful, especially with a cold Tiger beer, to wash it all down and cool the fire.

Because Singapore has always been a world leader in technology and in the passing of information by electronic means (75 percent of Singaporeans own computers, and 65 percent of them are on the Internet), we would be lax if we didn't provide you details of the hawker website: www.makansutra.com.

Run by Mr. K. F. Seetoh, (aka Makansutra), the website rates hawker food and stands. Seetoh, the godfather of hawker culture, produces a cable TV show that visits a new stand every episode, offers hawker updates on a cell-phone audio and video link, arranges hawker food tours, publishes a paperback guide to the best of Singapore hawkers, and offers a printed brochure featuring pictures, menus, and locations, of what he calls "15 Hawker Legends."

What's next? The "Superstars of Satay" or "Legendary Hawkers of Singapore" trading cards? I'll trade you one Ah Hock Fried Oyster for a Si Yang Steam Soup or an An Ji Famous Fishhead Noodles.

BACON-WRAPPED SCALLOPS WITH SOY SAUCE GLAZE

I sampled this dish in Basement 2, right under the Takashimaya Department Store at one of the dozens of hawker stands found there. The scallops were huge, and they were cooked perfectly. In Singapore, you buy fresh scallops still attached to one side of their shell and you grill them just as they are, simply brushing sauce on the meat, then cooking them in their shell. Serve this dish with steamed rice or buttered noodles.

- 3 tablespoons tamari (dark soy sauce)
- 3 tablespoons brown sugar
- 1 teaspoon butter
- 1 tablespoon freshly squeezed lime juice
- 1 teaspoon lemon pepper
- 1/2 teaspoon garlic salt
- 2 tablespoons freshly squeezed lemon juice
- 2 tablespoons olive oil
  Pinch of cayenne pepper
- 16 large scallops (about 1 pound)
- 4 (12-inch) branches fresh rosemary, stripped of leaves
- 16 slices bacon, halved lengthwise

In a small saucepan, combine the tamari, brown sugar, butter, lime juice, lemon pepper, and garlic salt, and bring to a boil over high heat. Decrease heat to medium and cook at a low boil for 4 minutes, or until the liquid is reduced by half. Cover and refrigerate.

In a large shallow dish, combine the lemon juice, oil, cayenne, and scallops. Let stand, turning frequently, for 15 minutes.

Preheat a charcoal or gas barbecue to 375°F. Make sure the grill rack is clean and oil it thoroughly with nonstick cooking spray.

Sharpen the ends of each rosemary branch with a sharp knife. Drain the scallops, discarding the marinade. Wrap 1 strip of bacon around each scallop, transferring the wrapped scallops to a plate, seam-side down. Thread the scallops crosswise through the edge and through the bacon seam, (see Note, below), onto the rosemary skewers. Transfer to the prepared grill rack over direct heat and cook for 4 minutes. Turn each skewer, brush the wrapped scallops with the glaze, and cook for 3 to 4 minutes longer, until the bacon is cooked through and crisp around the edges.

Transfer the skewers to a platter, brush with more glaze, and serve immediately.

SERVES 4

NOTE: Threading the scallops sideways (though the diameter instead of the thickness) makes the skewers easier to turn and helps them cook evenly on both sides, since the scallops can lay flat on the grill. With this method, you can get 4 to 5 scallops on each skewer.

BEEF SATAY WITH SPICY PEANUT SAUCE

Although recipes and ingredients vary, satay usually consists of chunks or slices of meat on skewers that are grilled over wood or charcoal fires. Among the spices used in the preparation of satay are garlic, palm sugar, galangal leaves, peanuts, coriander, cumin, shallots, and turmeric (which is used to give the food a characteristic yellow color). Meats used include: beef, lamb, venison, fish, shrimp, chicken, and even tripe (cow stomach). Because Singapore is primarily a Muslim country, pork satay is seldom seen. Satay is also usually served with a spicy peanut sauce, or peanut gravy, accompanied by slivers of onion and cucumber in vinegar. Serve the satay with fried rice and sautéed Chinese long beans.

- 4 tablespoons smooth or chunky peanut butter
- 6 tablespoons dark soy sauce
- 6 tablespoons freshly squeezed lime juice (about 3 limes)
- 1 tablespoon sweetened rice vinegar
- 3 tablespoons chopped cilantro leaves
- 2 tablespoons brown sugar
- 2 teaspoon Sriracha or other Asian hot chile sauce
- 3 green onions, white and green parts, minced
- 1 (1-inch) piece fresh ginger, chopped
- 2 cloves garlic, minced
  Zest of 1 lime
- 1 tablespoon vegetable oil
- 1 (1½ pound) beef steak (round, sirloin, rib-eye, or chuck)

Soak 6 bamboo or wooden skewers in water for 1 hour.

For the sauce, in a bowl, combine the peanut butter, 4 tablespoons of the soy sauce, 4 tablespoons of the lime juice, vinegar, cilantro, 1 tablespoon of the sugar, and 1 teaspoon of the chile sauce, stirring until a smooth, thick, gravylike consistency is reached. Cover and set aside. (Store in an airtight container in the refrigerator for up to 1 week.)

For the marinade, in a food processor, combine the green onions, ginger, garlic, the remaining 1 teaspoon of the chile sauce, the remaining 2 tablespoons of lime juice, lime zest, remaining 2 tablespoons of soy sauce, remaining 1 tablespoon of brown sugar, and the oil. Process until pureed. Set aside.

Cut the beef against the grain into pieces 6 inches long and ½ inch wide. Thread the beef lengthwise onto the prepared skewers. Transfer the skewers to a large, shallow pan and pour the marinade over the meat; cover and refrigerate for 3 to 4 hours.

Preheat a charcoal or gas grill to 400°F. Place a strip of heavy-duty aluminum foil across the top front of the barbecue. Make it deep enough so the satay skewers can lie on it. This will keep the ends of the skewers from burning.

Remove the skewers from the marinade and drain, discarding the marinade. Transfer the skewers to the foil-covered grill rack and grill over direct heat for 2 minutes per side, or until cooked through.

Meanwhile, warm the peanut sauce in a small saucepan over low heat just until it barely begins to bubble.

Serve the satay on the skewers with small bowls of the warm peanut sauce on the side.

SERVES 4 TO 6

NOTE: **For a special treat, try flavored skewers from Callison's Fine Foods. They come in flavors like garlic herb, citrus rosemary, Thai coconut lime, Indian mango curry, Mexican fiesta, and honey bourbon.**

GRILLED COCONUT FISH

I had this dish at a hawker stand at the Makansutra Gluttons Bay and it was one of the best seafood dishes I had during my visit—crispy outside, tender and moist inside, with a superb coconut. Lemongrass is one of the most commonly used culinary herbs in Southeast Asia. It has a strong flavor of the fruit it's named after, and can be used fresh or in its dried and powdered forms. Only the soft inner part of the stalk is used in cooking. Serve this fish with rice that you've cooked in coconut milk instead of water for a delicious change.

- 3 stalks fresh lemongrass, peeled, trimmed, and minced
- 1 small bunch cilantro
- 5 shallots, minced
- 3 cloves garlic, minced
- 1 (1-inch) piece fresh ginger, minced
- 2 small hot chiles, seeded and minced
- 1 tablespoon turmeric
- 2 cups coconut milk
- 1 teaspoon freshly ground black pepper
- 1 teaspoon salt
- 1 (3¹/₂-pound) whole Pacific red snapper (see Note)
  Thinly sliced lime, for garnish
  Thinly sliced lemon, for garnish

In a bowl, combine the lemongrass, cilantro, shallot, garlic, ginger, chiles, turmeric, coconut milk, pepper, and salt, and stir.

On a counter, lay a large piece of heavy-duty aluminum foil. Place the fish in the middle of the foil. With a spatula, spread one-third of the marinade inside the cavity of the fish, and top with the rest. Wrap the foil around the fish, sealing all edges by double-folding the foil. Transfer to the refrigerator for 2 hours.

Remove the fish from the refrigerator and let stand for 1 hour, or until at room temperature.

Preheat a charcoal or gas grill to 375°F.

Transfer the foil package to the grill over direct heat. Cook on the first side for 15 minutes, then gently roll the package over and cook 15 to 20 minutes longer, until the fish is opaque all the way through. Do not overcook the fish. You'll need to open the package to check for doneness.

Remove the fish from the foil and transfer to a heated platter; garnish with lime and lemon slices, and serve.

SERVES 4 TO 6

NOTE: Since the common and overfished red snapper is on the Seafood Watch list (www.mbayaq.org/cr/seafoodwatch.asp), I suggest you use Pacific, rainbow, or black snapper, each of which are caught on hook and line, instead of in huge dredging nets.

HOISIN CHICKEN WINGS

Another favorite dish at Singapore's hawker stands, these wings flew me to culinary heaven. For some reason, Singaporeans love chicken wings. In fact, in the market there's one stand that sells only fresh chicken wings, and they are much bigger than those found in frozen bags in U.S. markets. Hoisin made from a combination of fermented soy, garlic, vinegar, chiles, and sweetener (honey, molasses, or brown sugar), is dark in color and thick in consistency. It has a very strong salty and slightly sweet flavor. Some call it Asia's barbecue sauce.

24	chicken wings (about 1³/₄ pounds)
¹/₄	cup water
2	tablespoons cornstarch
¹/₂	cup hoisin sauce
¹/₄	cup plum sauce (duck sauce)
¹/₄	cup tamari (dark soy sauce)
¹/₄	cup cherry jam
1	tablespoon ground ginger
1	tablespoon freshly squeezed lemon juice
1	tablespoon Sriracha sauce (or other Asian hot chile sauce)
	Salt
	Freshly ground black pepper

Preheat a charcoal or gas grill to 375°F. Make sure the grill rack is clean and oil it thoroughly with nonstick cooking spray.

Cut the wings into three sections, reserving the pointed wingtips for another use.

In a small bowl, combine the water and cornstarch, stirring until there are no lumps.

In a one-gallon resealable plastic bag, combine the cornstarch mixture, hoisin, plum sauce, tamari, jam, ginger, lemon juice, and chile sauce. Add the chicken wing pieces, shaking to coat. Let stand in the refrigerator for 6 to 8 hours.

Remove the chicken wings from the bag and pour the marinade into a small saucepan. Boil the marinade for 12 minutes and set aside to use as a baste and dipping sauce.

Transfer the chicken wings to the prepared grill rack over direct heat and cook, turning and basting often, until it reaches an internal temperature of 155°F, 20 to 30 minutes.

Transfer the chicken wings to a warmed platter, season with salt and pepper, and serve with the remaining sauce on the side.

SERVES 4 TO 6

NOTE: There are many varieties of Asian hot sauces, but Huy Fong Sriracha Hot Chili Sauce is about as good as it gets. It's in a bright red bottle with a white rooster on the front, and is usually available in Asian grocery stores, hot sauce shops, and in the Asian food section of many grocery stores.

EGGPLANT SATAY

This is a great side dish, or main dish for vegetarians. This recipe was inspired by a class in spices and satays at the at-sunrice culinary academy in Singapore. The eggplant, surprisingly enough, is a member of the same botanical family as potatoes. Smaller, young eggplants are best, as the older, larger ones are bitter. Only buy firm, smooth-skinned eggplants that are firm and solid, avoiding those that have mushy-soft areas or are dotted with brown spots or other discolorations.

2 medium eggplants, cut crosswise into ¹/₄-inch slices

Salt

¹/₄ cup coconut cream

1 tablespoon soy sauce

1 tablespoon freshly squeezed lemon juice

3 tablespoons crunchy peanut butter

³/₄ cup boiling water

2 sweet potatoes, peeled and cut crosswise into ¹/₄-inch slices

1 tablespoon light sesame oil

1 teaspoon ground cumin

¹/₄ teaspoon freshly ground black pepper

Soak 12 bamboo or wooden skewers in water for 1 hour.

Sprinkle the eggplant slices with salt and leave up to 30 minutes to remove some of the moisture and bitter taste. Rinse and pat dry before using.

In a small saucepan over low heat, combine the coconut cream, soy sauce, and lemon juice.

Gradually stir in the peanut butter and water until blended and smooth and warmed through. Set aside.

Preheat a charcoal or gas grill to 375°F. Make sure the grill rack is clean and oil it thoroughly with nonstick cooking spray.

Transfer the eggplant and sweet potato to a large mixing bowl. Add the sesame oil, cumin, ¹/₂ teaspoon of salt, and pepper, stirring to combine.

Thread the vegetables onto the prepared skewers. Transfer to the prepared grill rack over direct heat and grill for 20 minutes, turning occasionally, until the vegetables are tender and browned.

Transfer the skewers to serving plates and drizzle with the peanut sauce.

SERVES 4

NOTE: The at-sunrice culinary school in Singapore offers a unique experience for tourists in a five-day class that has students touring local markets, dining with some of the city's most famous chefs, and learning how to cook Asian dishes in their superb teaching kitchens.

COCONUT-PAPAYA TART

K. F. Seetoh shared a recipe similar to this with me, when I asked him his favorite hawker stand dessert. Unfortunately the stand that makes this was temporarily closed the last time I was in Singapore. Next time! Cream of coconut is a smooth, thick liquid made from fresh coconuts. It is thick and very sweet and is commonly used in mixed drinks; it can usually be found in liquor stores, and is available in liquid and powdered forms. Don't confuse it with coconut milk, which is a rich, creamy liquid made from water and pressed coconut pulp.

- 1   prepared piecrust (see Note)
- 1   tablespoon flour
- 1   (8-ounce) package cream cheese, at room temperature
- 6   tablespoons cream of coconut
- 3   tablespoons brown sugar
- 1   cup shredded coconut, lightly toasted
- 1/4   cup chopped crystallized ginger
- 1   (12-ounce) papaya, peeled, seeded, and thinly sliced
- 1/2   cup apricot-pineapple preserves
- 1   tablespoon butter
-     Whipped cream or whipped coconut cream (see Note)

Prepare a charcoal or gas grill for indirect grilling (it is not necessary to use a drip pan with this recipe). Preheat to 450°F.

On a floured work surface, unfold or unroll the piecrust (or remove it from the pie pan), pressing out the fold lines if necessary. Sprinkle with flour and roll out to a 12½-inch round. Transfer the dough, floured side down, to an 11-inch tart pan with a removable bottom. Using a fork, pierce the bottom and sides of the dough in 5 to 6 places.

Transfer the tart pan to the grill rack and cook over indirect heat until golden brown, about 12 minutes. Remove from the grill and let cool completely.

Meanwhile, make the filling. Using an electric mixer on high speed, beat the cream cheese until smooth. Add the cream of coconut, sugar, 3/4 of the shredded coconut, and the ginger. With a spatula, spread the mixture into the tart pan. Arrange the papaya slices on top of the filling.

In a small saucepan, melt the preserves over low heat, stirring frequently; add the butter and stir until smooth and completely melted. Let this glaze cool slightly and brush it over the papaya. Sprinkle the remaining shredded coconut over the top of the tart. Refrigerate until filling is firm, at least 1 hour.

Serve with whipped cream.

SERVES 4 TO 6

NOTE: You can buy frozen piecrusts in aluminum pans, but I much prefer Pillsbury's chilled crust, rolled and sealed in waxed paper bags. It unrolls into whatever pie or tart pan you wish to use. For a pastry-impaired person like me, it saves time and makes a perfect, flaky crust every time. For a special treat, whip up coconut cream just like whipped cream with an electric mixer and serve with additional coconut flakes sprinkled over each slice.

SOUTH AFRICA
Of Braai, Sosaties, and Potjiekos

In South Africa they don't barbecue—they braai. Like the word "barbecue," the word braai (pronounced "bry") is a both a noun and a verb. As a noun, it refers to the grill itself and as a verb you would "braai some spareribs." And the same way that you would host a barbecue, you would also host a braai. One big difference: in the United States, barbecue is generally done during the summer months, while in South Africa they get to braai the whole year round.

Braais started as spit-roasts at Dutch-African "fairs" or celebrations in the seventeenth century; they are now a cultural institution beloved by all South Africans—especially the men. Women rarely braai. The men gather round the braai, or braaistand (the fire or grill) and cook the food (usually massive quantities of meat) while women prepare the salads, desserts, and vegetables for the meal.

South African cuisine itself is a blend of diverse cooking styles and flavors that has evolved over centuries. Cape Dutch settlers had Malaysian slaves, and since they were in the kitchen, they had a great deal of influence on the national cuisine. Malay-inflected dishes include bobotie, a custard-topped minced meat pie seasoned with onion, curry, and fruit chutney; sosaties, or curry-marinated pork or lamb kebabs; and *bredie*, a meat or fish stew with vegetables and chiles. The Indians introduced their wondrous, and endless, array of curries to the Southern African kitchen; the Afrikaaners brought to the fire their succulent *potjiekos*, or stews of maize with tomato and onion sauce or rice, and festive *braais* of grilled seafood and meat; and the thrifty Dutch contributed their fried dough crullers, or *koek sister*, and *melkos* or milk pies. The British brought their native meat pies, and the Germans their pastries. Even the French made their mark, bringing with them *le* grape vine, as well as marinades and herbs for grilled meats and fish.

Some favorite traditional *braai* foods include:

Biltong, or dry salted meat, often taken from rump cuts of cows, game animals, or ostrich. The South African Boers (of Dutch origin) would marinate the meat in vinegar, adding various herbs and spices for extra flavor, and then dry the meat in thin strips in the sun.

Boerewors, which are spicy South African sausages made of beef, pork, and/or lamb. Fillings can include different combinations of spices, tomato paste, onions, chiles, tomato ketchup, or whatever other strongly flavored ingredient you fancy.

Sosaties, or mutton chunks marinated overnight in fried onions, chiles, garlic, curry leaves, and tamarind juice, then threaded on skewers, grilled well on both sides and served with *sate* (a spicy sauce).

An everyday backyard variety *braai* might include lamb leg chops marinated with garlic and rosemary; marinated chicken, onion, and pepper kebabs; *boerewors*; mealie pap (cornmeal pie) with tomato and onion sauce; fresh home-baked bread rolls; potato and egg salad; a large Greek salad; fresh fruit skewers; and puddings or little tarts.

Mmmmm, please pass me a big bowl of that *potjiekos* and another *sosatie*, I've worked up a hunger here.

FRIKADELLER

Frikadeller are South African "fast food"—they are available everywhere and come in a variety of flavors. These meatballs are slightly flattened and look like sausage patties. You can serve them as an appetizer or as an entrée with mashed potatoes or basmati rice.

- 2 teaspoons fennel seeds, crushed
- 2 tablespoons coriander seeds, crushed
- 1$^1/_2$ pounds ground beef
- 1 pound ground lamb
- 1 cup soft, fresh bread crumbs (no crust)
- 3 beef bouillon cubes
- 1 large onion, chopped
- 2 cloves plus 1 teaspoon garlic, minced
- $^1/_2$ teaspoon garlic salt
- $^1/_2$ teaspoon sugar
- $^1/_2$ teaspoon ground fresh nutmeg
- $^1/_2$ teaspoon freshly ground black pepper
- $^1/_2$ teaspoon ground allspice
- $^1/_4$ teaspoon ground cloves
- $^1/_3$ cup balsamic vinegar
- 2 eggs, beaten
- 3 tablespoons olive oil
- 1 tablespoon minced onion
- 1 teaspoon curry powder
- 1 tablespoon butter
- 3 tablespoons coconut milk

In a large mixing bowl, combine the fennel, coriander, beef, lamb, bread crumbs, bouillon, onion, 2 cloves of minced garlic, salt, sugar, nutmeg, pepper, allspice, cloves, vinegar, and eggs. Mix thoroughly with your hands or a large spoon.

Use a $^1/_3$-cup measure to scoop out the meat mixture. Roll into 2-inch round balls; squash with the palm of your hand, flattening to about a $^3/_4$-inch thickness. Transfer the patties to a resealable plastic bag and refrigerate for at least 2 hours and as much as 4 hours.

Prepare a charcoal or gas grill for indirect grilling. Preheat to 350°F. Make sure the grill rack is clean and oil it thoroughly with nonstick cooking spray.

Remove the meat from the refrigerator and let it come to room temperature. Transfer the meatballs to the barbecue over direct heat and cook, turning, so that both sides are nicely browned, about 2 minutes per side. Transfer to a warmed platter or large skillet, cover, and set aside.

In a large cast-iron skillet over medium-high heat, heat the olive oil and cook the onion until just beginning to go from translucent to brown about 10 to 12 minutes Add the curry, butter, and coconut milk and cook, stirring constantly, for 2 minutes. Add the meat to the onion mixture in the skillet and move the pan to the cool side of the grill. Cook over indirect heat until the inside of the patties is no longer pink, about 12 minutes.

Arrange on a serving platter and serve with toothpicks.

SERVES 8 TO 10 AS AN APPETIZER

GRILLED LAMB WITH APRICOTS

South Africans enjoy their lamb kebabs, especially these, which are made with vegetables and smothered in a delicious curried apricot marinade. This tasty dish, called sosaties *in South Africa, has its origins in the Cape Malay culture, which is influenced by the spices and cuisine brought by Malaysian slaves.*

- 1 tablespoon minced garlic
- 1 tablespoon minced fresh ginger
- 1 tablespoon vegetable oil
- 1 teaspoon ground coriander
- 1 teaspoon ground cumin
- 2 bay leaves
- 1 cinnamon stick
- 2 whole cloves
- 3 tablespoons curry powder
- 1 teaspoon ground allspice
- 2 teaspoons turmeric
- 2 tablespoons sugar
- 1 cup white wine
- 1/2 cup apple cider vinegar
- 1/2 cup chicken stock
- 2 tablespoons apricot jam
- 1 cup tamarind juice (see Note)
- 2 pounds boneless lamb
- 1 cup dried apricots or dried prunes, softened in boiling water
- 2 large onions, cut into quarters

  Red or green bell peppers cut into 2-inch pieces (optional)

Two days before cooking, in a large skillet over high heat, sauté the garlic and ginger in the oil until softened, about 1 minute. Add the coriander, cumin, bay leaves, cinnamon, cloves, curry, allspice, turmeric, and sugar, and stir for about 30 seconds. Add the wine, vinegar, stock, jam, and tamarind juice, and bring to a boil. Decrease the heat and simmer for 5 minutes. Remove from the heat and let cool.

Skewer the meat, alternating with apricots, quartered onions, and bell peppers on steel or wooden skewers. (If you are using wooden skewers, soak them for 1 hour in warm water before using.) Transfer the skewers to a large roasting pan. Add the marinade, cover with plastic wrap, and refrigerate for at least 8 hours or up to 2 days.

Preheat a charcoal or gas grill or *braai* to 400°F. Make sure the grill rack is clean and oil it thoroughly with nonstick cooking spray.

Just before cooking, drain the marinade and pour into a saucepan. Boil for 12 minutes to use as a basting liquid.

Transfer the skewers to the prepared grill rack over direct heat and cook, brushing with the basting liquid and turning frequently, for 4 to 5 minutes, until the meat is browned all over and just pink inside. If using wood skewers, put a piece of aluminum foil on one side of the grill to protect the handle part of the wood from burning.

SERVES 6 TO 8 AS AN APPETIZER

NOTE: Tamarind juice can often be found in specialty health food stores, Asian or Latino food markets, or online. If you can't find it, substitute 1/4 cup orange juice mixed with 2 tablespoons lime juice.

SAVORY MEAT PIE

The African name for this dish is bobotie, *and its origins can be traced back to Asian influences on South African culture. The fruit and chutney contrast with the curry flavoring very nicely, while the milk-soaked bread adds moisture to the dish. This is usually served with saffron rice, and you can add a green salad to round out the meal.*

3	slices of white bread, crusts removed
1	cup milk
1	tablespoon vegetable oil
1	clove garlic, minced
2	onions, chopped
1	tablespoon curry powder
2 1/2	pounds ground lamb
1/4	cup vinegar
1	tablespoon freshly squeezed lemon juice
1	teaspoon brown sugar
2	tablespoons apricot jam
1	tablespoon mango or onion chutney
6	bay leaves
1	orange, sliced
1	lemon, sliced
3	eggs

Prepare a charcoal or gas grill for indirect grilling (it is not necessary to use a drip pan for this recipe). Preheat to 325°F. Grease a 10-inch pie pan with nonstick cooking spray.

Combine the bread and 1/2 cup of the milk in a small bowl and soak for 10 minutes.

In a large skillet set on the grill over direct heat (or over medium-high heat on the stove top), heat the oil. Add the garlic, onion, and curry power and cook, stirring occasionally, for 3 minutes; add the ground meat and cook, stirring frequently, until no longer pink, about 10 to 12 minutes.

Using your hands, squeeze the milk from the bread. Discard the milk and add the bread, vinegar, lemon juice, sugar, apricot jam, and chutney to the meat. Cook for about 1 minute; remove the pan from the heat.

Transfer 3 of the bay leaves and 3 slices each of the orange and lemon to the bottom of the prepared pan. Cut the remaining orange slices in half crosswise and arrange the rest of the fruit around the sides of the pan, rounded-side up.

Beat the eggs and the remaining 1/2 cup milk together in a small bowl. Spoon the ground lamb mixture into the pie pan; add the beaten egg mixture and stir well to incorporate. Decorate the top with the remaining 3 bay leaves. Transfer the pan, uncovered, to the grill rack over indirect heat and cook for about 30 minutes, or until it's browned on top and a meat thermometer registers 160°F.

Remove from the grill and let sit, covered, for about 10 minutes before serving.

SERVES 4 TO 6

GRILLED TILAPIA WITH GROUNDNUT SAUCE

The farming of tilapia is recorded as far back as ancient Egypt. Tradition holds that the tilapia was the fish that Jesus used to feed the five thousand by the Sea of Galilee, thus one of its common names: St. Peter's fish. True tilapia are only native to Africa and the Middle East. This fish is popular with subsistence African fisherman, who fish with hand-thrown nets, arrows, and fish spears. Serve this dish with steamed rice or buttered noodles.

- 1 whole (4 ¹/₂-pound) tilapia
  Salt
  Freshly ground black pepper
- ¹/₄ cup olive oil
- 1 large onion, finely chopped
- ¹/₂ cup natural, unsweetened peanut butter
- 1 teaspoon curry powder
- ¹/₂ teaspoon ground nutmeg
  About 1 cup water

Prepare a charcoal or gas grill for indirect grillling (it is not necessary to use a drip pan for this recipe). Preheat to 375°F. Make sure the grill rack is clean and oil it thoroughly with nonstick cooking spray.

Make 2 or 3 deep cuts into each side of the fish; rub salt and pepper into the cuts and over the rest of the fish. Drizzle with 2 to 3 tablespoons of the olive oil.

Transfer the fish to the prepared grill rack over direct heat and cook, turning only once with long-handled tongs, for about 5 minutes per side, until browned and crisp on both sides.

Transfer the tilapia onto a piece of aluminum foil placed over the cool side of the grill. Cover the fish with another piece of foil and grill 2 to 3 minutes longer, until the flesh flakes when tested with a fork. Transfer the fish to a heated platter.

In a cast-iron skillet over direct heat, sauté the onions until browned in the remaining 1 or 2 tablespoons of oil, 10 to 12 minutes (see Note). Pour the onions over the fish and cover to keep warm. In the same skillet set on the cool side of the grill, combine the peanut butter, curry powder, and nutmeg and slowly stir in enough water (about 1 cup) to make a smooth sauce.

Pour the sauce over the fish and onions and serve immediately.

SERVES 4

NOTE: If you would like to, you can add tomatoes, green pepper, chopped celery, shallots, chives, finely chopped peanuts, hot chile peppers, and/or garlic when frying the onion.

MEALIE PAP

Many of us love crusty cornbread. A dark pan will make crustier cornbread than a metal or glass pan. For the crustiest cornbread, use a cast iron skillet. You will find versions of mealie pap *(cornmeal pie) on every restaurant menu in the country—it's the equivalent to our mashed or baked potatoes.*

- 1 cup yellow cornmeal
- 3/4 cup water
- 2 cups buttermilk
- 3 tablespoons butter, melted
- 1/2 cup sugar
- 1/4 cup honey
- 1/2 teaspoon salt
- 2 eggs
- 2 teaspoons baking soda
- 1/2 cup shredded Cheddar cheese
- 1/2 cup chopped bacon (about 6 slices)

Prepare a charcoal or gas grill for indirect grilling (it is not necessary to use a drip pan with this recipe). Preheat to 375°F. Spray an 8- by 8-inch-square baking pan with nonstick cooking spray.

In a large saucepan over high heat, combine the cornmeal, water, buttermilk, butter, sugar, honey, and salt, and heat until boiling. Decrease the heat to low and simmer for 5 minutes, stirring constantly until very thick and the mixture heavily coats the back of a large spoon. Transfer the cornmeal mixture into a bowl and let it cool.

In a large bowl, combine the eggs, baking soda, and half each of the cheese and bacon. Add the cornmeal mixture, stirring to blend. Pour into the prepared pan. Sprinkle with the remaining cheese and bacon.

Transfer the pan to the barbecue and cook over indirect heat, with the lid closed for 30 to 35 minutes, until a toothpick inserted in several places comes out clean.

SERVES 6

NOTE: When mixing batter for cornbread or muffins, put away your electric mixer. Mixing by hand helps you avoid overmixing. It is desirable to have a few lumps in the batter. They will hydrate during baking and the lumps will help give a rustic appearance to your breads.

BOEREWORS

Boerewors translates as "farmer's sausage," and the dish is another inheritance from South African pioneering forefathers who used to combine minced meat and cubed spek (pork fat) with spices and preservatives (chiefly vinegar), which were available in the then–Cape Colony. The self-sufficient South African farming community wasted nothing. Letitia Prinsloo of the International Culinary Academy in Stellenbosch was kind enough to share this recipe.

3	tablespoons whole coriander seeds
1	teaspoon whole cloves
3	to 3^1/$_2$ ounces sausage casings
3	pounds coarsely gound beef
3	pounds coarsely ground pork
1	pound bacon, minced
^{1}/$_2$	cup red wine vinegar
2	tablespoons brown sugar
1	clove garlic, finely minced
4	tablespoons Worcestershire sauce
2	tablespoons salt
1	teaspoon freshly ground black pepper
^{1}/$_2$	teaspoon freshly grated nutmeg
^{1}/$_2$	teaspoon dried thyme
^{1}/$_2$	teaspoon ground allspice

In a small skillet over high heat, brown the coriander and cloves, shaking the pan gently from time to time, being careful not to burn them, about 5 minutes. Grind the spices with a mortar and pestle and strain with fine-mesh sieve to remove the husks.

Preheat a charcoal or gas grill to 350°F. Make sure the grill rack is clean and oil it thoroughly with nonstick cooking spray. Put the sausage casings into warm water and let them soak for 10 to 12 minutes.

In a large bowl, combine the meat, spice mixture, vinegar, brown sugar, garlic, Worcestershire sauce, salt, pepper, nutmeg, thyme, and allspice, and mix thoroughly with your hands, until all the spices are evenly distributed.

Drain the casings and place one over the mouth of a sausage mill. Gather enough of the casing so that about 3 inches is ready to be filled and tie a knot at that point. It is much easier to have an extra pair of hands; have an assistant hold the casing and guide the meat, while you feed the meat mixture into the casing. Add the meat to the mill in small amounts, while you lightly push on the stopper to control the flow of the meat into the casings. Form the *boerewors* with your hand so that it is equally thick all over.

Don't overfill the casings as this can cause the sausages to explode when cooking. Try to press out as many air bubbles as possible. Once the casing is full, remove it from the machine and set it aside. Continue to push the rest of the mixture out of the mill and into the casings. Knot the casings.

Transfer the sausages to the prepared grill rack over direct heat, turning often, until the skin is nicely browned but the inside is still moist, 12 to 14 minutes.

SERVES 8

AFRIKAANS MELKTERT

Melktert means "milk tart," and this most traditional of Dutch-Afrikaans desserts is a refreshing tart that has a dense creamy texture with just the right amount of sweetness. The simple ingredients and simple cooking method (you can also cook this in an oven) are direct descendants from the early South African settlers. If you don't want to make your own piecrust, a premade piecrust will work just fine.

CRUST

2¹/₂ cups flour
  2 teaspoons baking powder
¹/₄ teaspoon salt
  1 cup unsalted butter
  1 cup sour cream

CUSTARD

  2 cups milk
¹/₂ cup sugar
¹/₄ cup flour
  5 large eggs
¹/₄ teaspoon salt
  1 teaspoon vanilla extract
  1 teaspoon almond extract

  2 teaspoons cinnamon
¹/₂ cup firmly packed brown sugar

Prepare a charcoal or gas grill for indirect cooking (it is not necessary to use a drip pan for this recipe). Preheat to 400°F.

For the crust, combine the flour, baking powder, and salt in a food processor. Add butter and process until the flour resembles coarse cornmeal. Then add the sour cream and process until the mixture forms a ball.

On a floured surface, roll out the dough to fit a 10-inch tart pan, (about 12 inches). Crimp the edges to form a rim and pierce the dough with a fork in several places. Transfer the pan to the grill rack over indirect heat and bake the crust for 20 to 25 minutes until crisp and golden, then remove from the barbecue and let cool.

Make the custard by heating the milk to boiling. While the milk is heating, combine the sugar, flour, eggs, and salt in a blender. When the milk begins to foam, pour it slowly into the blender with the motor running at low speed. When the milk is well combined with the other ingredients, pour the custard back into the saucepan and cook over medium heat, stirring constantly until thickened, 3 to 5 minutes. Remove from the heat and stir in the vanilla and almond extracts. Let the custard cool for 20 minutes in the refrigerator.

Spread the custard filling evenly into the cooled tart crust, then generously sprinkle the top with the cinnamon and brown sugar. Return the tart to the cool side of the grill or to the oven for about 15 minutes, until the brown sugar melts and the top is firm.

This tart is best served warm, but also can be refrigerated and served the next day

SERVES 6 TO 8

Of Game and Men

(Author's note: After filming the South Africa episode for *Barbecue America: The World Tour*, we went deep into the interior for a visit to the Chinaka Game Lodge, where we filmed an authentic bush barbecue and the preparation of *potjiekos*, a traditional dish cooked slowly in cast-iron pot over an open wood fire. Chris Browne, the field producer on the segment, wrote this piece about the South African trip.)

If you are an American and you tell another American that you're planning a trip to South Africa, one of three things will happen: 1) the American will make reference to the lion cub Simba in Disney's *The Lion King*; 2) the American will begin singing (or if you're lucky, humming) Toto's 1982 pop hit, "Africa"; or 3) the American will furrow his or her brow with concern, envisioning the dreadful disease and/or war that might tear through Africa on the day that you, the hapless tourist, happen to be sightseeing on a Jeep-chauffeured safari.

While the Disney corporation certainly has its flaws, and most of Toto's back catalog is best reserved for the bargain bin, it's the last of these three reactions that bothers me the most. Comparing South Africa to any other country on the African continent is like equating Oregon and Nicaragua since they're both in North America.

South Africa has unbelievably beautiful scenery and, most importantly for this book's subject matter, unique and diverse cuisine. When you visit South Africa, the country politely asks you to give up your preconceived notions, to step outside your comfort zone and eat food you'd never consider, let alone be able to even pronounce. From marinated impala steaks to crayfish curry with basmati rice; sirloin kebabs to a traditional English breakfast of sausage and broiled tomatoes; creamed butternut squash to *mapone* worms sautéed in mango chutney—South Africa offers a bevy of delectable dishes.

And yes, you read correctly: *worms*. I believe that you can't truly say you have visited a new continent without trying something that makes you squirm—and ideally something that literally squirms itself. Would I repeat such a gastronomic delight? Probably not. But it certainly gives me at least a year's worth of bragging rights.

If the idea of munching on a soft-bodied invertebrate makes you queasy, rest assured: comfort food is abundant. Just like barbecue in the States, South African *braai* is an excuse to showcase one's well-honed ambidextrous skills—holding a bottle of beer in one hand and a pair of tongs in the other. If they held a worldwide competition for such skills, our hunting expert, Stefano, would surely take home the gold medal. He explained to us that the most popular items to grill

in South Africa are lamb shanks, homemade *boerewors* (beef sausage), and chicken. He also taught us how to properly load a rifle and hunt wildebeest, so he is a man to be trusted . . . and monitored closely.

Stefano helps run the Chinaka Lodge, a secluded game farm four and a half hours outside of Johannesburg. It was there that I stared down a pair of rhinoceroses, tracked leopard "spoor," and approached a herd of giraffes on foot. The culinary encounters at the lodge were equally memorable: cornbread baked by being buried in hot coals; the aforementioned wildebeest, sliced thin and chilled with pepper and lemon as an appetizer, and a springbok cocktail (half Amarula Cream liqueur, half crème de menthe) that mirrors the colors of South Africa's national rugby team. (Rugby, by the way, is a big deal there.)

Back in the city of Cape Town, a guy named Guy was our tour guide through a city full of delightful people and wonderful restaurants. Guy's job was to show us the best Cape Town has to offer, and that he did. We dined at the Wharfside Grill, where they heap dollops of garlic butter the size of Coney Island ice cream cones onto sole and kingklip fillets.

He led us downtown where we were treated to huge dishes of grilled meat and *mealie pap* stacked four layers high at Nyonni's Kraal, the interior of which is decorated like a real African village. Colin Nyonni, the owner and chef, was the source of the worm experience. The sauce was great, the worms . . . well, chewy.

And finally we went down to the shore, near the Cape of Good Hope, and had an incredible seaside lunch prepared for us by the Henricks family, gathered around a three-generations-old Dutch oven full of garlic-soaked shrimp, crayfish curry, and the best calamari any of us had ever eaten. With the crystal Atlantic Ocean behind us, Al, the humble chef, grilled a huge abalone that his daughter Shelene had dived for that very morning.

Every night we were treated to the African sky—a window to the universe that contained more stars than a constellation map from an observatory souvenir shop.

If you're looking for something new, if you're willing to mingle with the primates, carnivores, and ungulates, and if you're ready to experience something unforgettable, then prick up your ears, open your eyes, and prepare your taste buds for South Africa.

And just remember these wise words I heard from an African *braai* shaman, "Keep your warming on your grill, and off your globe."

SPAIN
Eating the Air

Warning! This chapter introduction is *not* about barbecue, grilling, smoking, or anything related to barbecue, grilling, or smoking. It's about ham. So if you don't want to read about one of the top eating experiences of a lifetime, move on to another chapter. Otherwise, grab a napkin and a glass of port, and read on.

My visit to Spain took me to Sevilla, capital of the Andalusian region and a city where restaurants, sidewalk cafés, and tapas bars crowd the narrow cobbled streets and wide generous plazas. But it was outside the city that I had my most exciting discovery. Roger Cross leads food and wine tours throughout the country

and brought me to the culinary heart of Andalusia, if not Spain itself.

Our trip began in the mountainous province of Huelva, an area famous for producing exceptional ham from exceptional pigs. These animals are long-legged Iberian hogs, also known as *pata negra* (black foot) for their distinctive appearance. They are allowed to range freely amid the local cork oak groves where they feed on dropped acorns. (So the region not only produces premium ham but also produces the corks for the wine that accompanies the ham!)

In the heart of the Sierra de Aracena lies the village of Jabugo. Cold and dry in winter, mild in spring and summer, Jabugo is home to Cinco Jotas (5J), the premium ham producer in the region, and perhaps all of Spain. Here we were given an incredible tour by Severiano Sánchez, master ham maker at 5J, who explained in great detail the wonders of Serrano (which means "from the mountains") ham.

According to Sr. Sánchez, only the ham from the *pata negra* pigs can be called *jamón Ibérico* and only makes up around 7 percent of Serrano hams. Jamon Iberico is further separated into three categories: *jamón Ibérico de bellota* (which means "acorn") is the highest quality and has the distinct nutty flavor imparted by the pigs' unusual acorn diet; *jamón Ibérico de recebo* is produced from pigs that are fed a combination of acorns and grain; and *jamón Ibérico* comes from hogs that are grain-fed. Not as luxurious as the *bellota* ham, the two latter varieties still offer superb taste and texture.

The curing process at Cinco Jotas is both a science and an art. The fresh hams are first trimmed and cleaned, then stacked like cordwood, covered with sea salt, and stored at 37°F and 90 percent humidity. This serves to draw off excess moisture and preserve the meat. After several days (the actual length of time varies), the salt is washed off and the hams are hung on ropes in cool, dry bodegas (store-rooms) to air dry. This is where the distinct, subtle flavors and aromas develop, and the hams begin to take on a golden sheen as well as a spotty coat of mold. While the average curing process normally lasts from six to eighteen months, depending on the climate, and the size and type of ham being cured, Sr. Sánchez shared a secret, "At Cinco Jotas, they are cured for three years!"

In one of the most astonishing experiences of my life, we were given a tour of the 5J bodegas. We walked through seemingly endless rooms hung with hundreds of thousands of curing hams. Golden in color, moist to the touch, the meat saturated every molecule of air with a rich, flavorful, buttery, and pungent scent. I literally wanted to eat the air.

Sr. Sánchez told us there were currently 1,500,000 Iberian blackfoot pig hams curing in their plant, and he smiled as he told us that they were "*all* pre-sold." Shortly after our visit, I checked online and found that a 7-kilogram (15-pound) Cinco Jota hind leg ham costs $558 (or $37 per pound), while a 4.5-kilogram (9.9-pound) shoulder ham rings in at $172 ($10 per pound). And those are bargains compared to the Maldonado company's *reserve jámon Ibérico*, which sells for $1,540 for a thirteen-pound hind leg or $489 for a nine-pound

shoulder ham. That's $118 and $54 per pound respectively. Because this curing method is so costly and slow, the hams available in local restaurants and for home consumption are usually the lesser-quality Serrano hams, 95 percent of which are derived from white hogs, crossbreeds like the Large White, Landrace, or Duroc strains.

Leading us back to a private office, Sr. Sánchez offered to demonstrate how to properly cut and enjoy the ham. He explained, "This is a 'room temperature' product. To get the best of flavor and aroma, serve it at room temperature and store it in a cool, dry place. Refrigerate it only if absolutely necessary and make sure to let it acclimate several hours before serving." He continued, "If you're serving it as a starter or snack, serve in very thin, freshly cut, bite-sized slices. (A "snack" at $37 to $118 a pound!) Exposure to the air dries and dissipates its special aromas, so please only slice just before you serve—and it's okay to eat with your fingers!"

Sr. Sánchez revealed a whole 5J hind leg ham displayed on a *jamonero*, (a specially designed stand), radiant in its golden glory. As he began slicing we began eating, savoring the subtle differences between the flavors and textures of meat cut from the knuckle, shank, or flank. A glass of port in one hand, paper thin slices of moist, chewy, intensely flavored meat in the other, I decided that this was as close to culinary heaven as I would ever get.

In seconds, we had dispatched about half of an Iberian ham. Severiano laughingly asked me if I still wanted to go back and "eat the air" in the bodega. With a mouth full of ham, I didn't bother answering.

(Author's Note: Great news! Starting in 2008, the U.S. will permit the importing of Parma, Serrano, and Iberian hams, pork shoulders, and loins into this country. At prices from $70+ a pound for bone-in and $130+ a pound for boneless, they're still a luxury. But at least now we don't have to sneak them into the country in our luggage. Not that I did, mind you. . . .)

GRILLED PORK PINCHOS

Pinchos *are a traditional Spanish appetizer cooked on a skewer, usually wood or bamboo, like Turkish kebabs or Singaporean satays.*

- ¼ cup olive oil
- 1 tablespoon paprika
- 1 tablespoon ground cumin
- 1 teaspoon allspice
- ½ teaspoon oregano (see Note)
- ½ teaspoon cayenne
- 2 tablespoons freshly squeezed lemon juice
- ½ teaspoon freshly ground black pepper
- ½ teaspoon salt
- 1 (1-pound) pork tenderloin, cut into 1-inch cubes
- 1 Spanish onion, cut into 2-inch pieces

In a bowl, combine the oil, paprika, cumin, allspice, oregano, cayenne, lemon juice, pepper, and salt. Transfer the tenderloin to a resealable plastic bag and pour in the marinade. Seal the bag, pressing out all the air, and shake to coat. Let stand in the refrigerator for 6 to 8 hours.

Soak about 8 wooden or bamboo skewers in water for 1 hour. Preheat a charcoal or gas grill to 375°F. Place a strip of heavy-duty aluminum foil across the top front of the barbecue. Make it deep enough so the skewers can lie on it. This will keep the ends of the skewers from burning.

Drain the pork and set aside. Pour the marinade into a saucepan and boil for 12 minutes to use for basting.

Thread the pork onto the skewers, adding a piece of onion between every 2 pieces of meat. Transfer the skewers to the foil-lined grill rack over direct heat and cook, turning once and basting occasionally, for about 8 minutes, until the meat is no longer pink and has just begun to char at the edges. Remove from the heat and serve immediately with the remaining sauce drizzled over the skewers.

SERVES 4 TO 6 AS AN APPETIZER

NOTE: For a wonderful way to use oregano, go to a health food store, or go online, and look for oil of oregano. Loaded with flavor and easy to use, it imparts a very special taste to sauces and marinades.

LA BARRACA MUSSELS

Feel free to use different varieties of mussels in this recipe, and you can even throw in your favorite clams as well. Just follow the process described below: clean, check for live shellfish, then add to the pot. Serve this dish with a fresh baguette to sop up the sauce.

- 2 pounds mussels
- 1 clove garlic, minced
- 4 shallots, minced
- 2 sprigs fresh thyme
- 3 tablespoons olive oil
- 2 tablespoons butter
- $2/3$ cup dry white wine
- $1/3$ cup water
- $1/4$ cup minced celery
- $1/4$ cup chopped carrot
- 5 tablespoons minced fresh parsley, plus more for garnish
- 1 bay leaf
- $1/2$ teaspoon freshly ground black pepper

  Pinch of cayenne paper
- $3/4$ cup fresh cream
- 1 lemon, cut in quarters, for garnish

If shells are slightly open, firmly tap them on the counter; if they close, go ahead and use them, if they stay open, discard them.

Preheat a charcoal or gas grill to 425°F.

Place a Dutch oven or deep cast-iron skillet over the hottest part of the grill and sauté the garlic, shallots, and thyme in the olive oil and butter until transparent, about 5 minutes. Do not let them brown. Add the wine, water, celery, carrots, parsley, bay leaf, black and cayenne peppers, and the mussels. Pour in the cream. Cover the pan and cook, shaking frequently, for about 4 minutes, until the shells open.

Remove from heat and serve the mussels and sauce immediately on a large platter, garnished with lemon and fresh parsley.

SERVES 4 AS A MAIN COURSE, 6 TO 8 AS AN APPETIZER

HERBED SEVILLA SWORDFISH

Swordfish are in jeopardy of serious overfishing (and the 250,000 sea turtles that are caught every year by accident in the same lines are already endangered). U.S. regulations are the strictest, so please, only buy U.S. long-line-caught swordfish, or substitute halibut, mahimahi, or striped bass steaks. A trip to Barcelona introduced me to this dish; the optional sauce made from Seville oranges is wonderful. (If you make it, skip the recipe steps for making the herb-onion sauce.)

- 4 (6- to 8-ounce) U.S.-caught swordfish steaks
- 3 tablespoons olive oil
  - Salt
  - Freshly ground black pepper
- 2 tablespoons chopped fresh parsley (optional)
- 1 tablespoon chopped fresh basil (optional)
- 4 shallots, minced (optional)
- 1 small onion, minced (optional)
- 1 clove garlic, crushed
- 3 tablespoons fine fresh bread crumbs
- 1 teaspoon chopped fresh oregano
- $1/2$ teaspoon chopped fresh chervil, preferably Spanish chervil (see Note)
  - Juice of half a lemon
- 4 large tomatoes, halved horizontally
  - Seville Orange Sauce (optional; recipe follows)

On a large plate, sprinkle the swordfish with 1 tablespoon of the olive oil and season with salt and pepper; let stand for 20 minutes.

Preheat a charcoal or gas grill to 375°F. Make sure the grill rack is clean and oil it thoroughly with nonstick cooking spray.

Heat 1 tablespoon of the olive oil in a small saucepan until it begins to shimmer. Add the parsley, basil, shallots, and onion, and cook until the onion becomes translucent and is just beginning to brown about 3 to 4 minutes, set aside.

In a bowl, combine the garlic, bread crumbs, oregano, chervil, and lemon juice. Season with salt and pepper, and set aside.

Transfer the tomato halves to a baking sheet and sprinkle them with the bread crumb mixture. Transfer the baking sheet to the grill rack over direct heat and cook for 10 to 15 minutes, until they begin to brown and soften. Set aside.

Transfer the swordfish to the prepared grill rack over direct heat and cook for 4 to 5 minutes per side, until golden brown, brushing with the remaining 1 tablespoon of olive oil if the fish starts to look dry.

Serve immediately with the tomato halves. Generously drizzle with either the herb-onion sauce or the Seville orange sauce.

SERVES 4

NOTE: **Spanish chervil has a stronger anise flavor than regular chervil. Seville oranges were the first and only oranges imported into Europe in the early 1500's and were the first oranges to be shipped to the New World. The wide, rough-surfaced fruit, with a fairly thick, aromatic, bitter peel, is famed for its use in marmalade, but can be used in cooking if you balance the bitterness with a sweetener.**

SEVILLE ORANGE SAUCE

- 1 teaspoon freshly squeezed orange juice, preferably Seville
- 1 teaspoon sugar
- $1/2$ teaspoon paprika
  - Zest of $1/2$ orange, finely chopped
- $1/4$ stick butter, melted
- 1 small shallot, chopped
- 1 teaspoon coarse sea salt

In a small bowl combine the juice, sugar, paprika, zest, and butter and stir. Using a mortar and pestle, grind the shallot with the sea salt until it's a paste and add to the bowl. Stir, cover, and set aside at room temperature until ready to use.

STEAK WITH BLUE CHEESE SAUCE

This sumptuous steak dish was described to me by a Mexican chef as "the best steak in Europe." This dish goes beautifully with saffron rice and grilled fresh asparagus, accompanied, of course, by a rich Spanish red wine from the Rioja district or a Catalonian Penedés.

8 ounces Spanish Cabrales or other blue cheese, crumbled

1 clove garlic, finely chopped

2 tablespoons red wine

Dash of cayenne

1 tablespoon olive oil

4 (^{1}/$_2$-pound) rib-eye steaks, 1 inch thick

Kosher salt

Freshly ground black pepper

^{1}/$_4$ cup water

2 tablespoons butter

2 tablespoons chopped cilantro, for garnish

Paprika, for garnish

Preheat a charcoal or gas grill to 375°F. Make sure the grill rack is clean and oil it thoroughly with nonstick cooking spray.

In a cast-iron skillet large enough to fit all 4 steaks, combine the cheese, garlic, wine, and cayenne over low heat, stirring frequently, until all of the cheese is melted. Set aside and keep warm.

Brush the olive oil on the steaks and season with salt and pepper. Transfer the steaks to the prepared grill rack over direct heat and grill, turning once, until they reach an internal temperature of 145°F for medium-rare, about 5 minutes per side. Add the water to the cheese mixture, stir until blended, then add the steaks. Place the skillet on the grill rack over direct heat until the sauce boils, turning the steaks several times to coat.

Immediately remove the skillet from the grill, put a pat of butter on each steak, cover, and let sit 5 minutes, then serve with the pan sauce. Garnish with cilantro and paprika.

SERVES 4

GRILLED GARLIC CHICKEN

Garlic is an essential ingredient in much of Spanish cooking. When buying fresh garlic, choose plump, dry heads that feel firm and are white to off-white in color. Garlic should be stored in a cool, dark place (though not a refrigerator) and can be kept for several weeks. Serve this dish with rice and thick slices of good bread, both of which will absorb the succulent juices. If you wish you may brush both sides of the bread with olive oil and then quickly grill the bread on both sides, just until it gets grill marks.

1 (3-pound) chicken, butterflied

3 tablespoons olive oil

1 onion, thinly sliced

4 green onions, white and green parts, minced

^{1}/$_4$ cup minced garlic, about 6 to 8 large cloves

3 plum tomatoes, seeded and chopped

^{1}/$_3$ cup chopped baked ham

^{1}/$_2$ cup golden raisins

^{1}/$_2$ cup port wine

^{1}/$_4$ cup brandy

1 tablespoon yellow prepared mustard

2 tablespoons tomato paste

1 tablespoon freshly squeezed lemon juice

1^1/$_2$ tablespoons cornstarch mixed with 2 tablespoons cold water

1 tablespoon balsamic vinegar

Salt

Freshly ground black pepper

Parsley sprigs, for garnish

Lemon slices, for garnish

Prepare a charcoal or gas grill for indirect grilling (it is not necessary to use a drip pan for this recipe). Preheat to 375°F. Make sure the grill rack is clean and oil it thoroughly with nonstick cooking spray.

Brush the chicken with 2 tablespoons of olive oil and transfer to the prepared grill rack over direct heat. Grill until nicely marked on both sides, about 5 to 7 minutes total. Remove to a large bowl and set aside.

continued

In a large roasting pan set over indirect heat, add the remaining 1 tablespoon of olive oil, then add the onion, green onion, garlic, tomato, ham, and raisins and stir while heating until the mixture is starting to brown, about 10 to 12 minutes.

Meanwhile, in a small bowl, combine the port, brandy, mustard, tomato paste, and lemon juice. Pour this sauce over the chicken and rotate it several times with tongs to cover all surfaces.

Transfer the chicken to the top of the onion mixture in the roasting pan. Cover the pan with a lid or aluminum foil and move it to the cool side of the grill. Lower the grill rack and cook the chicken for 4 to 5 hours, until a meat thermometer inserted in the thickest part of the thigh registers 180°F. Remove the chicken from the pan, cover, and keep warm.

On a stove top or side burner over high heat, skim the fat from the juices in the pan; add the cornstarch mixture and stir until thickened, about 8 minutes. Stir in the vinegar and season with salt and pepper.

To serve, quarter the chicken and transfer to a warm platter, drizzled with some of the sauce and garnished with parsley sprigs and lemon slices. Serve the remaining sauce on the side.

SERVES 4

GARLIC-ROASTED PEPPERS

Discovered by old Chris Columbus during his visit to the Americas, the green and red pepper plants were to have a huge effect on Spanish (and Italian) cuisine. In Europe, the red and green vegetables became known as "Spanish peppers," and their popularity spread along the Mediterranean coast and even to England. Pepper plants were cultivated in royal Spanish gardens and a brisk trade in peppers shortly followed.

12	large red bell peppers
1/4	cup olive oil
6	large cloves garlic, thinly sliced
1/4	cup sherry vinegar (see Note)
3	tablespoons minced orange zest
	Sprinkle of garlic salt

Preheat a charcoal or gas grill to 500°F. Make sure the grill rack is clean and oil it thoroughly with nonstick cooking spray.

Cut off the tops of the peppers and discard. In a large bowl, toss the peppers with the olive oil. Drain the peppers and reserve the oil. Transfer the peppers to the prepared grill rack over direct heat. Cook, turning every 10 minutes, for about 20 minutes, or until evenly charred and blistered.

Transfer the peppers to a brown paper bag, fold closed, and let stand about 15 minutes, or until the skin will easily slip off. Peel and seed the peppers and cut them lengthwise into 6 strips. Brush with the some of the reserved olive oil. Return the peppers to the grill rack and grill over direct heat, turning once, until the edges are charred, about 5 minutes per side. Set aside.

In a large cast-iron skillet, combine the garlic, vinegar, and reserved olive oil and simmer over medium heat, stirring frequently, until the liquid becomes syrupy, about 25 minutes. Add the peppers and cook for 5 minutes longer. Remove the skillet from the heat and let cool.

Transfer the peppers to a serving platter. Sprinkle with the zest and garlic salt, and serve.

SERVES 6 TO 8

NOTE: Both sherry and sherry vinegar have been produced in southern Spain since well before the sixteenth century. Like their Italian cousin balsamic, you'll find sherry vinegars aged for thirty, fifty, and sometimes up to seventy-five years. As with fine balsamics, the older, high-quality vinegars are sometimes used as an aperitif or digestif. Bring your wallet: like great wines, great vinegars are pricey—but worth every lip-smacking dollar.

TAHITI AND FIJI

Remembering Kava and Banana Cream Pie

Everyone has heard of amnesia. But how many have heard of Anglonesia? Or Micronesia? Or Melanesia? Perhaps a bunch of you have heard of Polynesia. The "'nesias," as I call them, are merely names of various island groups in the South Pacific, often referred to as Oceana. With an estimated 30,000 islands

in this part of the globe, I'd be writing for the rest of my life if I tried to catalog their varied culinary styles. So I picked two of my favorites for this chapter: Tahiti, which is in Polynesia, and Fiji, which is part of Melanesia.

Fiji is comprised of more than 300 islands and atolls, scattered across 200,000 square

197

miles of ocean, and is approximately the size of New Jersey. Fiji's two main islands, Viti Levu, and Vanua Levu, have vast tropical forests, superb beaches, a gold mine, and a mountain that reaches almost a mile high. Fiji's population of just under a million is comprised mostly of indigenous Fijians (54 percent of the population), East Indians and Indo Fijians (38 percent), and the rest a mixture of Europeans, other Pacific Island people, Chinese, and others.

Fijian cooking features many of the ingredients common in the South Pacific—fish, shellfish, breadfruit, taro, cassava, pork, beef, chicken, yams, rice, coconut milk, tropical fruits such as bananas, and various greens such as taro leaves or ferns. Then there is kava, a pungent, murky drink that is a vital part of the Fijian culture. Kava, a relative of the pepper plant, is pounded into a powder, mixed with water, and poured into coconut half-shells, then downed in one gulp. Frankly, and with all due respect, I thought it tasted like old gym socks, dipped in mud, and then steeped in old pond water. But like a good sport I downed three shells worth, and actually sort of enjoyed that last gulp. It's clearly an acquired taste.

In the kitchen, cooks rely on ginger, garlic, turmeric, fenugreek, coriander, cumin, and a huge assortment of Indian-Fijian curry blends. On the table, they provide salt, lemon juice, soy sauce, and hot chiles, leaving choice of condiments up to each person. Most Fijian salads, appetizers, soups, and beverages, are made with fruits such as mango, lime, guava, bananas, coconut, and pineapple. Meat is one of the key elements of many Fiji main dishes, and pork and cured or smoked hams, are often served as a main dish. And, naturally enough, fish and seafood is central to Fijian cooking. Fijians grill rock lobster, *palusami*, unicorn fish, shrimp, cod, mahimahi, haddock, snapper, grouper, albacore tuna, and a dozen or so other species of fish, over simple grills or, if it's a special occasion in an earth oven called a *lovo* which is used to cook whole pigs as well as chickens, seafood, and root vegetables.

The best place to taste local food, as in most countries, is in someone's home, if you are lucky enough to get an invitation. The first time I visited Fiji, the headwaiter at the resort I was visiting invited me to his home for dinner, and I eagerly accepted. Man, what a feed. Grilled fish in coconut curry, spicy rice, and grilled plantains and breadfruit, followed by a salad of fresh fruit. But you can also find good, local-style restaurants in the cities of Nadi, Suva, and Lautoka.

Tahiti, part of French Polynesia (which contains 118 islands and atolls), is the largest and highest of the islands located in the archipelago of the Society Island group, and has a population of a little over a quarter million people—78 percent of them from various nearby islands, 12 percent Chinese, and the rest mostly European (chiefly French). The island is a mere 28 miles long, but over 400 miles in area and is at the same time, lush, volcanic, and coral reefed.

Tahitian cooking has been affected by European influences beginning with the arrival of one Captain Bligh (the captain of the *Bounty* whose crew mutinied), who showed up to collect breadfruit trees. An invasion of British missionaries followed, then the French took over, declaring Tahiti a French colony, as it remains today. But thankfully traditional cooking, *ma'a Tahiti*, still predominates. Similar to the Hawaiian *imu*, Tahitians often cook in the *ahima'a*, from *ahi* (fire) and *ma'a* (food), an oven dug in the earth where dinner is grilled, braised, or steamed. Chicken, fish, pork, banana, papaya, taro, sweet potatoes, and other vegetables, are placed in woven coconut-leaf mats or baskets on top of porous volcanic rocks that have been heated in wood fires. Rocks, mats, and foods are then buried cooked for three to four hours until the food is cooked.

Dozens of varieties of fish (including: snapper, rockfish, tuna, halibut, and kingfish), beef, goats, lamb, pigs, chickens, a huge variety of root and garden vegetables, and rice form the basis of Tahitian cooking. And everything, and I mean everything, is fresh. I don't recall even seeing a freezer in the homes I visited.

The use of fruits, coconut, vanilla, and an occasional glug of rum, in both entrées and desserts is also typical in Tahiti, and the combinations are mouthwatering. I'll never forget a tiny roadside pie stand where Bridgett and Victoire Tahiata served up by far the most incredible homemade dessert I have ever tasted. A still-warm-from-the-oven banana cream pie so good I instantly decided to forego lunch and proceeded instead to eat a whole pie by myself.

And it was a big pie!

VANILLA-COCONUT PRAWNS

Tahitians love vanilla. Families often spice their rum with vanilla, which they then use to flavor food and drinks. They use vanilla in rice puddings, crème brûlée, banana and fresh fruit dishes, and with mahimahi or chicken in a cream sauce, among many, many others. Bourbon vanilla beans are long and slender, with a very rich taste and smell, a thick and oily skin, an abundance of tiny seeds, a strong vanilla aroma, and a creamy, sweet taste, with vanilla overtones.

2   pounds large prawns, peeled and deveined

1   tablespoon olive oil

1/2 cup dark rum

1   whole vanilla bean, preferably Bourbon, sliced open (see Note)

1   cup heavy cream

3/4 cup coconut milk

     Salt

     Freshly ground black pepper

1/4 cup packaged unsweetened coconut flakes

     Steamed white rice

Prepare a charcoal or gas grill for indirect grilling (it is not necessary to use a drip pan for this recipe). Preheat to 375°F. Make sure the grill rack is clean and oil it thoroughly with nonstick cooking spray.

In a bowl, combine the prawns and olive oil, turning to coat each prawn with oil. Set aside.

In an ovenproof skillet on the grill, combine the rum and vanilla bean and bring to a boil over direct heat. Boil until the rum is reduced to 2 tablespoons, about 10 minutes. Add the cream and coconut milk. Remove the vanilla bean and scrape the seeds into the skillet (save the pod and add to your sugar bowl for vanilla sugar). Continue cooking, stirring often, until the mixture is reduced by half, about 10 to 12 minutes more. Season with salt and pepper and stir in the coconut flakes. Move the pan to the cool side of the grill.

Transfer the prawns to the hottest part of the grill and cook until pink all over, 2 to 3 minutes per side. As each prawn is cooked, use tongs to transfer it to the skillet on the cool side of the grill.

When all the prawns are in the skillet, move it over direct heat and cook for 1 minute longer, until heated through. Remove from the heat and serve immediately over the rice.

SERVES 4 TO 6

NOTE: Because of its high heliotropin content, Tahitian vanilla is believed to be excellent for calming the nerves. It's even suggested that you carry the beans with you so that when you feel anxious, nervous, or harried, you can sniff their fragrance. After a medical study at Memorial Sloan-Kettering Cancer Center, doctors there began using the beans to calm cancer patients undergoing MRIs.

BARBECUE-BRAISED FISH AND PLANTAINS WITH PAPAYA SALSA

Also called "cooking bananas," plantains are very popular in much of Asia and the Pacific Rim—I ate them just about every day when I visited Tahiti. They are served as a vegetable rather than as a fruit, since they can't be eaten raw unless they are very ripe, when they turn completely black. Since they are often available in the produce section of a typical grocery store, anyone can try these. They're easy to cook, offer up a nice taste and consistency, and are very healthy. If you can find it, try the Hua Moa variety, a short, fat plantain that originated in Tahiti. The name is Polynesian for "chicken egg." They are very sweet (for plantains) and caramelize well when cooked. If you want to be authentic, instead of using foil to wrap the fish, use 4 large oiled banana leaves instead.

- 4 large (8-ounce) cod or haddock fillets
- 1 onion, sliced
- 4 tablespoons freshly squeezed lemon juice
- 4 ripe plantains, peeled and sliced into 1-inch-thick rounds
- 4 tomatoes, coarsely chopped
- 2 large green chiles, such as poblano or Anaheim, stemmed, seeded, and diced
    Salt
    Freshly ground black pepper
- 1 cup unsweetened coconut cream (see Note page 202)

SALSA

- 1½ cups cubed papaya
- ½ cup chopped red bell pepper
- 2 tablespoons chopped cilantro
- 1 tablespoon lime juice
- 1 tablespoon honey
- ¼ teaspoon red pepper flakes
    Steamed white or brown rice, to serve

Preheat a charcoal or gas grill to 350°F. Spray four 12- by 12-inch sheets of heavy-duty aluminum foil with nonstick cooking spray or brush with oil.

Transfer 1 fillet to the center of each foil sheet. Evenly divide the onion, lemon juice, plantain, tomatoes, and chiles among the fillets. Season with salt and pepper. Bring the edges of the foil up around the fish to form a bowl shape. Pour ¼ cup of the coconut cream over each fillet. Securely seal the foil packages by double-folding the edges.

Transfer the foil packages to the grill rack over direct heat and cook for about 25 minutes, until the fish is cooked through and flakes easily with a fork.

To make the salsa, in a small bowl combine the papaya, bell pepper, cilantro, lime juice, honey, and pepper flakes. Stir well, cover, and set aside until ready to serve.

Place 1 foil package on each of 4 serving plates, being careful when opening as the steam can burn. Serve with the papaya salsa and rice.

SERVES 4

VATULELE RESORT PORK LOIN

Turmeric, a leafy plant in the ginger family, is mildly aromatic and has scents of orange or ginger. By itself, it has a pungent, bitter flavor. Ground turmeric comes from fingers that extend from the plant root. These are steamed, and then dried and ground. This dish had its origins at one of the most incredible resorts in the South Pacific. Vatulele Resort (on Fiji's Vatulele Island) is small, intimate, luxurious, and gorgeous, with world-class food served communally under the stars. Serve this with garlic mashed potatoes and grilled pineapple.

1 (4- to 5-pound) pork loin roast

5 cloves garlic, thinly sliced

$^3/_4$ cup dry white wine

$^1/_2$ cup soy sauce

1 large onion, chopped

$^1/_4$ cup freshly squeezed lemon juice

2 cups unsweetened coconut cream (see Note)

1 teaspoon ground fenugreek

3 tablespoons brown sugar

1 teaspoon turmeric

1 tablespoon dry mustard

1 tablespoon ground ginger

With a sharp knife, cut numerous slits in the roast and insert a thin slice of garlic in each slit.

In a resealable plastic bag, combine $^1/_2$ cup of the wine, soy sauce, onion, lemon juice, coconut cream, fenugreek, sugar, turmeric, mustard, and ginger. Add the pork and shake to coat; seal the bag, pressing out any air, and refrigerate for 8 to 12 hours.

Prepare a charcoal or gas grill for indirect grilling (it is not necessary to use a drip pan for this recipe). Preheat to 375°F.

Remove the pork from the bag and transfer it to a roasting pan, fat side up. Pour the marinade into a saucepan. Boil the marinade for 12 minutes; set aside to use for basting.

Transfer the roasting pan to the grill rack over indirect heat and cook, turning and basting several times, for $2^1/_2$ to 3 hours, until the internal temperature reaches 170°F. Generously baste during the last half-hour of cooking. Remove the meat from the pan and let it rest, covered with aluminum foil, for 10 minutes. Meanwhile, deglaze the pan with the remaining $^1/_4$ cup of wine and pour into a sauce boat for serving on the side.

SERVES 8 TO 10

NOTE: You can easily find canned coconut cream in the ethnic foods aisle of the grocery store. But if you want to make it yourself, grate the meat from 1 coconut, reserving the milk. Heat the meat and the milk in a saucepan until boiling. Remove the pan from the heat and let it cool. Press the coconut mixture through a double thickness of cheesecloth set over a bowl; discard the pulp. The resulting liquid is fresh, homemade coconut cream. It will keep for a week or so, in a sealed container in the refrigerator. One medium coconut makes about $^1/_2$ to $^3/_4$ cup cream.

GRILLED EGGPLANT IN LEMON-COCONUT CREAM

Tahitian coconuts are very famous worldwide, but not, surprisingly, for cooking only. Tahitian coconut oil is famed for its cosmetic benefits and is said to be the closest oil to natural skin oils. But coconut cream is used in dozens of Tahitian recipes to cook everything from chicken and pork to vegetables and fruits. This dish also works well with carrots, turnips, and other firm-fleshed vegetables. First, blanch carrot or turnip strips for 1 minute in boiling, salted water, then proceed as you would for the eggplant. If substituting zucchini for the eggplant, follow the recipe exactly.

4　eggplants, cut lengthwise into ¼-inch-thick strips

1　tablespoon olive oil

2　tablespoons freshly squeezed lemon juice

1　cup coconut cream

6　green onions, finely chopped

2　tomatoes, diced

1　green jalapeño, stemmed, seeded, and minced

1　teaspoon grated lemon zest

　　Salt

　　Freshly ground black pepper

Preheat a charcoal or gas grill to 375°F. Make sure the grill rack is clean and oil it thoroughly with nonstick cooking spray.

Place the eggplant on the prepared grill rack over direct heat and cook, brushing once per side with oil, for 4 to 5 minutes per side, until nicely marked and beginning to char. Meanwhile, in a mixing bowl, combine the lemon juice, coconut cream, green onion, tomato, chile, and zest, and season with salt and pepper. Mix well.

Transfer the eggplant to a serving dish, pour the coconut cream mixture over the top, and serve immediately.

SERVES 4

FIJIAN SOY-COCONUT CHICKEN THIGHS

Similar to a Hawaiian imu *feast, Fijians have their* lovo. *Food is wrapped in and cooked under native leaves and buried in a fire pit. Dishes like corned beef, whole fish, pork, seafood, chicken, taro, sweet potatoes, cassava, and even breads are cooked in this underground oven. This dish was part of the banquet prepared for my wife, Kate, and me on the occasion of our tenth wedding anniversary at Vatulele Resort on Vatulele Island. Serve this with jasmine rice, grilled sweet potatoes, and grilled corn on the cob.*

¾　cup soy sauce

¾　cup mirin or sherry

¼　cup coconut cream

2　tablespoons light sesame oil

3　tablespoons brown sugar

2　tablespoons freshly grated ginger

2　teaspoons ground cardamom

2　cloves garlic, chopped

3　green or red bell peppers, stemmed, seeded, and chopped

12　chicken thighs (see Note)

In a blender or food processor, combine the soy sauce, mirin, coconut cream, sesame oil, sugar, ginger, cardamom, garlic, and peppers, and process until smooth.

Place the chicken thighs in large resealable plastic bag and pour in the marinade. Transfer to the refrigerator for 2 to 4 hours, turning the bag once every hour.

Preheat a charcoal or gas grill to 375°F. Make sure the grill rack is clean and oil it thoroughly with nonstick cooking spray.

Remove the chicken from the marinade and wipe off the excess marinade. Pour the remaining marinade into a saucepan and boil for 12 minutes to use for basting.

Transfer the chicken pieces to the prepared grill rack over direct heat. Cook for 20 to 30 minutes, turning and basting often, until the thighs are browned and the internal temperature at the thickest part reaches 170°F. Serve immediately.

SERVES 4 TO 6

NOTE: If you wish, you can use turkey thighs and legs in this dish, increasing the cooking time by about 10 minutes.

PINEAPPLE AND SWEET POTATO BAKE

A popular dish at a Fijian lovo banquet, where food is cooked over burning coconut shells and heated stones, this mixture of ingredients may sound surprising but the tastes blend together perfectly.

This dish goes well with barbecued ham, grilled fish, roast chicken—or, if you go whole hog, a barbecue roasted suckling pig.

2	tablespoons butter
2	tablespoons flour
1¹⁄₄	cups milk
¹⁄₄	cup grated extra-sharp Cheddar cheese
¹⁄₈	teaspoon dry mustard
¹⁄₈	teaspoon cayenne
	Salt
	Freshly ground black pepper
2	medium sweet potatoes, peeled and cut into 1-inch-thick rounds
1	large fresh pineapple, peeled, cored, and cut into ¹⁄₄-inch rounds (see Note)
5	tablespoons freshly grated coconut or unsweetened packaged coconut
4	tablespoons minced green onions, green and white parts
1	tablespoon minced fresh parsley

In a saucepan over low heat melt the butter, but don't allow it to brown. Add the flour and stir until smooth. Cook over low heat for 2 to 3 minutes, stirring constantly, until it just begins to brown. Remove from the heat and add the milk, little by little, whisking after each addition to prevent lumps from forming. Return to the burner and increase the heat to high. Bring to a boil, whisking constantly until thickened, about 4 to 6 minutes. Remove from the heat and stir in the cheese, mustard, and cayenne, and season with salt and pepper. Stir until the cheese has melted. Set aside and keep warm.

Prepare a charcoal or gas grill for indirect grilling (it is not necessary to use a drip pan for this recipe). Preheat to 375°F. Grease a large cast-iron skillet.

Arrange the sweet potato, pineapple, 4 tablespoons of the coconut, and the green onion in 3 layers in the skillet, seasoning each layer with salt and pepper; top with the cheese sauce.

Transfer the skillet to the grill rack over indirect heat and cook, covered, for about 30 minutes, until potatoes are easily pierced with a fork. Remove from the barbecue and serve sprinkled with fresh parsley and the remaining coconut.

SERVES 4 TO 6

NOTE: Pineapples, like melons, do not have any starch reserves, so they do not get sweeter after they are picked. They must be harvested after they begin to ripen. Store at room temperature for 1 or 2 days before serving to allow the pineapple to become softer.

BARBECUED ORANGES

You can substitute just about any fruit in this refreshing dessert, which was inspired by one I was served at a party on Yasawa-I-Rawa Island in Fiji. Try apples, tangerines, bananas, pineapple, plums, pears, peaches, mandarin and blood oranges, tangelos, and even grapefruit (increase sugar by a third).

8	large oranges (see Note)
3/4	teaspoon cinnamon
1/2	teaspoon nutmeg
	Pinch of ground cloves
3/4	stick unsalted butter
6	tablespoons dark rum
6	tablespoons dark brown sugar
1	teaspoon confectioners' sugar

Preheat a charcoal or gas grill to 400°F.

Peel the oranges and cut into 1/2-inch-thick slices, reserving any juice. Transfer the orange slices and any juice to 6 large squares of heavy-duty aluminum foil and sprinkle with cinnamon, nutmeg, and cloves. Dot with the butter, and add 1 tablespoon of rum and 1 tablespoon of brown sugar to each package. Securely seal the foil package by double-folding the edges.

Place the foil packages in the center of the grill, close the lid, and cook for 15 to 20 minutes, until heated through.

Open the foil package, sprinkle with confectioners' sugar, and serve the foil packages right at the table, or pour the contents into bowls for a more refined presentation.

SERVES 6

NOTE: Oranges turn orange after being in cold temperatures. In the tropics, they stay a green to greenish-yellow color. Choose oranges that are firm, fragrant, and heavy for size. Avoid fruit with blemishes and shriveled or moldy spots. If you store at room temperature, use within a week. Storing them in the fridge helps them last for up to two weeks.

THAILAND

The Fork, the Spoon, the Spice

With China to the north and Malaysia to the south, you would rightly expect both countries to have made significant contributions to Thai cuisine. Chinese immigrants brought stir-frying and noodles; Muslim merchants from Malaysia contributed curries. In addition, British colonials brought their stews, and Portuguese traders introduced the use of eggs in sweet Thai desserts. But, perhaps surprisingly, the most pervasive of the Western influences does not involve ingredients or cooking techniques but eating utensils.

The story goes that King Chulalongkorn (Rama V), who was the first Siamese monarch to visit Europe and who is largely credited with modernizing Thailand in the late 1890s, ordered the royal kitchen to prepare a multi-course meal to be served with Western-style cutlery. To this repast, he invited a British diplomat for the express propose of observing the Englishman "eat as they do in Europe" so that he could evaluate Western table manners and implements.

His majesty found no use for the knife, as most ingredients were already bite-sized, but found the fork and spoon handy, and so he initiated their use throughout the country. Nowadays the fork is used in the left hand to push food onto the spoon (in the right hand), which then goes to the mouth. (The fork never does.)

Chopsticks are used for noodle dishes, but a spoon is usually provided to help. And when meat isn't prepared in bite-size pieces, Thais use a fork to hold the meat and a spoon (in the dominant hand) to push against the fibers in order to cut it, as sawing with a knife is thought to be too barbaric. So the next time you go to a Thai restaurant, ask for chopsticks if you've ordered noodles, but ask for a spoon if you're having a rice dish.

Thai cuisine can be summed up in five words: spicy, sour, sweet, salty, and bitter. Northern Thai dishes include vegetables, steamed sticky rice, chile sauces (which come in many varieties), chile soups (*gang*); and steamed, stir-fried, and grilled sausage, beef, pork, chicken, and duck. The northern Thais have a penchant for medium-spicy flavors with a touch of salt, almost to the exclusion of sweet and sour tastes. The famous regional dish of the Northeast is (*gai yang*, grilled chicken with sticky rice, eaten with one's hands. Also green papaya salad (*som tam*). These two dishes are so beloved, there are folk songs about them that everyone knows.

Regional dishes from central Thailand almost always include rice paired with vegetables, *nam prik* (chile sauce), *platoo* (herring), or perhaps a Thai-style omelette, grilled beef, or roasted pork.

Except for the Muslim curries, which use lots of cardamom and cinnamon, southern curries tend to be intensely hot, pungent, and spicy. Thailand's extensive southern coastline makes seafood a staple, and when it's tossed on a charcoal grill fueled by coconut husks and served with hot-and-sour chile dipping sauces, it's exceptional.

Many spices and herbs are used in Thai cooking: hot chile peppers, lemongrass, coconut milk, tamarind, galangal, cilantro, basil, palm sugar, garlic, coriander, ginger, onions, turmeric, and cumin. The hottest dishes are usually accompanied, and cooled, by steamed rice, mild noodle dishes, sweet Thai teas and coffees, sweet desserts, and fruits.

To sum up the meaning of Thai cuisine and hospitality, I offer a very brief lesson in the language: the phrase you will often be greeted with is "*Gin khao reu yung*?", which means "Have you eaten rice yet?" My kind of country!

THAI CHICKEN WINGS

This recipe calls for both cilantro and coriander, which are different parts of the same plant, which is a member of the carrot family. The stem and leaves are called cilantro, while the seeds, considered a spice, are called coriander. Coriander was mentioned in the Bible, and the seeds have been found at archeological sites dating back to 5000 BC.

1/2   cup honey

5   tablespoons soy sauce, preferably tamari

3   tablespoons fish sauce

Juice of 2 limes

Grated zest of 2 limes

1   tablespoon ground dried chile

1   tablespoon grated fresh ginger

1   teaspoon Sambal red chile sauce

Pinch of sea salt

2   cloves garlic, minced

1 1/2   teaspoons ground coriander

24   whole chicken wings (about 2 pounds)

1/2   cup coarsely chopped cilantro

Prepare a charcoal or gas grill for indirect grilling, placing a drip pan under the cool side of the grill rack (see page 3). Preheat to 375°F. Make sure the grill rack is clean and oil it thoroughly with nonstick cooking spray.

In a bowl, combine the honey, soy sauce, fish sauce, lime juice and zest, ground chile, ginger, chile sauce, salt, garlic, and coriander, stirring to mix. Place the wings in a resealable plastic bag and add the marinade. Seal the bag, pressing out the air, and refrigerate 4 to 8 hours.

Drain the wings, set aside, and let them come to room temperature. Meanwhile, pour the marinade into a saucepan and boil for 12 minutes to use as a baste.

Transfer the wings to the prepared grill rack over indirect heat. Cook, basting once or twice per side and turning often, until the wings appear sticky but the sauce isn't burning, 20 to 30 minutes. (A thermometer inserted in the wing should read 160°F.)

Serve immediately garnished with the cilantro.

SERVES 6 TO 8 AS AN APPETIZER

SWEET CHILE AND LEMONGRASS SHRIMP WITH PAPAYA-MANGO SALSA

Lemongrass, a native of India, is widely used in both Thai and Vietnamese cooking. It's loaded with citral, the active ingredient in lemon peel. Select fresh stalks that don't look dry or brittle, and store in the refrigerator wrapped in a paper towel, in a tightly sealed plastic bag for up to three weeks.

1	cup diced fresh papaya
1	firm mango, diced
$^1/_2$	cup diced red bell pepper
$^1/_2$	cup diced red onion
4	tablespoons chopped cilantro
4	teaspoons freshly squeezed lime juice
2	tablespoons honey
4	tablespoons olive oil
	Salt
	Freshly ground black pepper
1	clove garlic, minced
2	teaspoons minced lemongrass (white part only)
2	tablespoons chopped fresh basil
2	tablespoons sweet Thai chile sauce
1	pound (about 20 to 24) large shrimp, shelled and deveined

In a large bowl, combine the papaya, mango, red pepper, onion, 2 tablespoons of the cilantro, 2 teaspoons of the lime juice, 1 tablespoon of the honey, and 2 tablespoons of the oil, and season with salt and pepper. Stir, cover, and set aside.

In a resealable plastic bag combine the garlic, the remaining 1 tablespoon of honey, the remaining 2 teaspoons of lime juice, 2 tablespoons of the oil, 2 tablespoons of the cilantro, the basil, and chile sauce. Add the shrimp, shaking to coat, and refrigerate for 1 to $1^1/_2$ hours.

Soak bamboo skewers in water to cover for about 1 hour. Preheat a charcoal or gas grill to 375°F. Make sure the grill rack is clean and oil it thoroughly with nonstick cooking spray.

Drain the shrimp, discarding the marinade. Thread the shrimp, lengthwise, on the skewers. Transfer the skewers to the grill and cook for 2 to 3 minutes per side, until the shrimp are pink and firm to the touch.

Serve on a warm platter with the salsa on the side, and lots of chilled adult malt beverages.

SERVES 4 TO 6 AS AN APPETIZER

NOTE: For a bit of color, alternate the shrimp with mango, papaya, pineapple, or other fruit. Before serving the skewers, drizzle the fruit with honey.

GRILLED KOH SAMUI TILAPIA

Tilapia cultivation was first described five thousand years ago in Egyptian hieroglyphs. Hardy and fast-growing, tilapia are now widely cultured in other parts of Africa, as well as in Asia and South America. Serve this dish with Thai jasmine rice (see Note).

8   to 10 cloves garlic, minced

1/3   cup coarsely chopped cilantro leaves

1/4   cup olive oil

1/4   cup freshly squeezed lime juice

2 1/2 tablespoons fish sauce

2   teaspoons white pepper

2   teaspoons brown sugar

1   teaspoon ground coriander

1   teaspoon sea salt

4   (5- to 6-ounce) tilapia fillets, skin on

In a blender or food processor, combine the garlic, cilantro, oil, lime juice, fish sauce, pepper, sugar, coriander, and salt, and process until a thick paste forms.

Place the tilapia in a shallow dish and coat the flesh side with the garlic paste. Cover the dish with plastic wrap and transfer to the refrigerator for 1 to 2 hours.

Prepare a charcoal or gas grill for indirect grilling (it is not necessary to use a drip pan for this recipe). Preheat to 375°F. Make sure the grill rack is clean and oil it thoroughly with nonstick cooking spray.

Transfer the fillets paste side up to the prepared grill rack over indirect heat. Cook, without turning, for 10 to 13 minutes, until the fish flakes easily with a fork but is still moist in the center. Place a sheet of heavy-duty aluminum foil, shiny side down, over the fish and cook for 5 minutes longer.

Serve immediately.

SERVES 4 TO 6

NOTE: Steam fragrant rices like Thai jasmine rice, instead of boiling, as the steam fluffs up the rice and retains its full fragrance and flavor.

BEAU THAI CHILE PORK CHOPS

If you ever have a chance to visit Thailand, make sure you take a couple of days to visit Chiang Mai, where you must take a one-day class at the world-famous Chiang Mai Cookery School. Opened in 1993, the school has taught more than 100,000 people the art of preparing Thai soups, curries, stir-fries, carved vegetables, noodles, fish cakes, and rice dishes. This pork dish was created in one of the classes. Serve this dish with stir-fried zucchini, tiny Thai eggplant, baby corn, and rice noodles. Powdered lemongrass is available online.

4   (8- to 10-ounce) pork chops, about 1 1/2 inches thick

1   teaspoon grated lemon zest

4   cloves garlic, crushed

1/2   cup grated fresh ginger

1   tablespoon chili powder

1/2   teaspoon powdered lemongrass

1/4   teaspoon cinnamon

1/2   teaspoon ground coriander

1/2   teaspoon freshly ground black pepper

1/2   teaspoon crushed red pepper flakes

3   tablespoons water

Rinse the pork chops and pat very dry. Set aside.

In a blender, combine the zest, garlic, ginger, chili powder, lemongrass, cinnamon, coriander, black pepper, red pepper flakes, and water and blend to a smooth paste. Spread about 1 teaspoon of the paste on each side of the chops. Cover refrigerate for 8 to 24 hours.

Preheat a charcoal or gas grill to 375°F. Make sure the grill rack is clean and oil it thoroughly with nonstick cooking spray.

Remove the chops from the refrigerator and bring to room temperature. Transfer the chips to the prepared grill rack over direct heat and cook for 7 to 8 minutes per side, or until they are barely white-pink in the center and the internal temperature reaches 155°F.

SERVES 4

FRAGRANT GRILLED PORK

This recipe is from Chef Jet Tilla, owner of the Royal Thai Cuisine Restaurants and Bangkok Market. It is a traditional northern and eastern Thai dish. The grill really brings an amazing caramel flavor out of the soy and molasses, and the cilantro provides a bite that balances the flavorful, fatty quality of the pork. Serve with sticky rice and stir-fried vegetables.

- 1 (2-pound) pork shoulder or pork butt
- 4 cloves garlic, minced
- 2 tablespoons minced fresh cilantro
- 1 teaspoon white pepper
- 2 tablespoons fish sauce
- 1 tablespoon Chinese light soy sauce
- 2 tablespoons dark molasses
- 1 tablespoon brown sugar

Using a very sharp knife, cut the pork into strips about 3 inches wide. Don't trim too much fat off, but it's okay to trim any silver skin away.

In a food processor, combine the garlic, cilantro, pepper, fish sauce, soy sauce, molasses, and sugar, and pulse until slightly mealy. You don't want the garlic and herbs to disappear into the liquid; you want to see some small pieces of each.

In a resealable bag, pour the marinade over the pork and massage well until the pork is completely coated. Place the bag in a wide shallow pan and marinate in the refrigerator for 4 hours or overnight.

Preheat a charcoal or gas grill to 375°F. Make sure the grill rack is clean and oil it thoroughly with nonstick cooking spray.

When ready to grill, remove the pork from the marinade and pat the slices dry. Discard the marinade. Transfer the pork to the prepared grill rack over direct heat and grill until just cooked through, about 2 minutes per side. Be careful not to overcook, as the pork can easily become dry. Cut into slices against the grain and serve.

SERVES 4 TO 6

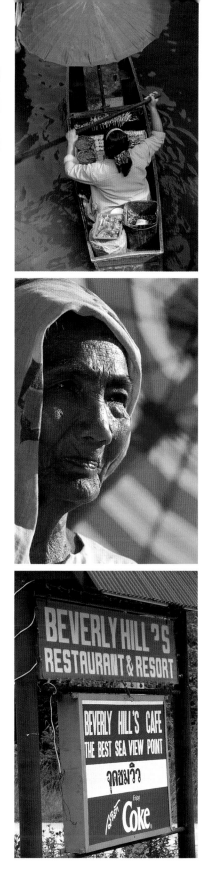

STREET VENDOR NOODLES

A close relative of ginger, galangal is an important ingredient in Thai cooking. The flavor is similar to ginger, but is more flowery and intense, and combines well with ginger and lemongrass. Ground galangal is easier to work with than whole galangal. This recipe is written for the stove top, but you can also make it on the grill over a hot (450°F) flame, or on your grill's side burner.

4 tablespoons oyster sauce

1 tablespoon fish sauce

1 tablespoon light soy sauce

1 teaspoon dark soy sauce

2 heaping teaspoons cornstarch, dissolved in 1/2 cup water

2 to 3 tablespoons peanut oil

3 cloves garlic, minced

1 (2-inch) piece galangal, grated, or 1 teaspoon powdered

1 small red Thai chile, diced

1 cup sliced shiitake mushrooms, caps only

3 boneless chicken breasts, cut into 1-inch cubes

4 green onions, green and white parts, cut into 1-inch lengths

1 cup small broccoli florets

1 package fresh Asian wheat noodles (see Note)

2 cups fresh mung bean sprouts

1/2 cup chopped fresh cilantro

1/2 cup chopped fresh basil

2 limes, quartered

In a small bowl combine the oyster sauce, fish sauce, and light and dark soy sauces. Add the cornstarch-water mixture, stir well, and set aside.

In a large wok or sauté pan over high heat, heat the oil until a drop of water sprinkled in the wok sizzles. Add the garlic, galangal, chile, mushrooms, chicken, and cornstarch-soy sauce mixture. Stir-fry until the chicken is cooked through, about 5 to 6 minutes. Add the green onion and broccoli, and continue to cook 1 to 2 minutes longer, adding a teaspoon of water to the pan if it becomes too dry, until the vegetables are just becoming soft.

Add the reserved sauce, then the noodles, tossing the noodles with a large spatula or wooden spoon. Continue cooking, tossing the noodles until the sauce is evenly distributed and the noodles are soft, 3 to 4 minutes.

Add the bean sprouts, stir once, then remove the wok from the heat immediately.

Transfer to a large warmed platter, sprinkle with the cilantro and basil , and serve with the limes on the side.

SERVES 4 TO 6

NOTE: I recommend using Chinese long wheat noodles in this dish. These round or flat noodles are made with wheat, water, and salt, and are available in various thicknesses, either dried or fresh. This recipe calls for the fresh variety, which usually can only be found in Asian markets.

PINEAPPLE FRIED RICE

Usually served in a carved-out pineapple, this is a signature rice dish of Thailand, where the average person eats 300 pounds of rice a year. In America, we consume a paltry 20 pounds. There are more than 80,000 varieties of rice, and it is grown on every continent except Antarctica. Fifty percent of all the world's rice is eaten within eight miles of where it is grown. This is essentially a stir-fry, and can be made either on the stove top, over a hot (450°F) flame in your grill, or on your grill's side burner.

1	whole pineapple
4	tablespoons peanut oil
3	cups cooked rice (best if 2 to 3 days old)
2	shallots, thinly sliced
3	cloves garlic, minced
1	green jalapeño chile, minced
3	tablespoons water
3	tablespoons chicken or vegetable stock
1	egg
2	tablespoons fish sauce or soy sauce
2	teaspoons Thai curry powder
1/2	cup frozen peas
1	small carrot, grated
1/2	cup chopped raw, unsalted cashews
1/2	cup golden raisins
	Salt
	Freshly ground black pepper
3	green onions, white and green parts, minced, for garnish
1/3	cup minced cilantro or mint, for garnish

To create a pineapple "bowl," slice off about one-quarter of the pineapple, lengthwise, keeping the leaves intact. Carve out the flesh with a melon baller or grapefruit knife. Cover the hollowed-out pineapple with plastic and refrigerate. Cut the pineapple flesh into enough bite-size pieces to make 1 cup and set aside; reserve the rest for another use.

Mix 1 tablespoon of the oil with the rice, breaking up any chunks so the rice grains are mostly separated. Set aside.

Place a wok or large nonstick skillet over high heat and add the remaining 3 tablespoons of the oil. Add the shallots, garlic, and chile, and stir-fry until fragrant, 2 to 3 minutes. Add the water and stock, stir, then add the egg, stirring quickly to mix it into the vegetables. Then add the fish sauce, curry powder, peas, carrot, and cashews, and cook for 2 minutes. Add the rice, pineapple, and raisins, stirring to combine. Cook until the rice pops, (you'll hear and see this), 1 to 3 minutes longer. Season to taste with fish sauce, salt, and pepper.

To serve, mound the rice into the hollowed-out pineapple. Top with green onions and cilantro.

SERVES 4 TO 6

GRILLED RED VEGETABLE CURRY

Red curry paste, which is used widely in many Thai dishes such as tod mun *and satay, is a mixture of dried chile pepper, shallot, garlic, galangal, lemongrass, cilantro root, peppercorn, coriander, salt, shrimp paste, and kaffir lime zest.*

- 1/4 cup plus 2 tablespoons peanut or sesame oil
- 6 cloves garlic, chopped
- 1 tablespoon sea salt
- 1 tablespoon red curry paste
- 2 teaspoons dark soy sauce
- 1 teaspoon fish sauce
- 2 tablespoons freshly squeezed lime or lemon juice
- 1 1/4 cup chopped fresh cilantro, loosely packed, including stems
- 1 eggplant, cut lengthwise 1/2-inch spears
- 2 red bell peppers, seeded and cut lengthwise into 1/2-inch strips
- 2 yellow or orange bell peppers, seeded and cut lengthwise into 1/2-inch strips
- 1 bunch green onions, white and pale green parts only
- 1 pint cherry tomatoes

In a glass or nonreactive metal bowl, combine the 1/4 cup oil, the garlic, salt, red curry paste, soy sauce, fish sauce, lime juice, and 1 cup of the cilantro. Let stand for at least 1 hour, but preferably 2 to 3 hours, in the refrigerator.

Preheat a charcoal or gas grill to 375°F.

In a large bowl, combine the eggplant, peppers, green onions, tomatoes, and 2 tablespoons oil, stirring to coat evenly. Transfer the vegetables to the barbecue and cook over direct heat, turning several times with long tongs, until softened and lightly browned, 10 to 15 minutes.

Transfer the vegetables to a heated platter, sprinkle with the remaining cilantro, and serve.

SERVES 4 TO 6

NOTE: Using a grilling basket to cook vegetables means nothing slips through onto the flames, and the vegetables are easy to turn so they cook evenly.

TURKEY

A Gastronomic Magic Carpet Ride (along with a Kebab or Two or Three)

The name of the country we know as Turkey should be spelled "Turkiye" and pronounced "Turk-ee-ya!" It seems some Latin cartographer wrote "Turchich" on his map and this was later changed to "Turkey."

When my television crew and I visited Turkey, we were in Istanbul, a center of world trade since the Byzantine era, and today as cosmopolitan as any city on earth. But despite its worldliness, Turkish cuisine stresses pure, unadulterated foods that are lightly spiced simply to bring out certain flavors.

Turkish breakfasts include olives, bread, and butter and jam—and tea. Turks drink tea like Americans drink coffee, reserving coffee for after dinner. Lunch is often at a *hazir yemik*, or "fast food" place, where thin slices of lamb or beef cooked over coals are inserted into fresh flatbread and eaten like a sandwich.

Dinner usually begins with a large assortment of *mezes* (appetizers), small shared dishes made with vegetables (sometimes including rice), drizzled with olive oil, and served at room temperature. Warm appetizers usually feature lamb, beef, chicken, or fish. Because so much attention is paid to the starters, main dishes are often portioned much smaller than you'd expect. And there is always room for dessert, especially Turkish desserts. More on these later. (And, by the way, the breads here—including the everyday *pide*, or flatbread, and *ekmek*, or white bread—are as good as any I've had anywhere.

Everywhere there are the kebabs (also known as *kebaps*, *kepabi*, and *kibobs*). Kebab means "meat on a skewer," and Istanbulis enjoy them in staggering varieties. They're made with beef, chicken, vegetables, and especially lamb. There must be dozens of lamb kebabs, including *bahçivan* (lamb shoulder kebabs combined with chopped onions and tomato paste); *kofte* (minced lamb meatballs with herbs, often parsley and mint); *orman* (lamb on the bone, cut into large pieces, and combined with carrots, potatoes, and peas); *tandir* (lamb pieces baked in an oven called a *tandir* and served with bread and raw onions); and on and on and on.

Mahmet, a professor at a local university and one of our guides, took us to a neighborhood restaurant for a typical Turkish lunch. Tucked away on a back street, Urfali Haci Usta restaurant gave us a memorable dining experience, starting with a tour of the kitchen where the staff were assembling kebabs, baking flatbread, chopping vegetables, and preparing a special dessert. We adjourned to the back room, which was festooned with birdcages housing singing canaries. (Locals are encouraged to bring their birds to lunch.)

As soon as we were seated, the table was quickly covered with a variety of dishes, including julienned cucumber, chopped tomatoes and cucumber, raw spinach leaves, pickled beet slices, several bowls of a tangy sauce, a plate of raw ground beef infused with onion and lots of paprika, and a plate of fresh lettuce leaves to wrap our selections. There was a Turkish "pizza" (a small flatbread covered with a tomato-based spicy paste), and two large loaves of the freshly baked round flatbread.

After devouring our *mezes*, we gasped as a huge tray arrived crammed with grilled chicken wings, more pizzas, and an array of kebabs, including stuffed eggplant, red peppers, lamb meatballs, green peppers, ground beef in a long sausage form, lamb, chicken livers, and marinated beef cubes. Mahmet showed us the proper form for filling the flatbreads with the kebab combos and fresh condiments, topping them each with a dollop of tangy sauce, and rolling them up like a burrito or wrap.

Most Turkish meals are followed by local fresh fruit, but you cannot visit Turkiye without sampling the baklava, a confection of paper-thin pastry sheets that are brushed with butter and folded, layered, or rolled after being filled with ground pistachios, walnuts, or heavy cream, then baked, and finally topped with sugar or honey syrup. Whether you select a "sultan," a "nightingale's nest" or a "twisted turban" will depend on the type of nut filling, their size and shape, how they are folded and formed, and the moistness or dryness of the pastry. They are all marvelous.

However, our lunch concluded with the aforementioned special dessert. It was called *knife* (pronounced nee-*fay*) and was made with (no kidding) angel hair pasta, butter, salt-free feta, pistachios, and cream. It was baked in what looked like a waffle iron (minus the grid) and served piping hot. The taste was extraordinary—light and refreshing and unlike any dessert I had ever had.

I left the restaurant with difficulty (barely made it to the car), stuffed like . . . you know I'm going to say it, don't you? . . . a turkey!

GRILLED BLOOD ORANGE FISH

Maltese, or blood oranges, have a flavor that is an interesting mix of oranges, raspberries, and concord grapes. Their pulp ranges from red to reddish purple, and the rind from orange to an orange deeply suffused with red. Blood oranges are cultivated in Malta, southern Europe, North Africa, and, recently, in California.

Juice of 1 large navel orange

Juice of 1 large lemon

1 teaspoon dried savory

Salt

Freshly ground black pepper

2 tablespoons olive oil

4 onions, halved lengthwise

1 tablespoon sesame oil

1 (3- to 4-pound) whole bluefish, mackerel, or bream

2 large blood oranges, cut crosswise into $^{1}/_{4}$-inch-thick slices

In a small bowl, combine the orange and lemon juices with the savory and season with salt and pepper. Add the 1 tablespoon of the olive oil, and whisk into mixture. Set aside.

Cut the onion halves into $^{1}/_{4}$-inch-thick slices. Transfer half the onions to a shallow roasting pan, setting aside the rest.

Preheat a charcoal or gas grill to 375°F. Make sure the grill rack is clean and oil it thoroughly with nonstick cooking spray.

In a small bowl, combine the remaining 1 tablespoon of olive oil and the sesame oil. Set aside. Place the fish on a work surface and place a layer of onion and a layer of blood orange in the body cavity of the fish. Using kitchen string and a darning needle, sew the cavity closed, or tie the fish closed with kitchen twine. Brush the fish with the oil mixture and season with salt and pepper.

Transfer the fish to the prepared grill rack over direct heat and cook for about 5 minutes per side, until it flakes when tested with a fork. Transfer the fish to the roasting pan, on top of the onions. Alternate the remaining onion and blood orange slices to cover the fish, reserving a few slices for the garnish. Pour the reserved sauce over the fish. Place the roasting pan on the barbecue for 5 minutes, until the sauce bubbles.

Remove fish, oranges, and onions to a serving platter, and garnish each serving of fish with a blood orange slice and an onion slice.

SERVES 4

BEEF KEBAB

If you want to grill more vegetables along with the peppers and tomatoes here, try zucchini, cauliflower, broccoli, carrots, and tiny new potatoes. Parboil the denser vegetables and cook them on skewers.

- 1 pound ground beef or lamb
- 1 onion, chopped
- 1 teaspoon crushed red pepper flakes
- 1 teaspoon ground cayenne
- 1 teaspoon ground cumin
- 1 tablespoon dried oregano
- 4 large tomatoes, halved lengthwise
- 4 green bell peppers, seeded and halved lengthwise
- Olive oil
- Salt
- Freshly ground black pepper
- Pita bread, for serving
- 1/2 cup chopped fresh parsley, for garnish

In a large mixing bowl, combine the beef, onion, pepper flakes, ground cayenne, cumin, and oregano, and mix well. Cover the bowl with plastic wrap and refrigerate for 8 to 10 hours.

Soak wood or bamboo skewers in water to cover for an hour. Preheat a charcoal or gas barbecue to 375°F.

Shape the meat mixture into 8 to 10 oblong pieces, about 1 inch thick by 4 inches long; chill for 20 minutes. Thread the meat lengthwise onto the skewers. Transfer to the grill and cook over indirect heat, 4 to 5 minutes per side for medium-rare. If you have a large grill you can cook the vegetables at the same time, otherwise do the meat first and keep it wrapped in foil.

Brush the tomatoes and peppers with olive oil and season with salt and pepper. Place the vegetables on the grill rack over direct heat. Cook, turning once, until the tomatoes are bubbling and start to get charred, about 10 minutes. Meanwhile, warm the pitas on the cool side of the grill, turning them frequently; do not burn them.

Remove the meat from the foil, sprinkle with parsley, and serve with the vegetables and warmed pita bread as an appetizer.

SERVE 4 TO 6 AS AN APPETIZER

TURKISH TURKEY WITH PISTACHIO STUFFING

To keep them at their freshest, store pistachios in a refrigerated, air-tight container, or keep them in the freezer for long-term storage. To restore crispness to pistachios that have lost their crunch, toast them at 200°F, for 10 to 15 minutes.

4	tablespoons plus 4 teaspoons unsalted butter
$1/2$	cup chopped pistachio nuts
1	cup chopped leek, white and pale green parts
2	teaspoons cinnamon
$1/4$	teaspoon ground cloves
2	cups cooked basmati rice
$1/4$	cup turkey or chicken stock
1	plum tomato, chopped
$1/2$	cup fresh mint leaves, finely chopped
$1/2$	teaspoon ground allspice
$1/2$	teaspoon dried oregano
$1/2$	teaspoon ground cumin
$1/2$	teaspoon garlic powder
	Salt
	Freshly ground black pepper
1	(10- to 12-pound) turkey
3	tablespoons unsalted butter, melted, for basting
2	cups water
4	tablespoons flour

In a small skillet over medium heat, melt 2 teaspoons of the butter; add the pistachios and cook until just beginning to brown, about 4 minutes. Remove with a slotted spoon and drain on paper towels.

In a large skillet over medium heat, melt the remaining 2 teaspoons of butter; add the leek, cinnamon, and cloves, and cook for about 7 minutes, until the leek is just soft. Add the rice, stir in the stock, tomato, mint, allspice, oregano, cumin, and garlic, and season with salt and pepper; decrease heat to low and cook, stirring often, for 10 minutes over low heat. Stir in the pistachios. Remove from the heat and let stand for 15 minutes.

Prepare a charcoal or gas grill for indirect cooking (it is not necessary to use a drip pan for this recipe). Preheat to 325°F.

Rinse the turkey under cold water and pat dry. Set the turkey on a rack in a roasting pan. Loosely pack the body cavity with the rice mixture. Use a skewer to secure the skin over the stuffing. Baste the top and sides of the turkey with the 3 tablespoons of melted butter. Season with salt and pepper and pour a half-inch of water into the bottom of the roasting pan.

Transfer the roasting pan to the grill rack over indirect heat. Lower the barbecue lid and

cook, basting occasionally, until the internal temperature of the breast reaches 165°F, about $3^1/4$ hours for a 10-pound turkey and $3^3/4$ hours for a 12-pound turkey.

Remove the turkey from the barbecue; transfer the stuffing to a serving bowl. Cover the turkey with foil and let rest for 15 minutes before carving.

Meanwhile, drain the fat off the pan drippings. Transfer 2 cups of the drippings to a saucepan over medium heat. Add the flour and the 4 tablespoons of remaining butter, whisking until smooth. Cook, whisking constantly, for 3 to 4 minutes, until the gravy is smooth and coats the back of a spoon.

Serve the turkey with the stuffing and gravy on the side.

SERVE 6 TO 8

GRILLED CHICKEN WITH YOGURT AND POMEGRANATE

Ayran, a yogurt-based drink, is so popular in Turkey that even international fast food chains feature it in their standard local menu. If you can find it, use it in this recipe; if not, plain yogurt will do just fine. Pomegranate syrup or molasses is usually made from a tart variety of pomegranate not grown in the U.S. Typically it's as thick and brown as molasses, and has a distinct sweet-sour flavor. It's available at Middle-Eastern grocery stores.

- 2 tablespoons cumin seeds
- 1 small onion, coarsely chopped
- 5 cloves garlic, finely minced
- 1 tablespoon paprika
  Juice of 1 lemon
- 1 cup ayran or plain yogurt
- 1/2 cup pomegranate seeds
- 2 (3- to 4-pound) chickens, halved, backs removed
  Salt
  Freshly ground black pepper
- 1/4 cup pomegranate molasses

In a small skillet over medium heat, toast the cumin seeds until fragrant and starting to pop, about 5 to 7 minutes. Remove from the heat and grind in a spice mill or with a mortar and pestle.

In a food processor or blender, combine the ground cumin, onion, garlic, paprika, and lemon juice and pulse to puree. Add the yogurt and pulse just until blended. Add half of the pomegranate seeds.

Prick the chickens in several places with a sharp fork and transfer to 1 or 2 resealable plastic bags. Pour in the marinade and shake to coat. Press to remove the air and seal the bag; refrigerate for 8 to 10 hours.

Preheat a charcoal or gas grill to 375°F. Make sure the grill rack is clean and oil it thoroughly with nonstick cooking spray.

Remove the chicken from the bag and wipe off excess marinade. Pour the marinade in a saucepan and boil for 12 minutes; set aside to cool.

Season the chicken with salt and pepper. Transfer to the prepared grill rack over direct heat and cook until the juices run clear when pierced with a fork, about 14 to 16 minutes per side, turning often, or until the internal temperature at the thickest part of the thigh reaches 180°F.

Remove the chicken to a heated serving platter and let stand, covered, for 10 minutes.

Add the pomegranate molasses and the remaining pomegranate seeds to the cooked marinade, stir, pour over the chicken, and serve.

SERVES 4 TO 6

WHOLE SMOKED LAMB

Lamb is the third most popular meat in Turkey, after chicken and beef, and this is an impressive way to cook it, if your grill is large enough. In one Turkish restaurant, I saw cooks putting peeled, quartered potatoes in the dripping pan and cooking them along with the lamb. They were wonderful, if a bit high on the cholesterol scale. Have your butcher prepare the lamb for this recipe (you could also substitute a goat here). Lamb is usually tender because it is from animals less than 1 year old. Look for good marbling (white flecks of fat within the meat muscle) and meat that is fine textured and firm. The flesh should be pink in color and the fat should be firm, white, and not too thick.

5	large onions (about 1¹/₂ pounds), minced
¹/₂	cup chopped fresh cilantro
2	teaspoons ground cumin
¹/₄	teaspoon ground allspice
3	tablespoons fresh thyme
5	tablespoons salt
2	teaspoons freshly ground black pepper
1	(22- to 24-pound) whole lamb, head and front legs removed
2	cups fresh bread cubes
2	large eggs, lightly beaten
¹/₄	cup freshly squeezed lemon juice
¹/₄	cup chopped fresh mint
2	tablespoons fresh rosemary
4	tablespoons tomato paste
2	cups plain yogurt
1	tablespoon minced garlic
¹/₂	cup olive oil
3	tablespoons balsamic vinegar
1	cup red wine

Preheat a charcoal or gas grill or smoker big enough to hold the whole lamb to 400°F. If using a large charcoal grill, mound the coals along the back of the grill only. Whether you are using a smoker or a charcoal or gas barbecue, put a large water pan on the grill rack, and a drip pan (or pans) under the entire length of the grill rack to collect the drippings. Make sure the grill rack is clean and oil it thoroughly with nonstick cooking spray.

In a bowl, combine half of the onions with the cilantro, cumin, allspice, thyme, salt, and pepper, and rub the inner cavity of the lamb with this mixture.

In another bowl make the stuffing by combining the remaining onions, bread cubes, eggs, lemon juice, mint, and rosemary. Using your hands, mix thoroughly.

In another bowl, combine the tomato paste, yogurt, and garlic and stir well. Spread this mixture all over the outside of the lamb.

Loosely pack the stuffing mixture into the lamb's body cavity. Using a trussing needle and kitchen string, sew the cavity closed. Combine the olive oil, vinegar, and red wine in a spray bottle for basting.

Lower gas flame, open vents, or close firebox vents to decrease heat to around 350°F. Place the lamb on the prepared grill rack, spray with the basting spray, close the grill lid, and cook for 3 to 4 hours, or until the internal temperature at the thickest part of the leg reaches 145°F for medium-rare. Spray once or twice per hour during cooking.

Remove the lamb from the barbecue, scooping the stuffing into a bowl, and let the lamb rest, covered, for 10 minutes. Carve and serve.

SERVES 8 TO 10

GARLIC-STUFFED GRILLED EGGPLANT

Turkey produces about 14 percent of the world's eggplants, ranking fourth of all countries, with the U.S. a distant twentieth. The best eggplants are firm and shiny with unbroken skin. Male eggplants tend to have fewer seeds, and are therefore less bitter than females. To sex an eggplant, look at the indentation at the bottom. If it's deep and shaped like a dash, it's a female. If it's shallow and round, it's a male.

- 4 baby eggplants (about 1 1/4 pounds total)
- 2 1/2 teaspoons flaked sea salt or kosher salt
- 1/4 cup olive oil
- 1 small yellow onion, finely chopped
- 8 cloves garlic, minced
- 1 small tomato, cored and chopped (about 3/4 cup)
- 1/2 cup chopped fresh parsley
- 1 1/2 teaspoons fresh tarragon
- 1/2 teaspoon sugar
- 2 teaspoons grated lemon zest
- 1 teaspoon freshly squeezed lemon juice
- 1 tablespoon cider vinegar
- 1/4 cup chicken stock
- 1/4 cup chopped cilantro, for garnish
  Paprika, for garnish

Using a small paring knife and starting in the middle, cut a lengthwise slit 3/4 of the way through each eggplant, to within 1/2 inch of each end. Using the 2 teaspoons of salt, salt each eggplant inside and let stand on paper towel for 45 minutes. Rinse the eggplants under cold running water, and pat dry.

Prepare a charcoal or gas grill for indirect grilling (it is not necessary to use a drip pan for this recipe). Preheat to 375°F. Make sure the grill rack is clean and oil it thoroughly with nonstick cooking spray.

To prepare the stuffing, heat 1 tablespoon of the oil in a large skillet over medium heat. Add the onion and sauté until softened, 5 to 7 minutes. Add the garlic and sauté for 1 minute longer. Add the tomato, parsley, tarragon, sugar, remaining 1/2 teaspoon of salt, zest, juice, and vinegar, and stir to combine, cook for 3 to 4 minutes longer.

Brush the eggplants with some of the remaining oil and transfer to the prepared grill rack over direct heat. Cook, turning, until both sides are nicely marked and they are beginning to soften, about 10 minutes.

Transfer the eggplants, slit-side up, to a large cast-iron skillet. Spread open the eggplants and fill each with the stuffing. Drizzle with the remaining oil, add the stock to the pan, and cover it tightly with a lid or aluminum foil. Place the skillet on the grill over indirect heat and cook, replenishing the stock when it cooks off, until the eggplants are tender and browned, about 1 hour.

Remove the skillet from the heat and let cool. Serve the eggplants on a warm platter, sprinkled with cilantro and a dash of paprika.

SERVES 6 TO 8

ORANGE–PINE NUT CAKE

Pinus pinea, *the stone pine tree, grows throughout the Mediterranean region, including Turkey, and produces soft nuts, ivory in color and shaped like a torpedo, with a sweet, delicate flavor. The ancient Greeks and Romans considered pine nuts an aphrodisiac, and pine nut recipes were found in the ruins of Pompeii.*

- 3 large oranges
- $1/2$ cup ground almonds
- $1/2$ cup firmly packed brown sugar
- 1 teaspoon baking powder
- 3 drops almond extract
- 3 large eggs, beaten
- $1/4$ cup pine nuts
- $1/4$ cup confectioners' sugar
- 1 pound fresh loganberries or raspberries

Place 1 whole orange in a small saucepan, cover with water, and simmer for 2 hours. Pour off the water and let the orange cool.

Prepare a charcoal or gas grill for indirect grilling (it is not necessary to use a drip pan for this recipe). Preheat to 350°F. Grease a shallow 9-inch cake pan and line the bottom with a cut-out round of waxed paper.

Cut the cooked orange in pieces and discard the seeds. Transfer it to a food processor. Process to a smooth puree and set aside.

In a large mixing bowl or the bowl of a stand mixer, combine the almonds, brown sugar, baking powder, and almond extract. Using an electric mixer on high speed or a stand mixer with the paddle attachment, add the eggs one at a time, beating for 1 minute between each addition. Add the pureed orange and beat for 1 minute longer, until thoroughly mixed. Add half of the pine nuts, stirring with a wooden spoon to incorporate.

Pour the batter into the prepared cake pan and top with the remaining pine nuts. Transfer to the grill rack over indirect heat, close the grill lid, and cook for 35 minutes, or until a toothpick inserted into the center of the cake comes out clean. Let cool slightly, then transfer to a wire rack to cool completely.

Peel the remaining 2 oranges and slice, crosswise, into $1/4$-inch slices. Lay them on a large plate and sprinkle with 2 tablespoons of the confectioners' sugar.

Just before serving, remove the waxed paper from the cake bottom and sprinkle the top with the remaining confectioners' sugar. Garnish the top of the cake with the sugared orange slices and fresh berries.

SERVES 4 TO 6

UNITED STATES

Barbecue: It Ain't Just for Breakfast Anymore!

Barbecue is as American as . . . you guessed it: apple pie! In fact, at the end of this chapter, I'll show you how to cook an apple pie right on the barbecue.

But barbecue is more than just a cooking method in America. It's a noun, a verb, and a part of the social culture in some parts of the country. This chapter's subtitle (a riff on the title of a Kansas City Barbecue Society cookbook) expresses what every serious barbecue fanatic secretly feels inside: everything goes better with 'cue.

It seems that just about everyone is barbecuing these days. In fact, a whopping 91 percent of American families of four or more own outdoor grills, according to the Hearth, Patio, and Barbecue Association. Yup, it's a bonafide national phenomenon. Championship 'cue can be found in Seattle, Syracuse, or Sacramento. Black as a meteorite and mouth-wateringly tender Texas-style brisket can be enjoyed in Houston, but also in Hannibal, Hartford, and Hershey. And pulled pork sandwiches topped with crunchy coleslaw are as likely to be found in northern outposts

like Minneapolis–St. Paul as Southern strongholds like Raleigh-Durham.

Barbecue, literally, is on fire across America. And a lot of the fire, and a whole lot of the smoke, is coming from the more than 10,000 barbecue restaurants igniting the nation. Some certainly qualify as shrines (that is, restaurants people drive more than 100 miles to get to). We'd love to list them all, but even we can't eat *that* much barbecue! (Did I mention there are more than 10,000 of these barbecue joints?) Suffice it to say that as far back as 1974, *New York Times* columnist and critic Calvin Trillin famously proclaimed Arthur Bryant's in Kansas City the "single best restaurant in the world."

If you'd rather stay home, there are thousands of tools and accessories, dozens of 'cue cookbooks, and hundreds of styles of grills for all budgets and abilities. It was interesting to learn during my travels that at some of the biggest barbecue contests in the country, there are amateur backyard grillers with $29 bullet smokers competing with and holding their own against the most accomplished professional barbecue chefs in the world using $30,000 custom-built, computer-controlled, high-tech smokers.

Many barbecuers are content to cook the same two or three tried-and-true dishes. A fellow I met in Nashville, who only grills ribs and burgers, confessed, "They're good, we know

how to cook 'em, and everyone loves 'em, so why not?"

Okay, but even if you live in Pensacola, *why not* smoke up a California tri-tip roast basted in olive oil, garlic, and balsamic vinegar? If you live in Bangor, try barbecuing an Alaska Copper River salmon fillet on a cedar plank. And if you live in Tucumcari, have a go at Owensboro-style grilled lamb with Kentucky-style black dip. Fargo grillers need to slop some Georgia yellow mustard sauce on their racks of St. Louis ribs, and pitmasters in Fort Worth should commit heresy by drizzling a Pacific Northwest hoisin-blackberry-soy sauce on their beloved brisket. Open those cookbooks, flip past those dog-eared pages, and try something new.

With thousands of bottled barbecue sauces, rubs, and marinades available, it's tempting to rely on them. Some grillers even insist that enhancements are necessary because our meat isn't as flavorful. Hogwash (which is what we do before we cook them)! Buy high-quality meat, cook it properly, and you'll only need a pinch or a drizzle instead of a tablespoon or a slather for great results. As you've already read, most of the world cooks their barbecue very, very simply.

All I have left to say is that, just about any day, any time, any place, any weather, it's time to . . . Barbecue America!

THREE BARBECUE SAUCES

For all the sauce loyalists out there, here are three regional classics.

TEXAS BARBECUE SAUCE

- 1 medium onion, minced
- 2 tablespoons bacon drippings
- 4 cloves garlic, chopped
- 3 cups canned crushed tomatoes
- 1 1/2 cups ketchup
- 1 cup freshly squeezed orange juice
- 6 tablespoons freshly squeezed lemon juice
- 6 tablespoons red wine vinegar
- 1/2 cup water
- 2 tablespoons dark molasses
- 1 tablespoon Worcestershire sauce
- 1/4 teaspoon Tabasco
- 2 tablespoons chili powder
- 1 tablespoon ground coriander
- 1 tablespoon dry mustard
- 1 teaspoon salt

In a large saucepan over medium heat, sauté the onion in the bacon drippings until golden brown; add the remaining ingredients, increase the heat to high and bring to boil. Decrease the heat to low and simmer for 1 hour, stirring frequently. Cool, bottle, and refrigerate for up to three weeks.

MAKES 8 TO 9 CUPS

KANSAS CITY–STYLE SAUCE

- 1 cup apple juice
- 1 cup tomato sauce
- 1 (6-ounce) can tomato paste
- 1/4 cup (1/2 stick) butter
- 1/2 cup Worcestershire sauce
- 1/2 cup firmly packed brown sugar
- 1/2 cup molasses
- 1/2 cup cider vinegar
- 2 1/2 teaspoons balsamic vinegar
- 1 tablespoon maple sugar pepper or citrus pepper
- 1 tablespoon prepared yellow mustard
- 1 tablespoon chili powder
- 1 teaspoon dried summer savory
- 1 teaspoon onion powder
- 1 teaspoon garlic salt
- 1 healthy dash of hot sauce

Combine the ingredients in a large saucepan over low and cook, partially covered, until the sauce thickly covers the back of a spoon, about 30 minutes. Cool, bottle, and refrigerate for up to three weeks.

MAKES 5 TO 6 CUPS

CAROLINA–STYLE SAUCE

- 4 cups cider vinegar
- 1/4 cup firmly packed brown sugar
- 4 teaspoons sea salt
- 4 teaspoons crushed red pepper flakes
- 2 teaspoons coarsely ground black pepper

Combine all the ingredients in a saucepan over low heat. Simmer for 15 to 20 minutes, stirring constantly. Do not boil! Cool, bottle, and refrigerate for up to three weeks.

MAKES ABOUT 4 CUPS

CEDAR-PLANK SALMON

Cedar wood, when used for cooking, actually becomes a natural flavoring. Native Americans would attach meats directly to a slab of wood and lay it against hot stones or the outside of the fire ring. Today, for cooking purposes, we use planks of alder, cedar, red cedar, cherry, hickory, maple, pecan, or white oak to achieve perfectly cooked, flavorful fish. The water-soaked planks steam the fish from the underside, evening out the heat from the coals or gas flames and making it almost impossible to burn or overcook.

1   (2¹/₂-pound) fresh salmon fillet, boned, skin on

1   tablespoon plus 1 teaspoon balsamic vinegar

1   tablespoon ground ginger

1   tablespoon garlic powder

2   tablespoons brown sugar

2   tablespoons chopped green onions, green part only

4   tablespoons extra-virgin olive oil

    Flaked or kosher salt

    Freshly ground black pepper

¹/₄ cup fresh raspberries

1   teaspoon granulated sugar

Soak an untreated cedar shingle or plank (large enough to hold the salmon fillet) for at least 4 hours in warm water.

Place the salmon in a shallow baking dish. In a mixing bowl, combine the 1 tablespoon of vinegar, the ginger, garlic, brown sugar, and green onion; pour over the salmon. Let stand for 30 minutes, turning the fish once or twice.

Preheat a charcoal or gas grill to 550°F. Fill a spray bottle with water to douse flare-ups.

Remove the salmon from the marinade and drain, discarding the marinade. Remove the plank from the water and brush with the olive oil. Place the salmon skin side down on the plank; season with salt and pepper. Transfer the plank to the grill rack over direct heat. Close the lid and cook for 20 to 25 minutes, basting 2 to 3 times, until the fish is cooked: white fat will bubble to the surface, the edges will just start to turn brown, and the center will be medium-rare. Near the end of cooking, the plank may flare up around the edges. This is okay; spray with water to douse flames and continue cooking.

Meanwhile, in a mixing bowl, combine the raspberries with the water, the 1 teaspoon of balsamic vinegar, and the granulated sugar; let stand until the salmon is cooked.

Remove the plank from the barbecue and place it directly on a serving tray. Drain the raspberries and sprinkle them over the fish, and serve.

SERVES 4 TO 6

BEER-BUTT CHICKEN

This author was dubbed by People *magazine "The Godfather of Beer-Butt Chicken," but I humbly admit that I borrowed the technique from a barbecue contest competitor who cooked a chicken on a beer can. When I asked him what it was, he said: "Why it's beer-butt chicken." Admittedly I was the first in the country to publish the recipe in a barbecue cookbook, and the first to prepare it on national TV. This position and method does two things: first, it helps drain off fat as the chicken cooks, and second, the beer steams the inside of the chicken, while the outside is cooked by the heat from the coals or gas flame, making this method the moistest way to cook a chicken. In addition to chicken, I have tried and succeeded in cooking turkeys, goose, duck, pheasant, game hens, and even quail on soda, fruit juice, iced tea, and beer cans. One day I'll cook up an emu sitting on a pony keg of beer, wait and see!*

- 1 teaspoon brown sugar
- 1 teaspoon garlic powder
- 1 teaspoon onion powder
- 1 teaspoon dried summer savory
- 1/4 teaspoon cayenne pepper
- 1 teaspoon chili powder
- 1 teaspoon paprika
- 1 teaspoon dry mustard
- 1 tablespoon finely ground sea salt or kosher salt
- 1 (4- to 5-pound) chicken
- 1 (12-ounce) can beer, plus 1 cup warm beer
- 1 cup apple cider
- 2 tablespoons olive oil
- 2 tablespoons balsamic vinegar

In a small bowl, combine the sugar, garlic powder, onion powder, savory, cayenne pepper, chili powder, paprika, mustard, and salt, and stir until well incorporated. Apply the rub all over the chicken, even in the cavity. Work the mixture gently into the skin and under the skin wherever possible. Cover the chicken and set aside at room temperature for 30 minutes.

Pour half of the can of beer into a spray bottle, add the cider, olive oil, and balsamic vinegar, and set aside.

Prepare a charcoal or gas barbecue for indirect grilling , placing a drip pan under the cool side of the grill (see page 3). Preheat to 375°F.

Hold the beer can in one hand and slide the chicken, tail-side down, over the can. Place the chicken on the can over direct heat on the barbecue and cook, using the spray bottle to baste once or twice, for 20 minutes, until it's just beginning to brown all over. Move the chicken to the cool side of the grill over the water pan. Lower the lid and cook, spraying with the basting spray several times, for 1 to 1 1/2 hours until the internal temperature at the thigh reaches 180°F and the chicken is very brown (can be almost a mahogany color).

Using a barbecue glove, remove the chicken from the barbecue and present it on the can to your guests. After they have reacted appropriately, remove the chicken from the beer can with tongs. Be careful, as the can and the liquid inside are very hot.

Spray the chicken once more with the basting spray, carve, and serve. Or, wearing barbecue gloves, pull the chicken apart with your hands and serve.

SERVES 4 TO 6

CAROLINA-STYLE PULLED PORK BUTT (SHOULDER)

The roast on the top end of the shoulder is also known as the pork butt, Boston butt, and even pork blade roast, because the roast contains part of the shoulder blade. Bone-in is preferred for smoking, since the bone helps to transfer heat into the roast and adds flavor.

- 1/2 cup bourbon
- 2 tablespoons molasses
- 1 1/2 cups cider vinegar
- 1 cup water
- 2 chipotle chiles, rehydrated and chopped (see Note page 56)
- 2 tablespoons salt
- 1 tablespoon crushed red pepper flakes
- 2 tablespoons freshly ground black pepper
- 1 (5- to 6-pound) boneless pork butt (shoulder)
- 1 cup wood chips
- 2 tablespoons salt
- 2 tablespoons paprika
- 1 tablespoon garlic powder
- 2 tablespoons cayenne
- Hamburger buns, for serving
- Cole slaw, for serving

In a large bowl, combine the bourbon, molasses, vinegar, water, chipotles, salt, red pepper flakes, and 1 tablespoon of the black pepper, and stir well.

Place the pork shoulder in a large resealable plastic bag and pour the marinade over it. Seal the bag, pressing out the air, and refrigerate for 6 to 9 hours.

Remove the pork from the bag and pour the marinade into a saucepan. Boil the marinade for 12 minutes to use for basting and as a sauce. Set aside.

Place the wood chips in a bowl or can, cover with water, and soak for at least 2 hours.

In a small bowl, combine the salt, paprika, garlic, the remaining 1 tablespoon of black pepper, and cayenne, and stir to mix. Generously sprinkle the spices on all surfaces of the pork, cover, and refrigerate for 1 hour, then allow it to come to room temperature while you fire up the grill.

Prepare a charcoal or gas barbecue or smoker for indirect cooking, placing a water-filled drip pan under the cool side of the grill rack (see page 3). Preheat to 250°F. Make sure the grill rack is clean and oil it thoroughly with nonstick cooking spray.

Put the soaked wood chips on a piece of heavy-duty aluminum foil and fold it over like an envelope to enclose the wood. Using a pencil, poke 3 or 4 holes in the top of the foil envelope (don't poke all the way through). Place the foil directly on the coals or gas jets and when the wood inside starts to smoke, transfer the pork butt to the prepared grill rack over indirect heat. Lower the lid rack and cook until the internal temperature reaches 190° to 200°F, about 5 to 6 hours. Baste with some of the reserved sauce every 30 minutes during the last 2 hours, and regulate the gas or add more charcoal to maintain the temperature throughout the cooking time. (Note that you can lose 15 minutes of cooking time each time you open the lid of the barbecue or smoker.)

Remove the pork from the grill and, using 2 large forks or a "bear claw," shred or pull the meat and transfer to a large bowl. Stir 3 to 4 tablespoons of the sauce into the meat (or up to 1/2 cup if you really like saucy meat) and serve on hamburger buns with cole slaw either on top or on the side.

SERVES 6 TO 8

BROWN SUGAR PORK SPARERIBS

There are two styles of spareribs: whole and St. Louis style. A whole slab still has part of the breastbone attached, as well as a strip of cartilage along the edge of the slab. If you cut away the sternum and cartilage, you have St. Louis–style spareribs. You can use either in this recipe. Serve this dish with cole slaw, baked beans, and cornbread or corn muffins.

2	racks (1^1/$_2$ pounds each) pork spareribs (see Note)
1^1/$_2$	cups firmly packed brown sugar
3	tablespoons coarse salt
2	cups warm water
2	cups light beer
	Juice of 1 lemon
	Juice of 1 lime
3	tablespoons olive oil
2	tablespoons dried summer savory
2	tablespoons granulated garlic
2	tablespoons paprika
^{1}/$_4$	teaspoon ground cloves
1	teaspoon cayenne pepper
1	teaspoon dry mustard
1	cup prepared yellow mustard
1	cup (alder, pecan, hickory, oak, or fruitwood) wood chips

The night before cooking, place the ribs in a two-gallon resealable plastic bag. In a large bowl, mix 1 cup of the brown sugar, the salt, water, beer, lemon and lime juices, and olive oil. Stir well and pour into the bag over the ribs. Seal the bag, shake to coat the ribs, and refrigerate for 8 hours, turning occasionally.

In a small bowl, combine the savory, garlic, paprika, cloves, and ^{1}/$_4$ cup of the brown sugar; set aside. In another bowl, combine the remaining ^{1}/$_4$ cup brown sugar, cayenne, and dry mustard; set aside.

Place the wood chips in a bowl or can, cover with water, and soak for at least 2 hours.

Drain the ribs, discarding the marinade, and pat the ribs dry. Slather the ribs with prepared yellow mustard, rubbing it into the flesh on both sides; set aside for 30 minutes.

Sprinkle half of the savory-garlic rub on the ribs, concentrating on the meat side of the rack. Cover and set aside for 2 hours in refrigerator. Remove the ribs from the refrigerator and rub with the remainder of the savory-garlic rub and let ribs come to room temperature.

Prepare a charcoal or gas barbecue or smoker for indirect grilling, placing a drip pan under the cool side of the grill rack (see page 3). Preheat to 375°F. Make sure the grill rack is clean and oil it thoroughly with nonstick cooking spray.

Put a handful of soaked wood chips on a piece of heavy-duty aluminum foil and fold it over like an envelope to enclose the wood. Using a pencil, poke 3 or 4 holes in the top of the foil envelope (don't poke all the way through). Place the foil directly on the coals or gas jets and when the wood inside starts to smoke, place the ribs on the grill rack over the drip pan, with the membrane side down and the thick end toward the back of the grill. Lower the grill lid and grill the ribs for 2 to 3 hours, turning 2 or 3 times, until the ribs are tender, and the meat has shrunken back from the bones by ^{1}/$_4$ inch or so.

Transfer the ribs to a sheet of doubled-over heavy-duty foil big enough to enclose the ribs. Sprinkle the meat side only with the cayenne-mustard rub. Seal the ribs in the foil and return them to the grill for 20 minutes longer. To test for doneness, grab 2 bones in the middle of the slab and give them a pull. If the meat offers some resistance but then begins to tear, the ribs are done.

Remove the ribs from the grill, cut them apart, and serve on a heated platter with your favorite barbecue sauce on the side.

SERVES 6 TO 8

NOTE: Look for pork ribs with no large areas of surface fat, but rather lots of red meat showing. Avoid "shiners," or places where the meat has been cut so close to the rib bones in spots that it exposes whole sections of bone.

BUFFALO RIB ROAST WITH AN ORANGE-MOLASSES GLAZE

Buffalo meat tastes similar to fine beef, with a slightly sweeter and richer flavor. Today most buffalo is farm raised and fed on grains and natural grasses, so there should be no "gamey" or "wild" taste. Because the meat is low in fat, it's also very low in cholesterol.

1	(7- to 9-pound) buffalo rib roast or top sirloin roast
1	tablespoon olive oil
1 1/4	cups minced red onion
3	tablespoons finely minced garlic
	Freshly ground black pepper
1/2	cup balsamic vinegar
1 1/4	cups freshly squeezed orange juice
1	cup root beer
1	tablespoon grated orange zest
1/3	cup molasses
1	tablespoon crushed toasted coriander seeds
1/4	cup yellow mustard seeds
1	tablespoon chili powder
1	cup dry red wine
2	cups beef stock
	Salt
	Freshly ground pepper

Place a rack in a roasting pan. Carefully trim the roast to remove all but a thin layer of fat, then place the roast in the rack in the roasting pan and set aside.

In a saucepan, heat the oil over medium-high heat. Add the onion and garlic and sauté until just beginning to color. Add 1 tablespoon of black pepper and the vinegar, orange juice, root beer, zest, molasses, coriander, mustard seeds, and chili powder and bring to a boil. Decrease heat and simmer for 8 to 10 minutes, or until slightly thickened. Let cool.

Generously brush the roast with the glaze and transfer to the refrigerator to marinate for 6 to 8 hours. Refrigerate any remaining glaze to use for basting.

Before roasting, bring the meat to room temperature, about 30 minutes. Prepare a charcoal or gas grill for indirect cooking, placing a water-filled drip pan under the cool side of the grill rack (see page 3). Preheat to 450°F. Make sure the grill rack is clean and oil it thoroughly with nonstick cooking spray.

Transfer the roast to the prepared grill rack over direct heat and cook for 15 minutes, turning often, until it begins to brown on all sides. Transfer the roast to a roasting pan placed on the cool side of the grill and continue to cook, basting occasionally with the reserved glaze, until the meat is browned all over with some edges slightly charred and the internal temperature in the center of the roast reaches 145°F to 155°F (rare to medium-rare); this will take about 1 1/2 to 2 hours.

Transfer the roast to a serving platter, cover with foil, and keep warm. Add the wine and stock to the roasting pan on the grill and bring to a boil over direct heat, scraping up any brown bits. Reduce the liquid slightly and then strain the juices. Add salt and pepper to taste.

Serve the roast sliced in individual rib chops with the sauce on the side.

SERVES 8

TEXAS BEEF BRISKET

Look for a brisket with good marbling, white fat, and a deep color in the meat. There should be good fat throughout the meat and not just in one place. If the fat cap is more than a third of an inch thick, you might want to trim it down. In this recipe, you will want the brisket to cook fat side up so that the melting fat will run over the meat and keep it moist.

2	cans plus 1/2 cup Coca-Cola (not diet)
2	beef bouillon cubes, dissolved in 1/2 cup of water
4	cloves garlic, minced
1	tablespoon Worcestershire sauce
2	tablespoons freshly squeezed lime or lemon juice
1	tablespoon A.1. steak sauce
1	(10- to 12-pound) untrimmed (packer) brisket

- 1 cup (alder, pecan, hickory, oak, or fruitwood) wood chips
- 1 tablespoon garlic salt
- 1 teaspoon chili powder
- 1 teaspoon freshly ground black pepper
- 1 teaspoon cumin
- 1 tablespoon paprika
- 1 tablespoon brown sugar
- 1 cup apple juice
- $1/4$ cup balsamic vinegar
- $1/4$ cup olive oil
- Prepared yellow mustard

Combine the 2 cans of cola, dissolved bouillon, garlic, Worcestershire, juice, and steak sauce in a bowl, stir and pour over the brisket in a shallow pan. Cover with plastic wrap and marinate for at least 8 hours.

Place the wood chips in a bowl or can, cover with water, and soak for at least 2 hours.

Remove the brisket from the marinade and discard the marinade. Let the meat sit at room temperature while you fire up the barbecue.

Prepare a smoker or charcoal or gas barbecue for indirect grilling, placing a drip pan under the cool side of the grill rack (see page 3). Preheat to 250°F. If using a charcoal or gas grill, put a handful of soaked wood chips on a piece of heavy-duty aluminum foil and fold it over like an envelope to enclose the wood. Using a pencil, poke 3 or 4 holes in the top of the foil envelope (don't poke all the way through). Place the foil directly on the coals or gas jets. If using a smoker, follow the manufacturer's directions to lay down smoke for the cooking period.

In a bowl, combine the garlic salt, chili powder, black pepper, cumin, paprika, and brown sugar, and set this rub aside. In a spray bottle, combine the apple juice, balsamic vinegar, the remaining $1/2$ cup of cola, and olive oil. Set aside.

Wearing rubber gloves, spread mustard all over the meat and rub it into both sides; generously sprinkle the meat on both sides with the rub, patting (not rubbing) the spices into the meat.

Transfer the brisket to the prepared grill rack over indirect heat fat side up. Lower the grill lid and cook for 4 to 5 hours, spraying with the baste once an hour, until the meat registers 155°F on a thermometer and the outside looked charred, but a fork still easily slides inside. Remove from the grill and let rest for 10 minutes.

To serve, slice across the grain and serve with your favorite Texas-style (not sweet) barbecue sauce on the side.

SERVES 8 TO 10

NOTE: Here's a schedule to follow for slow cooking a brisket: If you start about 7:00 a.m., cook the meat on the barbecue until about 10:00 p.m. Remove the brisket from the barbecue, double-wrap in plastic wrap, then in 2 layers of heavy-duty foil. Place the foiled brisket in a smoker, or in the oven, and cook at 150° to 160°F until 1:00 the next afternoon. The meat will have shrunk considerably and turned almost completely black outside, looking like a flattened meteor. But will be the best-tasting, juiciest, and most tender brisket you have ever eaten.

BROWN BAG APPLE PIE

This pie is cooked over a cookie sheet or several sheets of heavy-duty aluminum foil, in a large grocery store brown paper bag. I like to bring the bag right to the table on a serving tray, tear open the bag, and enjoy the reaction. Dole out succulent slices with a slab of extra-sharp Cheddar alongside each serving.

3   cups plus 2 tablespoons flour

$^1/_2$ teaspoons salt

$^1/_2$ cup shortening

5   tablespoons ice water

$^1/_4$ cup granulated sugar

$^1/_2$ teaspoon ground nutmeg

1   teaspoon cinnamon

$^1/_8$ teaspoon ground cloves

2   tablespoons freshly squeezed lemon juice

8   cups sliced apples

$^1/_2$ cup firmly packed brown sugar

$^1/_3$ cup ($^2/_3$ stick) unsalted butter

    Vanilla ice cream, for serving (optional)

    Extra-sharp Cheddar cheese, sliced thickly, for serving (optional)

Preheat a charcoal or gas grill to 400°F.

In a mixing bowl, combine $2^1/_2$ cups of the flour, salt, and shortening. Using an electric mixer, beat until the mixture resembles coarse crumbs. Stir in the water a little at a time, until the dough forms a ball.

On a lightly floured surface, roll out the dough to an 11- or 12-inch round and fit into a 9-inch pie pan, fluting the edges.

In a large bowl, combine the sugar, 2 tablespoons of the flour, nutmeg, cinnamon, cloves, and lemon juice. Add the apples, stirring to coat. Transfer the apple mixture to the pie pan, smoothing out the filling; set aside.

To prepare the topping, in a bowl, combine the brown sugar and the remaining $^1/_2$ cup of flour. Using 2 knives or a pastry blender, cut in the butter until the mixture resembles coarse crumbs. Sprinkle the topping evenly over the apple filling.

Place the pie in the brown paper bag and transfer the bag to a baking sheet; loosely fold the top of the bag under the pie. Transfer to the grill rack over direct heat. If you don't have a cookie or baking sheet, cut 3 large pieces of heavy-duty aluminum foil and cover the grill with this triple layer of foil. Close the grill lid and cook the pie until the apples are tender, 50 to 60 minutes.

Carefully remove the pie from the bag, avoiding the hot steam when you open the bag. Serve with generous scoops of ice cream and slices of cheese, if desired.

SERVES 6 TO 8

NOTE: **This works best with a metal pie pan. If all you have are aluminum disposable tins, put one inside the other so you have two layers of aluminum. For a fun effect, I sometimes use a propane lighter and call folks out to see the bag when I open the grill. Since it's extremely dried out, the bag ignites like flash paper and quickly burns away, while your guests are gasping, "Oh no— the pie is burning!" But the pie will be perfectly okay, emerging from the flames a delicious golden brown.**

DR. DAVIS'S BEST BARBECUED BEANS

Adding celery stalks to cooking beans does two things: first, it adds a nice bit of flavor. Second, the celery stalks absorb some of the sugars that we can't digest—sugars that bacteria in our nether parts gobble up causing them to pass their own gas, which builds up and makes us blush when it exits. This recipe was a collaboration between the author and Dr. John Davis, probably the biggest barbecue bean fanatic on earth. Man, oh man, how John loved his beans, and this was his favorite recipe. Get Bush's brand beans if you can: they hold their shape well, and are available in multiple varieties just about everywhere. Serve the beans with fresh homemade cornbread or garlic bread.

1 (14-ounce) can Bush's kidney beans

1 (16-ounce) can Bush's black beans

1 (16-ounce) can Bush's butter beans

3 (16-ounce) cans Bush's baked beans

1 (16-ounce) can Bush's garbanzo beans

1 pound smoked bacon, chopped in 1/4-inch pieces

1 large sweet onion, chopped

1/2 cup dark brown sugar

1 cup chile sauce

1 tablespoon chili powder

Dash of hot sauce

2 tablespoons prepared yellow mustard

2 tablespoons cider vinegar

3 stalks celery, leaves on, halved, lengthwise

Prepare a charcoal or gas grill for indirect cooking (it is not necessary to use a drip pan for this recipe). Preheat to 300° F.

Drain the kidney, black, and butter beans. In a Dutch oven or large pot, combine all the beans. Transfer to the grill, stove top, or side burner over medium heat and cook for 5 minutes, stirring often.

In a skillet, combine the bacon and onion, and sauté until the bacon is crisp and the onions are soft, about 10 to 12 minutes. Drain 1/2 of the bacon fat, then transfer the bacon, onion, and remaining bacon drippings to the pot of beans; add the remaining ingredients, burying the celery in the mixture.

Transfer the pot to the barbecue over indirect heat and cook for 20 to 30 minutes, stirring 2 or 3 times, until the beans are completely heated through and starting to bubble.

Remove the pot from the heat. Remove the celery stalks and discard.

SERVES 6

NOTE: If the bacon is too much, you can add leftover pulled pork, leftover brisket, or leftover grilled sausage (sauté the onions in 2 tablespoons of olive oil). I've also added apricot pieces, mandarin oranges, golden raisins, and bits of mango.

URUGUAY

Barbecue Heaven on Earth

Since this is the last chapter and the last country in this book, it's appropriate that I tell you this: it took eating my way through twenty-four other counties, but I finally found heaven—and in perhaps the most unlikely spot you can imagine. Not a smoky rib joint in Lexington. Not a historic barbecue pit in Kansas City. Not a dry-rub pork-rib restaurant in a Memphis alleyway. No *braai* in Cape Town is quite like this. No *vaca*, *cerdo*, or *pollo* in Buenos Aires goes out with such style. Not one of the many superb *churrascarias* in Rio de Janeiro can match the daily consumption of barbecued meats here.

Welcome to the Sitio Historico Gastronomia, Galleria de Arte y Artesanias: the Mercado del Porto in Montevideo—likely the most incredible barbecue venue on earth. Entering the vast hall was a culinary shock that I may never recover from. In front of me were blazing *parrillas* (barbecues), to the left were blazing barbecues, to the right were blazing barbecues, and, once I got twenty feet inside the building, behind me were blazing barbecues. With a ceiling that soars thirty to forty feet, the main hall holds fifteen *asado* (barbecue) restaurants, all with grills aflame, every inch of each one

239

covered with meat, punctuated by an occasional red pepper, whole onion, or slab of cheese.

I stood stunned, inhaling the wonderful smoke, watching dozens of chefs moving steaks and ribs on and off grills amid a blaze of Fellini-esque colors. There were whole lambs, suckling pigs, half chickens, and enough beef to feed all of Uruguay.

Wrapped in steam and smoke, I walked through the jammed aisles trying to select the best place for lunch, lured by the promise of *asado* nirvana. "The best *asado* in Montevideo!" proclaims a dark-eyed beauty, while next door a neatly dressed young man offers up "beef rib-eye steaks with garlic crispies," and across the way a well-fed cook beams as we watch him wrapping chicken breasts in caul fat.

The smell is intoxicating. The sounds of glasses clinking, orders delivered, acoustic guitars, and Spanish singers permeate the noisy conversations at hundreds of tables. Raw meat, sizzling meat, cooked meat, and smoked meat were being torn apart by fork and teeth and knives. Along with lamb, pork, and chicken, almost every cut of beef is represented, including this partial list (taken from the menu boards) of what was available on the day we visited: short loin, rib set, brisket, navel plate, rib plate, short ribs, eye round, outside flat, knuckle, rump cap, eye of rump, top sirloin, tri-tip, strip loin, tenderloin, skirt (thick and thin), flank steak, inside skirt, Spencer roll, rib-eye roll, chuck roll, neck, shoulder clod, blade oyster, chuck tender, shin shank, heel muscle, thick skirt, tongue, cheek meat, tail, liver, kidney, heart, sweetbreads, brains, tripe, honeycomb, spleen, tendons, head meat, lips, and intestines. Put all these pieces together and you could assemble an entire cow.

Vegetarians need not waste their time walking these corridors, although most restaurants sell nonprotein foods as well: cole slaw, lettuce salads, beet and carrot salads, cucumber and onion salads, potato salad, grilled red bell peppers, grilled onions, potatoes baked in foil, and French fries. But these are merely bit players.

Oh yes, and Montevideans, like nearly everyone in South America, drink (mostly red) wine. In fact, 90 to 95 percent of all the tables in the Mercado had an open bottle of red amid the trays piled with meat.

But it's the beef that captures the imagination, feeds the soul, and will remain a lasting memory in my mind. Beef from cows that live their whole contented, relaxed lives outdoors on grass. It's been said that for each of the thirteen million cows in Uruguay, there are two soccer fields worth of grass. That's a lot of open pasture, and a lot of contented cows. No overcrowded feedlots filled with stressed, chemically burdened creatures standing ankle-deep in excrement. Just happy, grazing cattle.

And the result is so outstanding that during a week in Uruguay, the only spice or preparation for beef that I saw was a sprinkling of coarse salt. That's it. No rubs, brines, marinades, or barbecue sauces to spoil the pure taste of red, succulent, tender, superb beef. There is a *chimichurri* sauce (a mix of olive oil, garlic, vinegar, parsley, bay leaf, oregano, and pepper), and a salsalike *criolla* sauce (chopped red and green peppers, onions, tomatoes, parsley, and salt), but I seldom saw anyone add anything to their steak or short ribs or tenderloin other than a contended sigh.

Sigh. I think I'll take an afternoon nap now. Gotta rest up for dinner.

SPICY CITRUS DUCK

Piercing the skin of the duck in several places with a fork or the tip of a knife allows the fat under the skin to drain while the duck is cooking. Always cook duck on a rack so it doesn't fry in its own drippings.

- 1 (4-pound) Peking, Moulard, or Muscovy duck
- 2 cups freshly squeezed lime juice (juice from about 16 limes)
- 1 cup freshly squeezed lemon juice (juice from about 5 lemons)
- 2 cups freshly squeezed orange juice (juice from about 6 oranges)
- 2 bay leaves
- 2 teaspoons flaked or kosher salt
- 1/2 teaspoon freshly ground black pepper
- 2 habañero chiles, seeded and minced
- 1 teaspoon garlic powder
- 1/4 cup Cognac
- 3 bananas, peeled and cut into 2-inch pieces
- 1 tablespoon cornstarch
- 1/4 cup slivered almonds
- 1/2 cup Cointreau or Triple Sec (see Note)

Rinse the duck with water and pat dry with paper towels; set aside.

In a large stockpot over high heat, combine the lime, lemon, and orange juices and bay leaves and bring to a boil. Decrease the heat to low, add the duck, and cook, covered, for 1 hour, turning the duck several times.

Prepare a charcoal or gas grill for indirect grilling (it is not necessary to use a drip pan for this recipe). Preheat to 450°F.

Drain the duck, reserving 3 cups of the cooking liquid. Skim off the fat from the liquid and set aside. In a small bowl, combine the salt, pepper, chiles, and garlic powder. Rub this mixture over the duck and into the cavity.

Place the duck on a rack in a shallow roasting pan. Transfer the pan to the grill rack over direct heat, cover the grill, and cook for 20 minutes until the duck starts to brown.

Add the reserved cooking liquid, Cognac, and bananas to the roasting pan. Move the pan to the cool side of the grill and cook, basting frequently, for 30 minutes longer, or until skin is crisp and brown all over. Transfer the bananas to a serving platter and keep warm. Transfer the duck to a carving board, cover, and let rest while you make the gravy.

Skim the fat from the pan and pour the drippings into a saucepan. In a small bowl, mix the cornstarch with a little water to make a smooth paste and add to the cooking liquid, stirring until thickened. Add the almonds and Cointreau and cook over low heat, stirring constantly, for 5 minutes.

Carve the duck, transfer it to the serving platter with the bananas, and pour some of the gravy over it, serving the rest on the side.

SERVES 4

NOTE: Of all orange-based liqueurs, Cointreau is arguably the most flavorful and most famous. It's made from dried bitter orange peels from the Caribbean, sweet orange peels from Seville and Valencia, spices, alcohol, and sugar. The recipe, however, is secret, having been passed down within the family since was first bottled and sold in 1875. It is known only to three family members who, incidentally, never travel together. If you don't have Cointreau, you can use Triple Sec or Curaçao.

GRILLED VEAL STEAKS WITH OLIVE-TOMATO RELISH

Look for veal with a fine grain and creamy pink color; any fat covering should be milky white. At the market, packages should be securely wrapped with no signs of leakage, and should be cold to the touch, without any tears or punctures. This recipe was inspired by one prepared by the chef at Casa Veronica in Montevideo, who gave me a shot at the grill in this tiny but bustling restaurant. Now I remember why I'm glad I'm a writer, TV host, and photographer: it was like working inside a blast furnace, and we were there in the autumn.

- 3 tablespoons chopped pitted green olives
- 3 tablespoons chopped pitted black olives
- 1 tomato, seeded and diced
- 1 clove garlic, minced
  Juice and zest of 1 lemon
- 2 tablespoons chopped parsley plus additional for garnish
- 4 tablespoons olive oil
- 2 ($^{1}/_{2}$-pound) veal steaks
  Salt
  Freshly ground black pepper

In a large bowl, combine the green and black olives, tomato, garlic, lemon juice, parsley, and 2 tablespoons of the oil. Mix well and set aside.

Transfer the veal steaks to a large piece of aluminum foil, setting them side by side. Using your fingers, rub the remaining 2 tablespoons of oil into the steaks on both sides and season generously with salt and pepper. Wrap the foil around the steaks, and let stand to marinate for 1 hour at room temperature.

Preheat a charcoal or gas grill to 400°F. Make sure the grill rack is clean and oil it thoroughly with nonstick cooking spray.

Remove the steaks from the foil package and transfer to the prepared grill rack over direct heat. Cook for 3 minutes, then rotate the steaks 90 degrees to make a criss-cross grill mark, and cook for 3 minutes longer. Flip the steaks over and cook for 5 to 7 minutes longer, until the internal temperature reaches 145°F for medium-rare. Transfer the steaks to a plate, grill-marked side up. Let stand, covered, for 5 minutes.

To serve, top each steak with 1 to 2 tablespoons of the olive sauce and garnish with chopped parsley.

SERVES 4

BARBECUED PORK CHOPS WITH BELL PEPPER SALSA

Molho campanha is a traditional Brazilian condiment served with barbecued meat. This Uruguayan version is a bit hotter than the Brazilian, so be ready with some cold adult beverages, like Uruguay's Patricia brand lager beer. The malagueta pepper is a small, tapered, green pepper that turns red as it matures. It is about 2 inches long at maturity and is very hot, with a range of 60,000 to 100,000 Scoville units (about the same as tabasco peppers). It's widely available online, or at stores featuring South American or Brazilian spices and condiments. If you can't find this pepper, you can substitute Thai peppers (they're in the same Scoville range).

4 (6-ounce) boneless loin pork chops

1 cup water

2 tablespoons salt

1/2 cup sugar

6 juniper berries, lightly crushed

2 fresh habañero chiles, chopped and seeded

1 teaspoon freshly ground white peppercorns

1 teaspoon freshly ground black peppercorns

1 teaspoon freshly ground coriander seeds

3 bay leaves, crushed

4 whole cloves

1 teaspoon dried thyme

2 tomatoes, coarsely chopped

1 large onion, finely chopped

1 small green bell pepper, seeded and coarsely chopped

1/2 cup red wine vinegar

3 to 4 dried malagueta (or Thai) peppers, crushed

2 tablespoons finely chopped cilantro

Place the pork chops in a large resealable plastic bag. In a mixing bowl, combine the water, salt, and sugar, stirring until dissolved. Add the juniper berries, habañeros, peppercorns, coriander, bay leaves, cloves, and thyme, and mix well. Pour the marinade into the bag with the pork chops and add additional water, if necessary, to cover. Seal, pressing out the air, and transfer to the refrigerator for 8 to 12 hours to marinate.

Preheat a charcoal or gas grill to 375°F. Make sure the grill rack is clean and oil it thoroughly with nonstick cooking spray.

Remove the pork, pouring the marinade into a small saucepan. Boil the marinade for 12 minutes to use for basting. Set aside the pork to come to room temperature.

Meanwhile, for the salsa, combine the tomatoes, onion, bell pepper, vinegar, dried chiles, and cilantro in a bowl, and set aside until ready to serve.

Transfer the pork to the prepared grill rack and cook over direct heat, basting and turning occasionally, for 10 to 12 minutes, until the chops are browned and the internal temperature reaches 155°F for medium-rare.

Remove the chops from the grill and let stand, covered, for 5 minutes. Transfer the pork to a serving platter and serve with the salsa on the side.

SERVES 4

THREE-MEAT MEATBALLS

For an alternative, instead of using the three different meats called for in this recipe, you can use just one. I prefer using all three to get the different flavors and textures in one meatball. You can also substitute ground turkey for the beef, and ground duck for the veal for a wonderfully complex flavor. I had meatballs like this—along with about a jillion other cuts of beef and veal—at a three-hour dinner at a farm called Aripuca, about an hour outside Montevideo.

- 3 tablespoons vegetable or olive oil
- 2 onions, finely chopped
- 1 1/2 cups beef stock
- 1 1/2 cups dry red wine
- 1/4 teaspoon dried thyme
- 1/2 teaspoon dried oregano
- 1 bay leaf
- Salt
- Freshly ground black pepper
- 1 large tomato, peeled and chopped
- 1/2 teaspoon crushed red pepper flakes
- 1 teaspoon sugar
- 1/2 pound finely ground veal
- 1/2 pound finely ground beef
- 1/2 pound finely ground pork
- 1 1/2 cups fresh bread crumbs
- 2 tablespoons minced garlic
- 4 tablespoons grated Parmesan cheese
- 1/2 cup small seedless currants or raisins
- 1/2 teaspoon grated nutmeg
- 3 eggs
- Milk
- Flour

In a saucepan, heat 1 tablespoon of the oil over medium heat. Add half of the onion and sauté until very soft, about 10 minutes. Add the stock, wine, thyme, oregano, and bay leaf, and simmer for a few minutes to blend the flavors. Season with salt and pepper and set aside to use for basting.

In a large skillet, heat the remaining oil over medium heat and sauté the remaining onion until soft, about 10 minutes. Add the tomato, pepper flakes, sugar, and salt and pepper to taste. Cook, stirring from time to time, until the mixture is thick and quite dry, about 15 to 20 minutes. Transfer to a large bowl and let cool.

To the bowl with the tomato mixture, add the veal, beef, pork, bread crumbs, garlic, Parmesan, currants, nutmeg, and eggs, and mix thoroughly with your hands. If the mixture is too dry to hold together, add a very small amount of milk; if too wet, add a bit of flour. Form the mixture into 3-inch balls around metal skewers (3 to 4 balls to each skewer), and chill for 20 minutes to firm the meat.

Preheat a charcoal or gas grill to 375°F. Make sure the grill rack is clean and oil it thoroughly with nonstick cooking spray.

Transfer the skewers to the prepared grill rack over direct heat. Cook for 5 to 6 minutes, turning once or twice and lightly basting with the sauce, until the meat is browned.

Remove from the heat and serve the meatballs with the remaining sauce as a gravy.

SERVES 4 TO 6

STUFFED SWEET POTATOES

The sweet potato has yellow or orange flesh, and its thin skin may be white, yellow, orange, red or purple. Some varieties are shaped like a potato (short and blocky with rounded ends), and some are longer with tapered ends. Most sweet potato dishes freeze well. Save time and energy by making one batch to serve and one to store in the freezer. This was a side dish I enjoyed in Punta del Este after a day of exploring the beaches, the "fingers in the sand" sculpture, and the world's only "roller-coaster" bridge.

- 4 large sweet potatoes, scrubbed
- 1/2 cup (4 ounces) cream cheese
- 1 egg yolk
- 2 teaspoons chili powder
- 3 green onions, chopped

  Salt

  Freshly ground black pepper
- 1/4 cup (1/2 stick) salted butter, cut into 1/4-inch pieces

Preheat a charcoal or gas grill to 400°F. Line the grill with heavy-duty aluminum foil.

Pierce the sweet potatoes in several places with a fork. Transfer them to the foil-lined grill rack over direct heat, close the grill lid and cook for 45 minutes, turning the potatoes two to three times, until easily pierced to the center with a knife.

Remove the potatoes from the grill and let stand until cool enough to handle. Cut the potatoes in half lengthwise. Using a spoon, scoop out the flesh into a mixing bowl, leaving a 1/4-inch shell of potato skin. Add the cream cheese, egg yolk, 1 teaspoon of the chili powder, and green onion to the sweet potato flesh and season with salt and pepper; mix well. Spoon the mixture into the potato shells, dot with the butter, sprinkle with the remaining chili powder, transfer back to the barbecue to heat through, about 6 to 8 minutes. Serve immediately.

SERVES 4

CHOCOLATE BREAD WITH DULCE DE LECHE FROSTING

In Argentina, Brazil, and Uruguay, dulce de leche is THE most popular dessert. It's layered between cookies, drizzled over ice cream, used in pies and cakes both inside and on top, and is by far the most popular sweet in South America. This recipe caused us to pass up lunch and just eat two more pieces each at a Montevideo sidewalk bakery.

- 1 cup confectioners' sugar
- 6 eggs
- 1 cup self-rising flour
- 1 cup unsweetened cocoa powder
- 1/2 teaspoon almond or vanilla extract
- 1/4 cup heavy cream
- 1 1/2 cups Dulce de Leche (page 15), warm

Prepare a charcoal or gas barbecue for indirect grilling (it is not necessary to use a drip pan with this recipe). Preheat to 375°F. Grease a loaf pan.

In a mixing bowl, using an electric mixer set on high speed, beat the sugar and eggs until light and fluffy; slowly add the flour, the cocoa powder, and the almond extract, and then the cream a couple of tablespoons at a time, stirring until well mixed, light and foamy. Pour into the prepared pan and transfer to the grill rack over indirect heat. Cook, with the lid closed, for 40 minutes, or until a knife inserted in the center comes out clean. Remove to a cake rack and let cool completely. Spread the warm dulce de leche on top of the cake and serve.

SERVES 4 TO 6

Acknowledgments

Particular thanks go to James T. Ehler at www. foodreference.com, Lynne Oliver at www.food-timeline.org, and Florence Sandeman at www. recipes4us.co.uk for their invaluable help in researching the twenty-five countries we visited, and for the permission they granted me to use materials from their websites in this book. Other special thanks go to Jackie DeKnock and Dan Duran at gourmetsafari.com for their invaluable help in getting us to some very special places in France, Morocco, and Spain. And, for spicing up my life for the past 10 years and generously providing spices, herbs, and special seasoning blends, a very warm and enthusiastic round of applause to Tom and Patty Erd of Chicago's famous Spice House (www.thespicehouse.com).

A special round of applause to food stylist Carol Ladd, and her two assistant chefs Dennis Sherron and Tony Brush, for making the studio food shots in this book look fantastic. And more thanks to Jerry Bocchino at AllFreshSeafood.com, Peter Kurfurst at Butcher Boys meats, and Kelly Beckwith at Pacific NW Best Fish Company, for helping provide the delicious meats, poultry, and seafood for the studio food shots.

There must be a special place in writers' heaven for the likes of Ten Speed editor Clancy Drake and art director Toni Tajima. Their enthusiasm, zest for excellence, great sense of humor, culinary savvy, and thorough professionalism kept me going and made me work even harder through the long proces of editing and proofing. Without them this book would not have happened.

Finally, my family: Kate, Trish, Reed, Emiko, Kara, Stephen, Christopher, Kevin, and Mary all get huge hugs and my deepest appreciation for their wholehearted support.

A Grelia Grill
Adam Lyal, Witchery Murder and Mystery Tour
Adem Colpan, Pudding Shop
Adrian Schirosa
Aida C. Nunez, TravelSmith
Airton Marchese, Galpao Crioulo
Akitoshi Asano, Asano Foundation for Taiko Culture Research
Alan Supraner
Alejandra Saggese, Pan Americano Hotel
Alejandro Cammarota, Oxford Hotel
Amanda Caygill, Mussel Inn
Andre Dang, Harrods
Andrew Roger, Matter of Communications
Andrew Waruszewski
Antonio Coucello, Restaurante O Fuso

Ashaun Bloch, Mariner's Wharf, Hout Bay
Benjamin Maxwell Flatt, Flatt's by the Sea
Bertus Fourie, KWV
Brent Burkhardt, Singapore Tourism
Bruno Ribeiro, Marriott Praia D'el Rey
Caroline and Graham Hamilton, Cairns Sheep Ranch
Caroline Ceretta, BBQ University, Lajeado
Casa Romana Hotel
Casey Rust, Royal Yacht Britannia
Chantal and Regis Sanglier, La Garanc en Provence
Chef Gilbert del Toro Coello, Pueblo Bonito, Mexico
Chef Lawrence Keogh, Roast
Chef Patrick Payet, Famous Provence Cooking School
Chef Peter Reinhart

Chef Shin-ichiro Takagi
Christopher Ivans-Brown, Compass Group
Christopher Robert Dennis Browne
Chris Peterson, Peterson Lakeshore Office
Chris Unsworth, Andrews Continental Delicacies
Christophe Megel, at-sunrice
Colin Nyoni, Nyoni's Kraal Restaurant
Coucoune Galerie
Cry Matsabola, Chinaka Lodge
Danielle Gambardella, Brazilian Wave Tours
Darina Allen, Ballymaloe Cookery School
Dario Queirolo, Uruguay Tourism
Derek Munn, The Ledges Inn
Dirk Crokaert, The Montague Hotel on the Gardens

247

Domaine de Marie

Doris Ho, Metropole Herbal Restaurant

El Palanque Restaurant

Elizabeth Bishop, Laura Davidson Public Relations

Erik Allin, Canon USA

Fellini Turismo

Fiona Stewart, Visit Scotland

Four Seasons Hotel

Frank E. Baxter, United States Ambassador to Uruguay

Garry Koh, Singapore Touring

Garry Rossen, Fish Works

Gordon Elphinstone, Edinburgh Touring

Gretchen VanEsselstyn, Chile Pepper Magazine

Grill on the Alley, London

Guy Reen, Platinum esCape Tours

Haci Baba Restaurant, Istanbul

Hector Herrera Landini, Sony Service Official

Heng Wai Leng, at-sunrice

Henk H. Evers, Cháteau Élan

Hisae Kojima, Hotel Nikko Kanazawa

Iain Simpson, George Watson's College

Ian Luck, Back Roads Touring Company

Ilda Cruz, Oeste Tourism

Ilustre Casa de Ramiro

Jabugo Cinco Jotus

Jackie and Dan Duran, Gourmet Safari

Jason Goodman, Chile Pepper Magazine

Jeff the Chef, Fetish for Food Bistro and Wine Bar

Jesus Ignacio Ortiz, La Cabana Restaurant

Jiro Takeuchi, The Kayotei Inn

Joanna Allen, VisitBritain

Joel Allen Schroeder

Johannes Maholola, Chinaka Lodge

John Davis

José de Brito, Marriott Praia D'el Rey

Juanico Winery

Justin and Kerri Clary

Kanaat Lookantase

Kara and Stephen Peterson

Kate Browne, Wishing Wells Productions

Kay Harte, Seven Hills Hotel

Kazutoshi Shoji, Fukumitsuya Sake Brewery

Kelly Rippa, Regis and Kelly Live

Kelly Smith, TravelSmith

Ken Bansho, Hotel Notokinpura

Kevin and Mary Lynch

K. F. Seetoh, Makansutra

Kiran Gowda, TravelSmith

Koji Yamade, Ishikawa Prefectural Govermment

Konyali Restaurant

La Cabrera Restaurant

Land's End

Lawrence J. Mayran, Cháteau Élan

Lemir Magnani, Churrascaria Na Brasa

Letitia Prinsloo, Institute of Culinary Arts

Lexar USA

Lic. M. Dolores Grassi, Argentina Tourism

Linda and Bob Buckley, Barbecue Mistress

Lisa Moreland Lyon, Visit Manchester

Liz Elman Feldman, Singapore Tourism

Luciele Alves, Das Araucarias Guest House

Marcela Sorondo, Buenos Aires

Marcelo Cigaina, El Federal Restaurant

Maria Dulce Rogue, Pastéis de Belém

Marian Goldberg, Japan National Tourist Organization

Marie Keane, Failte Ireland Tourism County Cork

Markus Hansen, South Africa Airways

Marriott Praia D'el Rey

Martin Yan, Yan Can Cook

Mary Darling, Glenkinchie Distillery

Mary Frances Fagan, American Airlines

Masanori Kamiguchi, Yamanaka Chamber of Commerce and Industry

Masanori Tanimoto, Governor of Ishikawa Prefecture

Mehmet Kayici, Tugra Tour Guide

Michael Gelman, Regis & Kelly Live

Michael Leonard, Christopher North Hotel

Minister Andrea Celoria, Deputy Consul General for Argentina

Miriam Berrios

Moira Quinn, Charlotte City Center

Mokgadi Mapaya, Chinaka Lodge

Morning and Jeff Stalcup

Moses Makotha, Chinaka Lodge

Motoyoshi Kaburaki, Kaburaki Shoho

Mushu Yamazaki, Kagamakie

Nan Deily, Compass Group

Nancy Vaughan, BMI

Natalie Shafer, Edelman

Nathalie Margan, Chateau la Canorgue

Nicole Moody, Cape Town Tourism

Noriko Nakarai, Expressions Interpretation

O Camelo Restaurant

Oscar and Kathy Tijerina

Pat and Tara Bennett

Patrick Mabolola, Chinaka Lodge

Pehlivan Restaurat

Penelope Horwood, KWV

Peter Fuchs, Harrods

Pousada Fazenda da Rinto

Rafik Kilardj, Dar Liqama House of Green Mint

Rapeepat Boriboon, at-sunrice

Regis Philbin, Regis and Kelly Live

Ricardo Perlini, Aripuca Bodego

Robert Krumbine, Charlotte City Center

Rob Newborn, Platinum esCape Tours

Roger Davies, A Question of Taste Food and Wine Tours

Rose South, Made in Oregon

Rowena Rose, Fetish for Food

Ruth Moran, Tourism Ireland

Sally Alfis, Booth & Associates

Sandra Yager, Hockinson High School

Sedona Fitzgerald, Ruder Finn

Seiichji Yamamoto, Yamato Soy Sauce and Miso Company

Sonoko Asaii

Stephen Peterson, BBQ Catering

Stefano D'Arrigo, Chinaka Lodge

Susan Bolger, Tourism Ireland

Takayuki Kamide, Ishikawa Prefectural Government

Takeshi Soda, Ishikawa Prefectural Government

Tawada Mushamiri, Chinaka Lodge

TravelSmith

Todd Hedrick, Viking

Treva J. Marshall, TJM Communications, Inc.

Turkish Ministry of Culture

Trish and Reed Kawahara

Vanitar Sindaya, Singapore Tourism Board

Veronica Gonzalez Pose, Cabana Veronica

Vista Do Vale Ranch

Wong Wee Tee, Singapore Tourism

Yasuhio Satake

Yvonne Goforth

Yuichi Kano, Yamanaka Chamber of Commerce

Index